# Praise for *Phantom Parks*

"It will shock and outrage us and move us to demand that the government live up to its promise to complete the park system by this millennium and to protect the biodiversity within existing parks."

—*David Suzuki*

". . . if what are supposed to be the most highly protected jewels in our national crown are tarnished, what does that say about the rest of the Canadian landscape?"

—*Monte Hummel, President, World Wildlife Fund Canada*

"This is a must read for every Member of Parliament and Canadian. Hopefully it will incite all of us to take action to maintain our parks unimpaired for future generations of all species."

—*Kevin McNamee, Canadian Nature Federation*

"Most Canadians will be shocked and saddened to realize that Canada's National Parks are at risk—that the diversity of species, the ecosystem functions, what is collectively called the ecological integrity, of the parks is eroding."

—*Elizabeth May, Executive Director, Sierra Club of Canada*

"Earth's intrinsic worth is symbolized in the National Parks, established because of their sublime beauties and protected with an intuitive sense that things other-than-human are vitally important. Rick Searle calls us back to this fundamental insight, stressing the inherent values of National Parks. Each one, a part of the marvelous Earth, reflects four billion years of creativity: bearing, evolving and preserving the inorganic and organic weave of life. To keep the vision alive, in a human world forgetful of its roots in the wild, is the sacred trust."

—*Stan Rowe, author of* Home Place

RICK SEARLE

# Phantom Parks

### The Struggle to Save Canada's National Parks

KEY PORTER BOOKS

**Canadian Cataloguing in Publication Data**

Searle, D. Richard (Donald Richard), 1951–
   Phantom parks : the struggle to save Canada's national parks

ISBN: 1-55263-160-5

1. National parks and reserves – Protection – Canada.  2. National parks and reserves – Canada – Management.  I. Title.

SB486.P76S42 2000          333.78'316'0971          COO-930003-1

Henderson Book Series No. 29

The Henderson Book Series honours the kind and generous donation of Mrs. Arthur T. Henderson, who made this series possible. The Canadian Parks and Wilderness Society gratefully acknowledges Mrs. Henderson's support of our efforts to build public support for protecting Canada's wilderness areas.

The Canadian Parks and Wilderness Society (CPAWS) is Canada's grassroots voice for wilderness. Since our founding in 1963, we have helped protect over 100 million acres of treasured wild places. We focus on establishing new parks and on making sure nature comes first in their management. Call us at 1-800-333-WILD for more information or to become a member.

The publisher gratefully acknowledges the support of the Canada Council for the Arts and the Ontario Arts Council for its publishing program.

We acknowledge the financial support of the Government of Canada through the Book Publishing Industry Development Program (BPIDP) for our publishing activities.

Key Porter Books Limited
70 The Esplanade
Toronto, Ontario
Canada  M5E 1R2

www.keyporter.com

Material for Chapter 3 previously appeared as "Standing Up for Riding Mountain," *Equinox*, April/May 1997; and "Riding Mountain Mystery," *Nature Canada*, Summer 1997.

Electronic formatting: Heidi Palfrey
Design: Peter Maher

Printed and bound in Canada

00 01 02 03 04  6 5 4 3 2 1

*For my grandfather*
*Irvine Baker*
*(1899–1976)*
*Who instilled in me a deep and abiding passion for all things wild, and*
*who, more than anyone, set my course in life.*

*And, for Parks Canada employees across the country and at every level of*
*the organization who remain committed to J.B. Harkin's vision of the*
*national parks: sacred places wherein ecological integrity and wildness are*
*to be protected, and the re-creation of the human spirit is made possible.*

There are so many people that deserved to be recognized and thanked for making this book a reality.

First of all, I want to thank all those organizations and individuals who provided much-needed financial support, enabling me to travel to twenty-eight of the thirty-nine national parks.

Research grants came from: National Component of the Public Service Alliance of Canada, World Wildlife Fund, David Suzuki Foundation, Royal Geographical Society, Riding Mountain National Park Biosphere Reserve Committee and Mountain Equipment Co-op.

Donations were received from: Ray Allard; Jo Anne Anderson; Doug Anions; Nora Arjis; Nancy Averil; Don Baker; Gladys Baker; Melanie Barnes; Joan Barrett; Ruth and Rueban Bellan; Judy Birch; Eric Bonham; Jim Borrowman; Keith Bowey and Sherida Milne; Mark Brown; B. Bruun; Jim Burgess; Michael Burns; Neil Cameron; Peter Campbell; Susan Carr; Audra Caughell; Bea and Laurie Cherniak; Karen Chester; Jim Chipperfield; Terri Chysowski; Jenny Clarke; Norm Cole; Jim and Leslie Corte; Donna Danyluk; Bruce Darwin; Celes and Sue Davar; Barb and Gene Degen; S. Dixon; Bob Dodge; Brian Dodge and Debra Koski; Garnet and Jay Dodge; Don Eastman; Yorke Edwards; Mac Estabrook; J. Etkin; Sheila Ferry; Stan Firby; Elizabeth Flemming; Bristol Foster;

Robin Fraser; Friends of Kootenay National Park; Friends of Yoho National Park; Lori Garcia-Meredith; Florence George; Gloria Goulet; Bill Graham; Micheal Greco; Brian Grison; Kira Guerwing; Elgin Hall; Gord Hammell; Gladys Hannah; Sue Hara; Aileen Harmon; S. Hewett; N.J. Hewitt; Michael Hoppe; Robin Hopper and Judi Dyelle; Barry Hughson; Bill Hunter; The Jacksons; Allan James; Thelma James; Brian Johnson; Donna Johnson; Verna Karpenic; Heather Keenan; Rich and Leslie Kerschtien; Robert Kidd; Barry Kingdon; Charlie Kingdon; Ken Kingdon; Robin Korthals; Bob and Dawna Lewis; Pat Lewis; Harvey Locke; Nik Lopoukhine; Colleen Malatest; Kathleen Maras; Jake Masselink; Ruth Masters; Lyn McCaughey; Catherine McClenaghan-Rowat and Randal Rowat; Bob and Nancy McMinn; Barry McNabb; Roy McNabb; June McPherson; Ed and Muriel Meadows; Gene Menzies; Bob Milne; Jonah Mitchell; Margot Moore; Mel Mummery; Kim Munson; Dave Newton; Susan Nonen; Fred and Jean Oberg; Leo O'Brien; Marion Ogbowski; M.L. Ogilvie; John Olafson and Linda Beare; Henry and Helen Oshust; Ralph Osterwold; Bob Peart & Mary Martin; Harvey and Carol Pengelly; Lois and Vern Phillips; Brian Pinch; Ev and Alec Potter; Ian Rogers and Judith Rosewilde; Susie Ross; Ron and June Routledge; Blaise Salmon; Charlie Saso; Kurt Saunders; Monika Schaefer; Marilynn and Frank Schwets; Lem Shuttleworth; John and Liz Simmons; Susan Staniforth; Jos Storm; Jackie Syroteuk; Merv Syroteuk; Duncan Taylor; Karen Taylor; Seymour Treiger and Betty Nickerson; Nancy Turner; W. Vandershuit; Marion and Sherry Wade; Ken Walker; Ken Wallace; N. Walmsley; Bill Webb; Taoya and Ian White; Don and Florence Whitmore; Ray and Marilyn Whittle; J.L. Wilkins; Suzanne Wilson; Kathleen Worral; Yellowhead Office Supplies; Jill Yukon; Doug and Joclyn Yurick.

While completing our 30,000-kilometre cross-Canada journey, many individuals and a couple of hotels provided my wife and I with accommodation and generous hospitality. To the following people, we say thank you: Mom and Dad (for allowing us to live and operate out of my old bedroom for several weeks); Jo-Anne Anderson and Alan Thwait (how can we ever thank the two of you for the incredible generosity, advice and assistance given during our three-week stay?); Keith Bowey and Sherida Milne; Catherine McClenaghan-Rowat and Randal Rowat; Liz Atkins; Jim Butler; Charlene and Bill Diehl-Jones; Shel and Stephanie Reisler; Ros and Phil Stooke; Tom and Heather Kovacs; Ted and Linda Mosquin; Donna and Bud Searle; Jill and Basil Seaton; Ron and June Routledge; Andrea and Brendan; Craig and Sheila Adams who own the Blue Bay Motel in Tobermory; and the management of the Hawood Inn in Waskesiu.

A special thank you to Tom Lee, chief executive officer of Parks Canada who not only permitted me an in-depth interview, but also sent out a system-wide memo asking that all national parks and historic sites waive their entrance fees for me and that all staff co-operate with my inquiries. I'm also deeply indebted to Parks Canada staff: superintendents, wardens, interpreters, visitor services personnel and maintenance workers who went out of their way, generously providing free camping, ease of access into the parks, by boat, canoe and helicopter, and critical information on the threats to ecological integrity. Most importantly, they took me into their confidence, revealing their deepest fears and hopes for the organization and for the national parks. Without their trust and involvement, this book could not have come into being.

Although the genesis for this book is entirely my own, I must acknowledge and thank several individuals who helped to develop my ideas into a detailed outline; they include: Bob Peart, Jim Christakos, Doug Chalk, Ron Malis, Kevin Van Tighem, Bob Lewis, Jonah Mitchell, Jim Butler, Harvey Locke, Ted Mosquin, Yorke Edwards, Paul Paquet, Jim Fulton and Monte Hummel. I am also extremely grateful to the following individuals who reviewed and provided comments on the manuscript at various points in its development: Bob Peart, Kevin Van Tighem, Jill Swartz, Clayton and Loreen Searle, Neil Munro, Nik Lopoukhine, Jim Christakos, Doug Chalk, Ted Mosquin, Harvey Locke, Brian Pinch, and Lori Garcia-Meredith. While each of these individuals provided invaluable suggestions for the book's improvement, I remain entirely responsible for its tone and content, including any errors.

At Key Porter, I wish to express my gratitude to Anna Porter for understanding the importance of my book's subject, for agreeing to publish it, and for assigning Patrick Crean to work with me. To Patrick, I offer my deep appreciation for his insightful guidance in restructuring and refining what was a very rough and rambling first draft.

Researching and writing this book has demanded nearly all of my attention over the past three years. During the latter half of the project, I was very fortunate to have Jen Paul as an associate. Without her, I simply could not have kept up with my numerous teaching, consulting, and journalism commitments. Therefore, she deserves a special thank you for her professional attitude, keen interest, and enthusiastic contributions to all of my various projects.

Two individuals who also deserve special recognition are Betty Nickerson and Seymour Treiger. Through their foundation, All About Us Canada, I was able to receive grants and donations to support the research and writing of this book. More importantly, they provided my wife and I with much appreciated encouragement, support and advice while we were travelling across Canada. Many times, they lifted our spirits when we ran into funding or logistical difficulties. Even now, they continue to be a source of inspiration to us for their compassion and desire to help others. It would not be stretching the point to say that this book would not have happened without their involvement.

I come now to my wife, Dianne, who shares my passion for the wild. She deeply understood and fully supported the research and writing of this book, every step of the way, by assisting with planning the cross-Canada trip, organizing fund-raising events, contacting the media, offering suggestions on the book's outline, structure, and content, and editing the final draft. I owe an immense and lasting gratitude to her for this freely given assistance, especially since I know that it sometimes came at a cost to her own work. Her willingness to do so is a reflection of the love we share for each other, and of her firm belief in the importance of protecting special places. Thank you Dianne, from the depths of my heart, for being an enduring source of strength, inspiration and love in my life.

If I have forgotten to thank anyone, please accept my apologies.

# CONTENTS

Before I read Rick Searle's remarkable manuscript, it had not occurred to me that the national parks of Canada were in such desperate trouble. One reason was that my favourite park—Point Pelee on Lake Erie—the one I visit every year to watch bird migrations—is an exception; it is the only park of its kind that has an ecosystem restoration plan. But, as this book makes only too clear, more than half of the thirty-nine national parks in Canada are victims of an ecological impact that is only one of several problems facing the wilderness areas that were supposed to be set aside for all time as part of our heritage.

As this book shows beyond a shadow of doubt, the great parks that used to be sacred places are dying from neglect, from a lack of vision, from mismanagement, from political interference, from developers and promoters and—worst of all in my view—from a dogmatic political philosophy, which insists that our national parks be used as commodities to make a profit—to be bought, sold and consumed like so many carnival rides. The cry has gone out that parks should be run like a business, complete with profit-and-loss statements issued annually, to promote the tourist trade, to pay for themselves through Disneyland-like gimmickry.

As a result, our first national park, Banff, is a disaster; more than half of Jasper has been destroyed or degraded through commercial enterprise, over use, government penny-pinching and sheer inattention. No Canadian has a God-given right to invade a protected area, trample over its native species and corrupt its wildlife. Yet that is the prevailing attitude. We have forgotten that the national parks of this country are sacred places and not cash cows for the entrepreneurs.

One of the points the author makes that caught my attention, was the need to put a ceiling on visitors to our dying parks. That is exactly the philosophy behind the restrictions on entry to the Thelon Game Sanctuary in the North West Territories. I well remember how difficult it was for me, when writing *The Mysterious North*, to obtain a permit to visit the sanctuary and observe the dwindling herds of musk oxen, which it protects.

Canada would do well to use similar techniques to save other conservation areas. We forget, sometimes, how valuable they are: the prospect of losing them is appalling. For unlike Disneyland, these last links with our wilderness past can never be replaced once we allow them to be destroyed.

*PIERRE BERTON*
*December 1999*

Canada's national parks system is a reflection of an approach to nature protection in North America that has evolved over the last 125 years. Mid-way through the industrial revolution, the national park idea was born as an antidote to the ugliness of unbridled commercial development. Our first, Rocky Mountains National Park at Banff, like the world's first, Yellowstone in the U.S., was created to preserve some of nature's beauty for people to enjoy.

Soon, national parks also came to be seen as places to conserve wildlife. The first wildlife study was done the year after the first reserve at Banff was created. Tourist facilities were not understood to conflict with wildlife and were built in some parks. Others, such as Nemiskam (Antelope), Buffalo and Wood Buffalo National Parks, were established explicitly to protect individual species.

In 1930 an explicit conservation objective was established for all of Canada's parks. The National Parks Act passed that year required the national parks to be used in a manner that left them unimpaired for future generations. In the 1960s, as our understanding of ecology grew, the first national parks policy was created to provide more guidance on nature protection and human use.

If the evolution of Canada's parks were truly progressive, one would expect that the strong policy from the 1960s coupled with the 1930 legislation had set our parks system firmly on the course of nature protection. Alas the truth is not so simple. A culture of confusion reigned which was exacerbated in the 1980s with the election of the Conservative government of Brian Mulroney. While some wonderful new parks were established, and the National Parks Act was amended to make ecological integrity paramount, this period will also be remembered for other reasons. Through a policy of tourism expansion, enormous pressure was put on Banff National Park to compete with tourism resorts outside parks in the rest of North America. A building boom ensued. The park's ecological integrity was deeply compromised. The cancer of commercialism threatened to spread throughout the parks system and a culture of allowing visitors to compromise ecological integrity did spread. Parks Canada was bounced around between the Departments of Environment and Canadian Heritage. When the government changed in the early 1990s, the national deficit was the leading preoccupation for the Liberals. Parks Canada's budget was severely cut. Privatization was pushed as the answer to Canada's fiscal challenges. It was a dark time.

However, there was some hope. The international outcry resulting from the Canadian Parks and Wilderness Society's campaign to halt commercial development in Banff National Park led to the Banff-Bow Valley Study. A group of experts was asked to assess the situation and provide solutions. Their report stated bluntly that Banff was a mess, and that the pace and scale of development put its future as a national park in doubt. By this time Sheila Copps was deputy prime minister and minister of Canadian Heritage. She had guts. She understood that national parks are nature reserves, not development zones.

After a very vociferous public debate across the country, the right decision was made. There would be an end to commercialization and a reaffirmation of the primacy of protection. Commercial development would be legally capped in all our national parks. The secretary of state for National Parks, Andy Mitchell, oversaw the establishment of Parks Canada as a separate agency with a clear conservation mandate so it would no longer be bounced from ministry to ministry. In 1994 the national park policy was strengthened further to make ecological integrity the overriding principle in public management. The period of confusion should be coming to a happy ending as I write this foreword. But one cannot be sure.

As Rick Searle has so thoroughly documented in this book, Parks Canada and all its political masters in the federal government have not yet fully embraced the need to protect nature in our parks. While there are encouraging signs at the ministerial, legal and rhetorical level, action on the ground is often inconsistent. This could simply be a case of the long turning distance required to steer the institutional momentum of a large organization or it could be a case of wilful resistance. Whatever the case, the result is not yet right. The push and pull between nature protection and exploitation in our national parks is not yet over.

As I write, the Panel on Ecological Integrity, a follow up to the Banff-Bow Valley Study, is reporting to minister Copps on the state of all our national parks and on the agency charged with safeguarding them. Advanced signals given in the media by Jacques Gerin, the panel's chair, indicate that the lingering behavioural and cultural problems that work against the protection of Nature in our parks will be vividly exposed.

These events bring us to a threshold of opportunity for our national parks. Their purpose has been clearly established, through law and policy, as places where people experience protected nature and where ecological integrity comes first. Their problems now identified can be addressed. The agency which is entrusted with their protection has a clear statutory mandate and has an opportunity to make a corresponding cultural commitment to the protection of Nature. The federal government has expressed a renewed interest in the environment and is now running budgetary surpluses. Although there is much to be done, there never has been a better time to do it.

Our park system is not complete. We still have the chance to create great wilderness parks in the Torngat and Mealy Mountains of Labrador, in the East Arm of Great Slave Lake, Northwest Territories, and in Yukon's Wolf Lake region, to name a few. We must also address the serious challenges which threaten the ecological integrity of existing parks, both inside and outside their boundaries. Solutions lie in better management of the areas around parks through stewardship zones combined with corridors to connect populations of wild things. We must also invest in undoing or mitigating the damage caused by infrastructure inside parks, many of which are bisected by roads and railways. And any species which has been lost to a park, like bison in the Rocky Mountains or lynx in Fundy, must be reintroduced. In short, we must rewild our damaged parks and keep wild those which still are.

Creating new parks and fixing past mistakes will require money. It is time for us to increase our investment in nature. Only future generations will be able to judge whether this period in national park history was a period of opportunity boldly seized or badly squandered.

This is a challenge for all of us, not just for our politicians and public servants. Rick Searle, moved by a deep love for our parks, decided to take it up. He took his writer's skills and keen sense of observation on a pilgrimage across Canada to celebrate and take the pulse of our parks. He found, as has the Panel on Ecological Integrity, that the patient is ill. This book makes his thoughtful diagnosis available to all Canadians. It is a labour of love and a call to action.

HARVEY LOCKE
*Vice President, Conservation*
*Canadian Parks and Wilderness Society*
*Calgary, Alberta and*
*Cambridge, Massachusetts*
*December 21, 1999*

My connection with the wild and with national parks runs very deep. I was born on the edge of Riding Mountain National Park in southwestern Manitoba.

My earliest memories are of lying on a blanket, staring up at the intense blue sky through a shimmering mosaic of green aspen leaves. As a toddler, I felt drawn to the forest that covered the lot next door, and made frequent attempts to enter its tantalizing depths. These efforts were inevitably thwarted by my mother, who grew weary of constantly having to keep her eye on me; she worried that I might become lost or be eaten by some wandering black bear. Despite my protests of "I come back" or "I be fine," she put me in a halter that was tied to a tree near the back steps on a rope just long enough to reach the sandpile a few metres away.

More than anyone, it was my grandfather who understood and encouraged my curiosity and love for all things wild. He had a long association with the natural world—and with Riding Mountain National Park. He had worked at a sawmill in a remote corner of the park while it was a forest reserve. After the reserve was converted to a national park in the early 1930s, he became foreman of the park's golf course. With the security of a good paying steady job, Grandfather fulfilled a wedding promise to my

Grandmother by building a modest two-storey house near the park's south gate. Here they lived for more than thirty years.

As I grew older, Grandfather began taking me on long rambling walks. Clasping his big warm hand, munching on peanuts that he always kept stashed in his pockets, and intrigued by the aroma of his pipe tobacco, I would follow him wide-eyed as we threaded our way along game trails that crossed back and forth over the park's boundary. Everywhere there was life. Squirrels chattered indignantly from limbs above our heads. Grey jays, chickadees and dark-eyed juncos with little pink feet and beaks flitted among the spruce boughs. Occasionally we would startle a ruffed grouse. With a flurry of powerful wingbeats, it would explode into the air, seemingly from beneath our feet, leaving our hearts pounding while we laughed from the surprise. Rare was the foray into the woods when we didn't encounter deer, moose, beaver or weasel. Through it all, Grandfather was there beside me, patiently answering my persistent questions about the natural world and telling me stories about the animals and plants around us.

As a young teenager, my rambles in the woods became longer and more solitary. I drew immense pleasure from plunging into the green chaos and then letting myself be guided by some invisible force in whichever direction it beckoned. These ramblings were never hurried; often I would sit with my back against the greenish-white trunk of an aspen and just quietly observe nature. Other times, I would diligently practise reading the signs animals had left on the trails, whether they were tracks, scat (droppings) or bits of fur. These habits I developed after reading books by naturalists such as Ernest Thompson Seton and Grey Owl. Never do I recall being frightened, even though I knew there was always a chance of encountering a black bear or moose. Instead, in the solitude, I experienced an at-one-ness with wildness that remains a fundamental part of my identity even all these years later, and though I now live in a modest-sized city on Canada's West Coast.

I'm not sure when I first began to realize that the wild world was threatened, but I do know that, by the time I decided to enter university, my overriding ambition was to save wildness from human carelessness and destruction. After completing my first year, I was presented with an opportunity that seemed almost too good to be true. The chief park naturalist at Riding Mountain National Park called to ask if I would like to be interviewed for a position as a museum attendant. In addition to answering the questions of visitors, I would care for the displays and present slide shows in the theatre. Originally, it had been a chapel, and my parents were married there. Although I had never heard of this work, I jumped at the opportunity as it seemed like a good way to become a park warden—the ultimate guardian of the wild in my mind. Besides, from the job description, I quickly deduced that the work was pretty much what Grandfather had done with me as a young boy, that is, sharing a love for and knowledge of the plants and animals found in the park. More importantly, it sounded as though I would have countless opportunities to educate the public on the need to protect the wild.

Over the next six years, from 1973 to 1979, I worked as a park naturalist (interpreter) at Riding Mountain and then at Kootenay National Park in the Rocky Mountains of British Columbia. At first, I was enthralled to be working for an organization dedicated to the goals I most cared about. More than anything else, Parks Canada represented a body of people committed to protecting species and ecosystems that had been placed under their care within the national parks. Among them I felt at home, part of an extended family. Many of the individuals I worked with during these early adult years remain good friends and colleagues today. However, with each passing season, I witnessed too many instances where economics and politics overrode ecology. In Riding Mountain, the number and size of boats on Clear Lake were allowed to grow, forcing Parks Canada to partially fill in a sensitive wetland ecosystem to accommodate the increase in vehicles and trailers around the launching docks. From what I heard through the grapevine, similar things were happening elsewhere in the system as well. In Yoho National Park, an interpreter stirred up trouble when his managers tried to cover up a CP Rail spill of crude bunker oil into the Kicking Horse River.

The inconsistencies deeply troubled me, as I know they did many others within the organization. When we asked about them, we were quietly warned by our supervisors to stay away from controversial issues. Some of my co-workers became bitter and cynical, saying that Parks Canada was too ready to put people above protection.

I left Parks Canada in 1979 to join the Manitoba Provincial parks branch, where I worked as regional interpreter and as a visitor services specialist until 1983. In the parks branch, I encountered even more frustrating inconsistencies, where protection of ecosystems and species was readily compromised to keep visitors or adjacent landowners happy.

In the summer of 1983, I left the branch and enrolled in a masters program to answer the burning question of why conflicts between use and preservation were usually resolved in favour of the former. Through the research, I learned about the influence of deeply held and largely unexamined beliefs, values and assumptions that inform attitudes and behaviours towards the environment. Simplistically, our view of the environment tends towards either anthropocentric or ecocentric. The first places humans at the centre of Creation, while the latter situates humans as merely one of many life forms existing on the planet. More to the point, anthropocentricism views humans as somehow separate from nature, while ecocentricism sees us as being inseparable from it. The anthropocentric perspective holds that humans are the sole arbiters of what has worth and what has not, with the decision being made on the basis of a thing's potential or actual utility in satisfying human wants and desires. Ecocentricism soundly rejects this idea, and instead argues that nature has intrinsic worth by virtue of being a part of Creation; it is recognized with respect and awe as something out of which humanity arose. As might be expected, anthropocentrism encourages exploitation while ecocentrism advocates protection.

While the academic studies helped to shed light on the underlying psychological, philosophical and spiritual dimensions of the ambivalence towards wildness I saw within Parks Canada and Manitoba Parks Branch, and indeed within Canadian society as a whole, they left me with more questions about what could be done to resolve the apparent dualities of humans versus nature, use versus protection, or economic growth versus environmental protection.

For the next ten years, I focused on one of the main questions left lingering after my graduate degree: whether or not a shift from an anthropocentric to an ecocentric world view could be facilitated. I felt certain that the human tendency to either domesticate or destroy wildness was not programmed into our genes but arose largely from a lack of understanding and caring. These shortcomings I believed could be overcome through environmental education, and I still believe this to be true. However, it had to be of a very different kind of education than that I saw being offered in the schools. While important, these forms fail to reach the middle majority of adult Canadians in a compelling and immediate way; consequently I delved deeply into the principles and practices of adult education, especially the fields of learning to learn, self-directed learning and transformative learning. This last area of study has been a gold mine of ideas about how adults can learn to transform even their most deeply held beliefs and assumptions. These ideas I have attempted to incorporate into my work as journalist, consultant and educator.

After my departure from Parks Canada, I continued to visit the national parks and kept in touch with many of the friends and colleagues I had met while working with the organization. Through them I remained informed of the mounting pressures of human activity in, around and well beyond park boundaries, as well as of the numerous reorganizations and budget cuts that threatened both the ecological integrity of the national parks system and the organizational integrity of Parks Canada itself.

In March 1996, an article by *Globe and Mail* columnist Michael Valpy struck a chord of terror deep in my soul. Under the headline

"The parks in the market," Valpy alerted his readers to the insidious changes occurring within Parks Canada, revealing that "[i]n bits and pieces over the past few months, the national government has been constructing the machinery to privatize and entrepreneurially transform many of its operations."[1] His article, plus several others that followed, galvanized me into action. I knew I had to do something to stop the desecration of Canada's national parks—sanctuaries for the wild that are the essence of Creation and of the human spirit.

In the fall of 1996, I travelled to the Yukon, where I visited and talked with staff at Kluane National Park and at the Klondike National Historic Sites in Dawson City to get some sense of just how bad the crisis was. I met with park staff after work hours or away from offices because the regional director of Parks Canada in Calgary, who had heard of my research, had sent out a directive that staff were not to speak with me. This directive, of course, backfired, making the staff even more suspicious of senior management and more willing to share with me their concerns about the changes occurring within the organization.

Throughout the winter of 1996–97, I continued to consult with former and current employees of Parks Canada, the head of the union representing them, executive directors of various environmental organizations—including the Canadian Parks and Wilderness Society, the World Wildlife Fund and the David Suzuki Foundation—and wildlife biologists. In May 1997, I was invited to attend an international forestry conference hosted by the World Wildlife Fund in San Francisco. While sitting on a sunny slope in Point Reyes National Park overlooking the Pacific Ocean, I discussed with my wife, Dianne, my desire to write a book about the loss of the wild from Canada's national parks and about what had to be done to restore it. To write the book, I felt I had to visit as many of the parks as possible to see them and to talk with people who knew them. After listening to me, she readily and strongly encouraged me to embark upon the project. With one condition: that she come along. Hardly a condition.

So, in mid-July 1997, we packed our aging 1981 Mazda hatchback and set out on what would become a five-month, 30,000-kilometre cross-Canada odyssey to enable me to learn first-hand what was happening in the national parks. Over the course of the journey (which could inspire a book in itself), we visited twenty-one of the thirty-eight national parks (one has been added since). At each park I met with key park staff, including wardens, ecologists, interpreters, visitor service officers and superintendents. I also made a point of talking with park visitors and representatives from local communities, business interests, First Nations and environmental groups. Wherever I could, I obtained and read through critical documents, such as management, conservation and business plans. Then Di would join me so we could get out into the parks to experience them for ourselves, sometimes on foot, other times by helicopter, boat or canoe. Since completing the cross-Canada trip, I have visited yet another six national parks, bringing the total to twenty-seven. All of the parks we visited, except Kluane, are southern parks; financial limitations unfortunately ruled out the possibility of visiting the remote northern parks.

I began writing in the spring of 1998, and the book you now hold attests to my personal commitment to do what I can to save wildness and the national parks. As indicated at the beginning of this preface, I cannot live without wildness. I am equally convinced that keeping the wild alive, even in our national parks, demands a much larger constituency of Canadians committed to this goal. My purpose, therefore, in writing this book is to alert as many Canadians as possible to the urgent crisis now engulfing their national parks and to encourage them to do whatever they can to reduce or reverse the loss of the wild from those parks.

A couple of disclaimers need to be made at this point. As indicated above, I was not able to travel to the northern parks, so I have restricted my observations and comments to the parks I have visited and know something about. Also, I have not addressed the topic of First Nations involvement within the national parks.

I recognize that they have subsistence rights in many parks, which allow them to hunt, fish, trap and gather herbs, berries and medicines. Nowhere in my research did I gain a sense that this activity is viewed as a serious threat to ecological integrity or wildness.

In closing, if the book's message can be reduced to any one simple idea, perhaps it is this: wildness is of inherent worth. It is sacred. It is the essence of who we are as Canadians and of this great northern wilderness called Canada. In destroying it, we destroy our soul. The national parks are part of the geography of hope for maintaining wildness both in the land and in our culture.

# ONE

# Death by a Thousand Cuts

Canada's national parks are dying. This is not an exaggeration. Throughout the system, ecosystems and species are succumbing to a relentless attack by forces within, around and well beyond individual park boundaries. In its 1994 State of the Parks report, Parks Canada bluntly acknowledged: "It is no longer enough to consider an area protected by just designating it a park . . . certain species that currently persist in parks may not survive in the long run."[1] Pine marten and woodland caribou populations have been so reduced in Cape Breton Highlands and Pukaskwa national parks respectively that their role in the ecosystem is "virtually absent." The last lynx spotted in Fundy National Park was in 1978. At least eleven species of reptiles and amphibians are no longer found in Point Pelee National Park. In Riding Mountain National Park, the wolf population has collapsed by more than 50 percent over the past twenty years. The grizzly bear is now a very rare sighting in the lower Bow Valley of Banff National Park. As the 1997 State of the Parks report makes frighteningly clear, despite many wonderful examples of maintaining and restoring ecosystems and species, the national parks are rapidly losing ground.

Tragically, the ecological deterioration of the national parks is going largely unnoticed by most Canadians. To many eyes, everything appears fine. I recall standing among a small knot of tourists who had gathered to watch a female grizzly and her two cubs in Waterton Lakes National Park. Our group was but one of several scattered along the road. In either direction there were scores of vehicles pulled over, clogging traffic. As vehicles crawled by, the occupants craned their necks upward to catch a glimpse of what was exciting so much interest. On spotting the bears on the high ridge above the road, many of them jockeyed their vehicles into place. Around me, people talked and pointed excitedly while others fumbled with tripods, cameras and lenses. While binoculars were being passed around, questions were flying: how big are they? can we see their hump? and is their fur really chocolate brown as it appears? In and around these questions there was much talk about the grizzly's reputed ferociousness, its threatened status and how good it was that the bear was protected in the park.

I was struck by how quickly and easily the presence of these three bears was taken as a general indication of a healthy population and a healthy park. I knew that these appearances were very deceiving. Perhaps as few as ten to fifteen grizzlies may be found in the park, a population so dangerously small that it cannot be self-sustaining. If it weren't for individuals moving in and through the park from Glacier National Park in Montana to the immediate south or from the eastern slopes of the Canadian Rockies to the immediate north, the grizzlies would very quickly vanish from Waterton Lakes National Park. At 525 square kilometres, it is already much too small to support even one adult male, which normally requires nearly twice that amount of habitat. Of deep concern to biologists on either side of the border is the fact that the bear faces an equally uncertain future in the broader regional landscape. Timber harvesting, cattle ranching, oil and gas drilling, and recreational subdivisions press in from all sides, destroying or fragmenting and degrading unprotected habitat.

The people who stood around me on that warm July evening, spellbound by the primal power of North America's largest carnivore, probably would have been shocked to know all this. We humans tend not to be very good at perceiving things like this because, in the words of Robert Ornstein and Paul Ehrlich, two American scientists, "our nervous systems evolved to select only a small extract of reality and to ignore the rest."[2] Instead of taking in everything about the world around us, our brains respond primarily to dramatic or sudden change. Unfortunately, this does not include such things as shifts in the acidity of rain, the breakdown of the ozone layer or the extinction of species—unless they directly affect us in some way. "As a result we are losing control of our future," warn Ornstein and Ehrlich. There is a deadly mismatch between perception and reality; both humanity and the rest of Creation are threatened by "changes taking place over years and decades, but changes over a few years or decades are too *slow* for us to perceive readily . . . At the same time the changes are too *rapid* to allow biological or cultural evolutionary processes to adapt people [and many other forms of life] to them."[3] Even as we rapidly change the world, we often do not see the dangers until we are suddenly confronted with "catastrophic evidence."

"Humans are creating vast changes: global warming, ozone depletion, genetic manipulation, etc.," urgently writes Bill McKibbon, author of *The End of Nature*, "that can and will radically alter our world and bring about the end of nature."[4] The changes occurring within the national parks are not yet obvious to most people, and so there is a very real danger that they may continue to the point where wild species and ecosystems become a thing of the past. Taken together, the changes amount to the domestication of the wild. In a world where nothing is quite what it seems to be, we are increasingly creating a legacy of phantom parks: places that still look beautiful, but where the essential quality of wildness is largely absent.

This is not what most Canadians want for their national parks; in fact, quite the opposite. Since the early 1960s there has been a mounting public demand for greater protection of ecosystems and species found within the national parks. The trend is reflected in the strengthening of the National Parks Act and Policy. "The National Parks of Canada are hereby dedicated to the people of

Canada for their benefit, education and enjoyment . . . [and] shall be maintained and made use of so as to leave them unimpaired for the enjoyment of future generations," says the Act, implying that parks are to be both used and protected.[5] But which comes first? The 1988 amendment of the Act leaves no room for doubt or uncertainty on this point: "Maintenance of ecological integrity through the protection of natural resources shall be the first priority when considering park zoning and visitor use in a management plan," it states categorically.[6] The 1994 National Parks Policy goes even further, stating that the protection of ecological integrity takes "precedence in acquiring, managing, and administering heritage places and programs. In every application of policy, this guiding principle is paramount."[7] Put very simply, protection is to override use.

The term *ecological integrity* may be unfamiliar to many people. The earliest reference to it appears to have been in the writings of Aldo Leopold, one of America's most ardent and eloquent defenders of wildlife and wilderness. In his classic essay "The Land Ethic," written sometime in the late 1940s, Leopold argued that "A thing is right when it tends to preserve the integrity, stability, and beauty of the biotic community. It is wrong when it tends otherwise."[8] It wasn't until the 1970s that the idea of ecological integrity began to appear within environmental laws and policies. The U.S. Water Quality Amendments, for example, aimed at restoring the "chemical, physical, and biological integrity" of that nation's waters. In 1979 the term popped up in Canada's revised National Parks Policy, which stated that ecological integrity must be perceived as a prerequisite to use, and, as stated above, by 1988 it had become fully embedded within the National Parks Act.

Despite its rise from obscurity to centre stage in the escalating drama of trying to protect and conserve the planet's rapidly dwindling biological diversity, ecological integrity remains a slippery and complicated concept. Parks Canada defines it as a state in which ecosystem structures and functions are unimpaired by human-caused stresses and where native species are present at viable population levels. This definition reflects some of the most recent advances in ecosystem science by moving beyond ideas that focused park management on single species.

Reed Noss, one of North America's leading conservation biologists, believes that it is "an integrating and holistic concept" that pulls together many related ideas. For him, ecological integrity includes ecological health, biodiversity, stability, naturalness and wildness. *Ecological health* is a term often used in place of ecological integrity. It suggests a comparison to something with which we are very familiar: our own health or that of our communities. In some ways, this is a useful analogy. We understand what it means to be sick or well, and can readily imagine what this might mean for an ecosystem or species. Some stress, for example, is normal and even healthy, but if it exceeds the ability of an organism or community to cope and respond, systems begin to break down and could eventually result in collapse and death. However, the comparison is not without its dangers. As Noss warns: ". . . although health is necessary for integrity, it is not sufficient. One can imagine many ecosystems that are quite healthy yet lack integrity. A tree farm, for example, might be considered healthy if it vigorously adds biomass [more and bigger trees], but surely it lacks integrity. Many species can be lost from an ecosystem before any overt signs of ill health are evident but with each loss of a native species the integrity of the ecosystem declines."[9]

Noss defines *biodiversity* as "the variety of living organisms, the genetic differences between them, the communities and ecosystems in which they occur, and the ecological and evolutionary processes that keep them functioning, yet ever changing and adapting."[10] At this point in time, the human race is causing the extinction of species and ecosystems on a scale and pace that is without precedent in the planet's history. There are strong moral, spiritual, political, biological and economic reasons to be concerned about this "death of birth," as one noted biologist has termed it. As Aldo Leopold pointed out more than fifty years ago, the first rule of intelligent tinkering is to keep all the parts.

Not surprisingly, the maintenance and restoration of biodiversity has become the primary focus for conservationists and ecologists worldwide over the past fifteen to twenty years; however, it too is not as simple as it may appear. As Noss points out, "Humans can easily increase species richness or diversity locally and perhaps regionally by fragmenting the dominant vegetation cover and facilitating invasion of opportunistic species."[11] Clear-cuts have been shown to increase the number of species in an area by creating openings and edges for species not adapted to closed canopy forests; however, as an even-aged forest matures, it no longer provides suitable habitat for many of the pre- and post-disturbance species, and so they are displaced.

*Stability* is an equally challenging ecological concept. For a long time we have tended to think of ecosystems as stable, a perception reflected in such ideas as the "balance of nature." Yet, as ecological science is now proving, the natural world is far more complex. Says Daniel Botkin, a professor of biology at the University of California: "Change now appears to be intrinsic and natural at many scales of time and space in the biosphere. Nature changes over essentially all time scales, and in at least some cases these changes are necessary for the persistence of life, because life is adapted to them and depends on them."[12] A good example of this is forest ecosystems that are adapted to, and depend upon, fire to maintain their health. If nature is in constant flux, does that mean there is no such thing as stability? Most scientists agree that nature operates within specific limits. Hence nature can be thought of as having a kind of dynamic stability: constantly changing and yet remaining the same.

As with all the previous concepts, the term *naturalness* must be used very carefully when talking about ecological integrity. The key question here is: what kinds of human activities are natural and which are not? Since humanity first appeared on the planet, it has been modifying and changing nature. As a result, all of Canada's national parks have been influenced to varying degrees by human activity. Waterton Lakes National Park in Alberta was the site of aboriginal activity, including the setting of fires to maintain prairies, dating back thousands of years. In Kouchibouguac National Park, large open meadows are a silent reminder of the Acadian people who lived here and whose land was forcibly expropriated by the New Brunswick provincial government more than twenty years ago to make way for the new park. Long before this, the forests were intensively harvested to provide for the ship building industry and for early settlement in the region. More recently, with the advent of acid rain, climate change and the long-range transportation of pollutants, none of the national parks remains in a pure or pristine state.

By virtue of culture and technology, humans seem to have gained a high degree of independence from the natural world. Humans live in the perpetually frozen Antarctic or the inky depths of space for longer and longer periods of time. With the computer and the electronic microscope, we have begun to crack the code of life hidden in the double-helixed strands of DNA and RNA, and to play God by cutting and splicing sections together in radically different patterns. Genetically altered life forms, space stations and thermal clothing all contribute to the illusion of being able to escape the limitations imposed by nature. Humanity appears to have very nearly lost a sense of deep connectedness to nature. Lacking the wisdom, humility and respect that this bond invokes, humans are increasingly driving species and ecosystems to the point of collapse (think of the East Coast cod or the West Coast salmon) and, in so doing, threatening our own well-being and survival. Surely this is "unnatural," even "mad" or "psychotic."[13]

The essence of nature is that it is a system of relationships in which no part takes precedence. Furthermore, as discussed above, this system fluctuates within a range that is generally conducive to the well-being of all the parts. Human-induced change, therefore, is natural to the degree that it respects the inherent worth of all other species and remains within the limits set by planetary and local ecosystems.

Last but not least, there is *wildness*. Webster's dictionary defines it as a state in which something grows or is produced independent of humans, in other words, not controlled, tamed or domesticated. More mundanely, it is the essential difference between a shopping mall and a wilderness area or between a cow and a grizzly bear. But the issue of control is a thorny one. Speaking about wilderness, Noss states: "I cannot agree that an area must be absolutely outside of human 'control' to possess integrity. Management is arguably a form of control, and many areas today require ecological management to maintain their native biodiversity and other 'natural' qualities, particularly when disturbance regimes and other natural processes have been disrupted."[14] York University professor of environmental studies Neil Evernden strongly disputes this position, contending that any management of wild animals or lands, whether to protect or to use, however wisely, is a form of domestication. "Wildness is not 'ours,'" he says. "Indeed, it is the one thing that can *never* be ours. It is self-willed, independent, and indifferent to our dictates and judgments. An entity with the quality of wildness is its own, and no other's."[15] He elaborates:

> Wildness, however, lies beyond the objects in question, a quality which directly confronts and confounds our designs. At root, it is *wildness* that is at issue: not wilderness, not polar bears, not whooping cranes or Bengal tigers, but that which they as individuals exemplify. These creatures are "made of" wildness, one might say, before they are made of tissue or protein. But perhaps even wildness is an inadequate term, for that essential core of otherness is inevitably nameless, and as such cannot be subsumed within our abstractions or made part of the domain of human willing.[16]

In the end, wildness can only be encountered and experienced, a theme echoed by John Livingston, a former colleague of

Evernden. Wildness, for him, is felt as "a tingling, prickling, participatory rekindling of the flesh."[17]

Ideally, wildness should be left to take care of its own affairs. Hence, I support a hands-off approach as suggested by Evernden wherever possible. However, I also recognize that humans can and do radically disturb natural systems thus necessitating, at times, hands-on intervention for the protection and restoration of wild lands and species. Therefore, I advocate a middle path that draws on whatever approach or combination of approaches ensures the greatest restoration and maintenance of wildness. At all times, our actions should be in congruence with the limits of our knowledge of what constitutes "right management," and with respect for the inherent sacredness of wildness.

As can be seen from the above discussion, ecological integrity is very complicated. There is no single "right" definition. However, enough is known for Parks Canada and the Canadian public to act in accord with the essence of ecological integrity when making decisions that affect our natural parks.

Let's return to Kouchibouguac National Park to gain an appreciation for the complexity and severity of this crisis. Several years ago, my wife, Dianne, and I toured the park with two park employees. They were keen on showing us the Tern Islands in the Saint Louis Lagoon. We climbed into an open runabout, which our guide eased away from the dock and swung towards the mouth of the Saint Kouchibouguac River, where the lagoon lay glistening in the sun.

After about a half-hour's ride, we slowly approached the islands, hundreds of common tern whirling and screeching over our heads. The colony is one of the largest in North America. Although the birds are not considered endangered, biologists have noted a worldwide decline in the species and have linked it to the invasion of breeding areas by gulls, which are becoming more numerous owing to the large amounts of garbage being generated by humans. About fifteen years ago, a colony of herring and great blackback gulls established themselves on a dune near the Tern Islands. Within five years, the colony had quadrupled in size, from 50 to 210 nests.[18] They increased by another 22 percent in the following year, but by then they had attracted the attention of some foxes, which moved into the dunes and quickly reduced the gull population to zero. Needless to say, the gulls never returned, but instead sought out more isolated islands on which to nest and breed.

In 1988, for the first time, one of their nests was spotted on Tern Island. Since then, their numbers have grown. "If they become too numerous, they could displace the terns altogether," one guide said as he piloted the boat among the shifting channels that lay alongside the island. "Trouble is, there is no other place in the park as well suited for the terns, especially given the constant pressure to make more dunes and islands accessible to park visitors."

The waters off the coast of Kouchibouguac are the warmest found anywhere north of the state of Georgia. As a consequence, thousands of people flock to the park each summer for the surf and sand. Not only do they inadvertently displace shorebirds from the beaches, but they also trample and damage the fragile dune ecosystem. To give the swimmers and sunbathers access to the beaches, Parks Canada built a boardwalk across a salt marsh and lagoon. The structure cuts these sensitive habitats into two smaller pieces, making them less effective in protecting birds and animals. Despite these known impacts, some park managers want to construct more boardwalks to other dunes and beaches to accommodate the ever increasing demand for more beach access. In addition, there is intense pressure to expand the park's campgrounds. One of the campground attendants told me that she and her co-workers turned away as many as two hundred vehicles a day during the peak summer months. While the construction of more campsites may relieve that pressure, it will put more stress on the park's ecosystems and species.

Swinging past Tern Island one last time before heading back upriver to the dock, I thought of how many times I had heard park staff vent their frustration that many managers were all too quick to put human needs above ecological protection. I recalled one park ecologist telling me: "The greatest threat to the park is management at all levels, which lacks a vision in harmony with maintaining ecological integrity. The pressure to develop is ever present, resulting in scarce dollars being spent on things which run counter to protection, such as new bridges, boardwalks, campgrounds or bicycle paths. Meanwhile, ecosystem science remains underfunded."

Later, as we were approaching the dock, our guide listed the threats to Kouchibouguac's ecological integrity: poor management decisions, adjacent land uses such as forestry, agriculture and peat bog harvesting as well as commercial fishing and clam harvesting.

As with Kouchibouguac, there is no one single cause of the decline in ecological integrity or wildness within Canada's national parks. Rather, the crisis arises from what can best be described as "death by a thousand cuts." Nowhere is this process made clearer than in the State of the Parks reports. Although there is some dispute among scientists and managers about the methods used to collect and interpret the data that provides the basis for the reports, there is very little disagreement over the general findings and conclusions.

The 1997 State of the Parks report lists exotic species, climate change, acid rain and heavy-metal pollution as some of the global threats to ecological integrity. Forestry, agriculture and mining are the most serious threats arising from adjacent land use, being linked to habitat loss and fragmentation, species loss, and significant negative impacts to air and water quality. Utility and transportation corridors are a source of significant ecological impact within twenty-five national parks, while urbanization is affecting twenty-four. Tourism and visitor service development, both inside and outside of park boundaries, however, wins the dubious distinction of being the greatest threat, implicated in the decline of ecological integrity in twenty-six national parks.

What about the issue of park management and infrastructure? The 1997 State of the Parks report indicates that the former is a significant problem in nineteen national parks, while the latter exerts a negative influence in eleven. However, based on my discussions with park staff, I would put the numbers much higher. The discrepancy probably arises because of a tendency within Parks Canada to filter out potentially bad news as it is passed up the organization's hierarchy. This is not conjecture on my part; I was told this by several park staff close to the State of the Parks reporting process.

There are still many instances of management decisions running counter to the requirement to maintain ecological integrity. In Wood Buffalo National Park, for example, the federal government and senior bureaucrats within Parks Canada recently buckled under pressure from local politicians to allow the construction of a winter road through the heart of the park. It is feared that this toe in the door will lead to a permanent, all-season road. Not only does the road carve up the vast tract of wilderness, but it also presents a greater opportunity for development of facilities which further fragment habitat. At Prince Edward Island National Park, Parks Canada and a land developer have jumped into bed together to construct an interpretive centre and forty-room hotel with associated shops on land very close to a sensitive dune ecosystem known as the Greenwich Dunes. The year before this arrangement was made, the dunes were transferred from provincial Crown land to Parks Canada to be added to the national park. To the horror of the local environmental groups, Parks Canada almost immediately began to develop the dunes for greater visitor use.

Why does Parks Canada behave in ways that are inconsistent with the mandate of "maintaining ecological integrity," as required by the National Parks Act and the National Parks Policy? Part of the problem can likely be attributed to the necessity to generate revenue to offset the debilitating effects of escalating budget cuts over the past fifteen years. This is a perspective shared by park advocates like Sharon Labchuk of Earth Action. Her group is one of those that worked hard to have the Greenwich Dunes bought and added to

Prince Edward Island National Park. "We're quite worried that with cutbacks to the Parks Canada budget, unqualified staff persons are making decisions that generate revenue through inappropriate and excessive development, which results in compromising nature protection," she told me. Her views echo those expressed by parks staff throughout the system. "There is a huge focus on promoting and increasing visitor use in the off-seasons and to keep people in the park longer," said one visitor services officer in Atlantic Canada. "The rationale is to increase revenue." A park warden in Western Canada bitterly acknowledged: "There is extreme pressure to generate revenue, which overshadows the mandate of maintaining ecological integrity. It's rarely stated, but we feel it all the time." These are not the opinions of whiners or troublemakers, as some senior managers have labelled them; rather, they are the clarion calls of dedicated staff who see the damage being done by running the national parks as if they were a business.

However, the roots of Parks Canada's inconsistent actions go much deeper. As a park ecologist summed it up: "There are essentially two schools of management philosophy within Parks Canada. The old school favours use and development while the new school believes in controlling and even decommissioning development, where appropriate and possible." The members of the old school, he said, tended to rise through the ranks with an operations and maintenance background, while the new breed were most often recent employees who were well educated in the sciences. What he suggested was the presence of a profound split deep within Parks Canada over critical questions concerning the organization's purpose and core values. This theme has come up time and again with other park staff elsewhere in the system, and among park advocates and wildlife biologists.

The expectations for Parks Canada are unquestionably very high. The organization has been entrusted with the care of something extremely important and irreplaceable. J.B. Harkin, the organization's first commissioner, believed that the Dominion Parks

Branch (the name of the organization at the time) should demonstrate leadership in the protection of wild lands and wildlife, a tradition reflected in current National Parks Policy. The second most important guiding principle in it, after maintaining ecological integrity, is leadership by example and by "demonstrating and advocating environmental and heritage ethics and practices . . ."[19] By embracing this principle, Parks Canada reinforces our high expectations, but it only does a fair job of meeting them. Regrettably, the glaring examples of compromised principles overshadow and set back the successes achieved in protecting and restoring park ecosystems and species.

Parks Canada's inconsistencies are not all of its own making; some of the compromises are forced upon the organization by larger political and public agendas. Since the mid-1980s there has been a hard swing to the right in reaction to a perceived national financial crisis. The majority of Canadians and their elected representatives have eagerly embraced an ideology of running government like a business in order to improve the bottom line by reducing the national debt and deficit. As a result, Parks Canada, like many other departments, has been subjected to massive budget cuts, forcing it to reduce some programs and generate revenue to support others. In addition, the organization is under intense pressure from a government intent on boosting tourism as a means of encouraging the expenditure of desirable foreign currencies in this country.

Like Parks Canada, the Canadian public appears to be philosophically dysfunctional on issues concerning national parks. On the one hand, they proudly profess their love for them; on the other, they have been accused of loving the parks to death. Nowhere is this more acutely true than in Banff National Park, as we shall see in the next chapter. The problem of overuse is a function of the number of visitors and the kinds of activities they engage in within a park. Too many visitors seem to expect all the amenities of home, including stores, restaurants, movie theatres, golf courses, tennis courts, gas stations and the best accommodation they can afford, and to be able to drive, boat or hike wherever and whenever they want.

Around and beyond the national park boundaries, Canadians are rapidly converting unprotected landscapes into tree farms, ranches, farms, mines and subdivisions in the relentless pursuit of greater economic prosperity. The net effect has been to reduce the national parks to islands of wildness in a vast landscape of domestication. However, they are too small, too few, too isolated and too fragmented to adequately protect the ecosystems and species found within their boundaries.

Sadly, the majority of Canadians are not even aware that there is a crisis within the national parks, nor do they know how their individual choices contribute to this crisis. The lack of awareness is perpetuated by the fact that everything *looks* fine. The parks still appear beautiful and seem to contain plenty of wild animals. Furthermore, Parks Canada is commonly believed to be doing a good job of managing the parks. Appearances can be very deceiving, however. This is the insidious nature of a death by a thousand cuts. Because most Canadians don't see the slow and silent bleeding away of wildness and ecological integrity from the national parks, they haven't reacted in a meaningful way.

To its credit, the government responded in 1998 by appointing a panel of highly respected scientists to study the crisis. Called the Panel on Ecological Integrity, this group is "to assess the approach Parks Canada is taking to maintain the ecological integrity of Canada's national parks" and to "provide advice and recommendations on how to ensure that ecological integrity is maintained across the system . . ."[20] The panel was asked to examine in detail six key areas: programs, technology, partnerships, level of investment, integration and awareness. The panel chose to add two more: organizational culture and science. These additions have not sat well with some of the senior managers and executives of Parks Canada.

In conducting its assessment, the panel visited seven national parks and held regional consultations with Parks Canada staff, stakeholders and other scientists across the country. From my discussion with the panel when it held consultations in Vancouver, and from their newsletter and press releases I have strong reason to believe that their findings, which are likely to be made public slightly ahead of the publication of this book, will be in close harmony with my own assessment and conclusions.

It will be interesting to see what the government does with the panel's recommendations. If past history is any indication, such as with the Banff–Bow Valley Study, there is a tendency to "cherry-pick" the ones that are easiest to implement and to indefinitely defer the more difficult ones. This brings us back to the crucial role that the Canadian public can, and indeed must, play in the maintenance and restoration of ecological integrity to the national parks. As J.B. Harkin fully understood more than sixty years ago: "What is needed in Canada today is an informed public opinion which will voice an indignant protest against any vulgarization of the beauty of our National Parks or any invasion of their sanctity. Negative or passive good-will that does nothing is of little use. We need 'fierce loyalties' to back action."[21] Only a strong constituency of public support will ensure that the government follows through with the panel's recommendations. The responsibility for maintaining ecological integrity cannot rest solely with the government or Parks Canada; they cannot do the job alone. If our national parks are to remain wild, then all Canadians must come to recognize how they share in this responsibility.

This will not be an easy goal to achieve. Not only do most Canadians not perceive a problem with the national parks, but they also harbour deeply held values and beliefs that conflict with those needed to maintain ecological integrity. These values and beliefs are a throwback to the Enlightenment period in Western history, a time when humanity's connection with the natural world was severed. Stan Rowe, one of Canada's leading plant ecologists and one of the country's wisest environmental thinkers, describes this way of thinking: "Back then, nature was divested of mind and soul and rendered at once dead and menacing."[22] This idea leaves nature devoid of any inherent value and open for exploitation. "The sole basis for ethical action is the greatest good for the greatest number of people. The values of all things lie only in their ability to serve us."[23] This "people first" or anthropocentric view of the world provokes this rebuttal from Rowe: "As long as we see ourselves as the centre of creation we will rationalize our proclivities to use, waste and destroy whatever parts of the world our technology qualifies as 'resources.' Only recognition of the world's inherent and exceptional worth can rescue the world from its most pushy creation."[24] This latter world view—the ecocentric—assigns the highest priority to the Earth. "The fundamental reason for preserving whatever wildness remains on land and in water is the symbolism of the act," continues Rowe, "the implicit recognition of values beyond humanity, something other than ourselves that ought not to be destroyed, an expression of wonder and awe before the marvelous world that created us and that, once gone, we cannot recreate."[25]

Like Rowe, I am utterly convinced that nothing less than a shift in world views is necessary to maintain and restore the ecological integrity of our national parks. I am equally certain that such a shift in fundamental values can be facilitated at both the individual and societal level. What is called for is a new kind of education, one that engages people in a self-directed process of inquiry and reflection on their relationship with the planet and with all other life forms. With such an approach they can move through the difficult process of uncovering deeply held values and engaging in the work of transforming them in accordance with an environmental ethic.

I am hopeful that this new approach to environmental education can be developed and effectively applied to the crisis within our national parks. Among the nations of the world, Canadians stand out as having been most strongly marked by the wild. Its presence is felt, albeit ever more faintly with the passing of time, deep within our individual and collective psyches. As long as wildness persists in the land and seas of Canada, and in the hearts and minds of Canadians, there is hope.

# The Battle Never Won

Every time I return to Banff, I am increasingly disturbed by the changes I see. If any single park can be said to be hemorrhaging the most from overuse and development within its boundaries, it's got to be Banff. On my most recent trip I suddenly came upon the high steel mesh fences designed to keep wildlife off the Trans-Canada Highway near Castle Mountain. I already knew that the freshly twinned, four-lane highway was being fenced, but I had no idea it had progressed this far from the park's east gate, more than fifty kilometres away. While the fence will reduce the number of animals injured or killed by the never-ending stream of vehicles hurtling through the park, this benefit is countered by the fact that the fence also contributes to the erosion of the park's ecological integrity.

As a growing number of biologists now recognize, roads, fences and railway lines—all present within Banff's Bow Valley—carve up the landscape into smaller and smaller islands of wildness. As these shrinking islands become more cut off from each other by resource extraction activities such as logging or mining (a process referred to as *insularization*), wildlife populations almost always collapse. With the free flow of individual animals, each with its unique genetic inheritance, impeded, and forced to compete for less available habitat, these populations become vulnerable to natural or human-caused disruptions.

Pulling off the highway and entering the townsite from the west, I passed by the Brewster/Greyhound bus terminal, a relatively new building constructed only fifteen years ago. Continuing south, I noticed a string of even more recently constructed hotels, but nothing prepared me for the shock when I turned the corner. There before me was an entire new block of stores and commercial services that hadn't been there just a couple of years before. Across the street stood a hotel so new that its rustic, peeled-log motif looked as though it had just been finished a few days before. A sign proclaimed it as part of the Brewster empire. I parked my car and walked down a once familiar street in stunned silence. To my left I passed a multi-storey modern car park, while in front of me towered another peeled-log structure of contemporary design incorporating steel and glass. A sign declared that it was the town administration office.

Overwhelmed by the changes in the commercial section, I returned to my car and drove through the residential areas. In every corner of the town, new single-family homes, townhouses and staff accommodations had sprung up, and in the southwest corner of the town I encountered several new subdivisions freshly hewn from the forested slope above the Cave and Basin hot springs, the very ones that were the primary reason for the creation of Banff National Park more than 110 years ago. Partially completed houses attested to the town of Banff's rapidly growing human population.

From the moment of its conception in 1883, when two construction workers with the Canadian Pacific Railway saw the economic potential of a few hot springs bubbling out of the base of Sulphur Mountain, the resort of Banff has achieved remarkable success as a year-round international tourist destination. Barely two years after a 26-square-kilometre federal reserve was established around the hot springs in 1885 to keep them from falling into the hands of developers or settlers, the resort and surrounding park were already attracting 3,000 visitors a year. By 1903, just sixteen years later, that number had grown to 10,000. In 1905 and 1906, it came close to doubling and then doubling again, swelling to over 30,000.[1] Most recent estimates put the annual visitation to Banff National Park at nearly 5 million.[2] During the peak summer months, as many as 60,000 people may be found within its boundaries on any given day. Over the past ten years, annual visitation has been growing by approximately 2.5 percent each year, and if present trends continue, it will hit 19 million in 20 years![3] The majority of visitors are Canadians, mostly from Alberta and British Columbia, but along Banff townsite's main street can be heard the banter of Americans, Japanese and Europeans, any time of the year.

As the flood of tourists has risen, so has the level of development within Banff townsite. Between 1986 and 1996, retail space grew by 104 percent and office space by 125 percent.[4] In 1986 there were nearly 600 businesses; by 1996 the number had grown to almost 900.[5] While the largest commercial-space category remains visitor accommodation in the form of hotels, motels and bed and breakfasts; shops and restaurants are not far behind. A visitor can purchase just about any product or service in Banff, from exotic furs to fine dining. In fact, the townsite offers a range of consumer options comparable to a city four times its size.[6]

The rapid growth in visitor facilities and services has been paralleled by an equally dramatic increase in the number of people living within Banff. According to official policy, devised to control what was widely perceived as runaway growth, only current employees and retirees who are or were employed within Banff National Park, along with their dependants, should reside in the park.[7] Despite this, the townsite's population of permanent and temporary or seasonal residents has risen to more than 7,500 by 1996 from about 5,000 in 1986, representing an annual average increase of 5 percent. If one takes an even longer-term perspective, say back to 1950, when the population was barely 2,400, then the rate of growth would be nearly 7 percent per year. No matter how you slice it, Banff townsite has become the largest community in any North American national park.[8]

Sir John A. Macdonald, the prime minister who created the original small reserve around the hot springs, would be staggered by Banff's success as an international destination and as a lucrative source of revenue for the government. In 1886, he and several members of his government accepted a complimentary ride on the CPR's freshly minted cross-Canada line. After his tour through the Canadian Rockies and a visit to the fledgling resort of Banff, Macdonald enthused:

> I do not suppose in any portion of the world there can be found a
> spot, taken all together, which combines so many attractions and
> which promises in as great degree not only large pecuniary
> advantage to the Dominion, but much prestige to the whole
> country by attracting the population, not only of the continent, but
> of Europe, to this place. It has all the qualifications necessary to
> make it a great place of resort.[9]

This was the original vision for Canada's first national park: it was to be for play and profit.

And profits Banff generates by the bundle. In 1995 more than $700 million were spent in the park, from which all levels of government extracted nearly $230 million in tax revenues.[10] But the people who are benefiting the most are the developers. Because the boundaries of Banff are fixed under the National Parks Act, and because demand exceeds supply, they can charge ludicrous amounts of money for commercial or residential space. A new single-family home typically sells for more than $500,000, while ten- to twenty-year-old houses can fetch as much as $450,000.

Banff's success as an international tourist destination has come at a mounting cost to the community and to the park, a trend that has angered long-time resident and former businesswoman Jos

Storm for many years. We first met several years ago, when my wife, Dianne, sold some of her work to Storm, who owned and operated the Quest, a high-quality arts and crafts store on the lower end of Banff Avenue, near the bridge over the Bow River. I took an instant liking to her; she exuded an unbounded energy and enthusiasm for life that was refreshing and inspiring. As a consequence I made it a point to look her up whenever I visited Banff. On this trip I found her particularly annoyed.

"Look at this town," she exclaimed, pointing out new buildings, malls and additions while setting a brisk pace along the busy noon-hour sidewalk. "It's changing and growing so fast, I hardly know it any more." Storm is not the only one who feels this way. The 1998 community plan revealed that the majority of residents believed the town was "out of balance" and "too many visitors, too much traffic, and too much commercial growth" were eroding "the very attributes that give Banff its unique character and sense of place."[11] "The problem seems to be that there are a few people who care more about making money than about the town or the park," Storm emphasized as we sat eating our soup and salad.

After a leisurely lunch with Storm, I drove over to the warden's compound on the northeastern edge of town to meet with Cliff White, the park's conservation biologist. If anyone could fill me in on what was happening with the park under the flood of visitors and development, I figured he would be the one who could do so. White was born and raised in Banff, and has worked for Parks Canada since 1973. After stints in Yoho and Ottawa, he returned to Banff National Park as the assistant chief warden in 1990. In 1996 he took over his current position.

Just before pulling up in front of the compound, I passed a small herd of elk grazing contentedly alongside the road. I had heard how common they had become around Banff, but nothing prepared me for how common and for the problems they were causing.

White appeared shortly after I introduced myself at the front desk and led me through a maze of cubicles and hallways to his office. He offered me a chair and a cup of coffee, while he cleared his desk so he could focus his attention on our discussion. He began to paint a very disturbing picture of the park. The large number of elk that I had observed in and around the townsite, far from being an indication of a healthy ecosystem, were actually a sign of an ecosystem in disarray. White estimated close to eight hundred elk now resided around the townsite; that's a density ten times higher than historic levels. "We call them the 'Banff Blob,'" he said as we studied a map of elk distribution in the Bow Valley from Lake Louise to the park's east gate, "and they are having a profound impact on the ecosystem and other species."

White and his colleagues first became alarmed when they noticed the declining vigour of aspen stands, one of the elk's pre-ferred food sources, around the Banff townsite. The animal, it quickly appeared, was eating itself and many other wildlife species literally out of house and home. Tender shoots, seedlings and branches were being consumed as fast as they grew, leaving only the old trees standing. In the Vermilion Lakes, the number of beaver lodges had declined by 90 percent since the 1970s, as aspen suitable for the beaver's food and dam-building materials has grad-ually vanished. The elk were even threatening their large, less gregarious cousin, the moose. "The habitat is so over-browsed by the elk," White explained, "that there is nothing left for the moose. There are no full-time resident moose in the lower Bow Valley any more." And who knows how many songbirds or small mammals were also suffering because of the exploding elk population.

The process by which this ecological crisis has unfolded is com-plex and subtle. Nevertheless, ecological research indicates that it is human-caused in at least a couple of important ways. "We used to have two wolf packs in the area," said White grimly, "but now there are maybe only one or two individuals." Several have been killed on the Trans-Canada Highway or CPR line, while others have moved away to avoid humans, whom they associate with danger. (The following spring, I read of the tragic death of the last wolf in the lower Bow Valley; she was another victim of the highway.) In the absence of predation, the elk have multiplied and become increasingly bold, grazing on the lush grass lawns in the townsite while also stripping the surrounding forests of any edible aspen.

There is a public safety concern related to this ecological problem. As the elk have become more numerous and nervy, there has been a worrisome rise in threatening encounters between humans and this large and potentially dangerous animal. Incidents of elk–human conflicts have risen dramatically, from "three in 1987 to a high of 75 in 1991," according to one Parks Canada study.[12] Needless to say, this is not acceptable to the organization, residents or tourists. As a consequence, aggressive elk have had their antlers shorn to reduce the risk of injury, and an education campaign has been initiated to warn people of the dangers of getting too close. Meanwhile, White and his co-workers are seeking ways to attract predators back into the region to naturally control the elk.

As for the possible reintroduction of fire into the lower Bow Valley to stimulate regeneration of aspen, this idea has been decisively ruled out for the time being because the elk quickly moved into a prescribed burn area and mowed down the new suckers about as fast as they sprang from the roots of charred stumps.

The problem is much bigger, however, than just an excessive number of elk taking refuge in and around the townsite. "The Bow Valley is a wildlife sink," White lamented. "We are simply losing too many animals from the corridor. Grizzly bears, for example, once resided in the lower Bow Valley, but now only the occasional one wanders through." His concern stems from the fact that the valley provides the best wildlife habitat in the park—it experiences less snow and warmer temperatures, and has lusher vegetation than the higher elevations that make up most of the park—yet very little remains intact. Known as *montane*, this critically important low-elevation ecosystem comprises less than 5 percent of the park's 6,640 square kilometres. Of this, more than 20 percent has been destroyed by the presence of Banff townsite, highways, rail lines, picnic sites, campgrounds and the like.[13] Even more disturbing, over half of it has been rendered ineffective in providing suitable habitat and protecting wildlife due to fragmentation and human use.

"What's critical here is that we find some way to restore the lower Bow Valley to ecological health," said White as I was about to leave. "We are making some headway. We now have a corridor near town closed to human use, which will hopefully allow large carnivores to begin controlling the elk, and we also have a couple of overpasses to allow wildlife to safely cross the Trans-Canada Highway. But there is still a huge problem looming with day use. With as many as sixty thousand people a day coming into the park during the summer and as many as thirty thousand in the winter, there are simply too many people and too many vehicles." His grim prediction is that by 2020, visiting Banff National Park will be like going to watch a football game: first you will have to buy a ticket to enter the stadium, and not everyone who wants in will get a ticket.

Banff is not the only national park suffering serious ecological impacts due to growth and development inside its boundaries. More than half of the thirty-nine national parks are experiencing similar problems. Each year in Riding Mountain National Park, more than 60 million litres of sewage from the Wasagaming townsite is pumped through a treatment facility designed to handle 21 million litres, with the excess spilling over into a nearby lake.[14] This lake and a small creek associated with the sewage lagoon feed Clear Lake, the park's largest lake and main attraction, with nitrogen- and phosphate-rich waters, triggering concerns about alga blooms. Water quality studies have also revealed elevated levels of chlorine in the lake, probably due to chlorinated drinking water reaching the sewers. If the levels of chlorine become too high, it could cause a serious decline in aquatic plants, invertebrates and fish. My mother, who has known it since her birth, says there has already been a significant decline: she no longer sees crayfish or clam as she once did. The lake has recently begun to be monitored.

Making matters worse, the number and size of boats on Clear Lake has reached a crisis point, causing park ecologists to worry about chemical contamination as well as disturbance of the lake's resident loon population.

In Cape Breton Highlands National Park, a 1993 study found that park infrastructure and activities were "increasingly at odds with the normal evolution" of Clyburn Brook.[15] Of particular concern were the impacts associated with the Highlands Links golf course; these included habitat loss and fragmentation, irrigation drawdown, which reduces the amount of water available for fish and other species, and the use of pesticides and herbicides. Very little is known about the combined effects of the eight different pesticides the golf course uses to stay green and weed-free. Individually, they have been shown to have negative impacts on terrestrial and aquatic ecosystems, to persist in sediments, to build up in the food chain and to develop resistance in plants and insects generally regarded as pests. The golf course also contributes substantially to habitat loss within the park's already threatened Acadian Forest region. The same 1993 study stated that "understory vegetation and dead timber" are routinely cleared from "forested areas adjacent to the fairways in order to make it easier for golfers to retrieve wayward balls."[16] Unfortunately, this action also destroys or degrades critical habitat for songbirds and small mammals.

As mentioned in the previous chapter, in Kouchibouguac National Park there is an ever increasing demand for more recreational access to the beaches. At the same time, there are equally strong concerns about how visitor use impacts on the park's ecosystems and species. The beaches provide crucial nesting habitat for the endangered piping plover; the dunes are susceptible to blowouts and slumping caused by trampling feet; and the boardwalks encourage the succession of the lagoons from open water to saltwater marshes.

Of Jasper National Park's 11,000 square kilometres, less than 7 percent is montane and more than half of it has been destroyed or degraded by the hamlet of Jasper, facilities, roads and rails. As in Banff National Park's Bow Valley, these developments are pinching off the crucial flow of wildlife through Jasper's three principal valleys.

The situation in Banff National Park had already become so bad by the early 1990s that it was in danger of losing its status as a national park.[17] Prompted by a potential international embarrassment, the federal government announced the creation of a special task force in the spring of 1994 to study the crisis in the Banff–Bow Valley Corridor and to make recommendations for its improvement. The task force consisted of five individuals with recognized expertise in ecological sciences, tourism, public policy and management, and it utilized a multi-stakeholder round table, numerous public information meetings across the country and copious ecological, economic and social research. After two years of intense discussion and reflection, the task force submitted its report to Sheila Copps, the Minister of Canadian Heritage.

Entitled "Banff–Bow Valley: At the Crossroads," the report presented the plain, unvarnished truth behind the park's misery. "While Parks Canada has clear and comprehensive legislation and policies, Banff National Park suffers from inconsistent application of the *National Parks Act* and Parks Canada's policy," the task force stated. "Despite the fact that ecological integrity is the primary focus of the *National Parks Act* and Parks Canada policy, we have found that ecological integrity has been, and continues to be increasingly compromised."[18] Indeed, the report went on to state, "We believe Banff National Park is clearly at a crossroads and changes must be made quickly if the Park is to survive."[19] Even more worrisome, it added, "If this crisis is not resolved in Banff, it will spread throughout the entire national park system."[20]

In the task force's opinion, the reasons for Parks Canada's inconsistency and loss of control over development in Banff came down to two key things: money and values. Since the early 1980s, Parks Canada had been hit with an escalating series of budget cuts, the most devastating being a 25 percent reduction commencing in 1995 and spread over five years. To offset the impact on programs and personnel, the organization engaged in an aggressive campaign to double the revenue generated by the national parks—from $35 million to $70 million—through such things as new user fees and corporate sponsorships. To the task force, this direction represented a profound shift from a public service to a business ethos, and created the danger of the protection of ecological integrity being sacrificed to the need for revenue generation.

The task force also observed that changes were occurring "at a pace faster than the organization's ability to adapt" and were affecting "its focus and, at times, its effectiveness."[21] At the time, one of the biggest changes was the move towards establishing Parks Canada as a special operating agency. Something akin to a Crown corporation, this new status would give the organization greater flexibility in generating and spending revenue.

The task force also identified problems with the organization's ability to implement open and shared decision making involving the public. Based on my own research, I strongly agree with the task force's analysis as far as it goes. However, the crisis *has already* spread throughout the system, and the roots of the problem go much deeper than they suggest.

To address the urgent crisis in the Banff–Bow Valley, the task force presented the government with more than five hundred recommendations, many of them very controversial, such as fencing the town of Banff and all campgrounds accessible by vehicle, reducing or capping human use in key areas, constructing wildlife overpasses along the Trans-Canada and removing horse corrals and airstrips near the Banff townsite. Taken together, the recommendations were perceived by some as an indication that people were no longer welcome in the park or town. Nevertheless, the task force was adamant. "There is no doubt of the urgency for action—work should begin immediately; a delay can lead to irreversible impact. There is no doubt about the need—simply put, it is saving the Park for future generations," they wrote. "There is no doubt about who has the responsibility to provide leadership—it is Parks Canada."[22] Ad hoc decision making had to come to an end, ushering in a new era in management—"one that puts the Park ahead of human needs and desires."[23]

It was possible, the task force found, to protect and even restore the ecological integrity of the Banff–Bow Valley and still provide opportunities for visitors to enjoy a world-class tourism destination. However, the key to achieving this harmony was very much dependent upon visitors and residents understanding Banff's ecosystems, the impacts on these ecosystems of inappropriate human use, and the urgency for change. According to the task force, if people fully comprehend these factors, they will be more willing to make the necessary changes in their attitudes and behaviours, and become more responsible and caring towards the park. Unfortunately, education, awareness and interpretation programs in Banff—indeed, throughout the entire system—had been the first victims of budget cuts, and were left so weakened that their ability to effect the necessary changes is questionable.

Upon the release of the Banff–Bow Valley Task Force report in the fall of 1996, the federal government, through deputy prime minister and minister of Canadian Heritage Sheila Copps, responded unequivocally. "Banff is the heart of our country's National Park System. And the Bow Valley is the heart of Banff," she proclaimed. "[It] is a place for nature . . . That means there are clear limits to growth." From now on, she promised, there would be "no new land made available for commercial development in Banff National Park." In addition, the government intended to legally designate key areas as "wilderness"; close and rehabilitate the airstrip, bison paddock and cadet camp; relocate public and park horse corrals; construct wildlife overpasses across the Trans-Canada Highway; cap the population of Banff at ten thousand; implement reservation systems for the most popular or fragile trails; and lastly, demand major revisions to the Banff National Park management plan.[24]

Reaction to her announcements was mixed. The environmental community was, for the most part, pleased. Said Kevin McNamee, conservation director for the Canadian Nature Federation: "While the decisions already announced are somewhat modest given the threats to the park, they signal a change in political attitude toward Banff, a swing that bodes well for its ecological future. It holds the promise of at least drawing a line against further development in the park, and the erosion of the philosophical underpinnings of Canada's national parks."[25] The general manager of the Banff Springs Hotel felt that the business leaders were onside. However, the president of an association representing the interests of the owners and users of Banff's three downhill ski areas wanted assurances that their interests would be considered and included in any implementation plans. The mayor of Banff townsite said that he could support the cap of ten thousand "as long as we are talking ballpark rather than counting individual heads."[26] The least supportive person was the Reform Party Heritage critic and MP for Kootenay West, Jim Abbott, who protested, "I think it absolutely goes too far. This report slams the gate on ordinary Canadians. I don't think it's fair and I don't think it's right."[27]

Despite protests from some quarters, the forces for change were gathering strength and momentum. A month after the release of the task force's study, Parks Canada received yet more criticism over their mismanagement, not just of Banff but of the entire system of national parks. This time the remarks came from no less than the Auditor General of Canada. In a special report to the House of Commons on how well they were doing at maintaining ecological integrity, the Auditor General found areas of concern. Management plans were either outdated or not completed. Those in place "emphasize social and economic factors over ecological factors," which could influence "decisions relating to the development of park facilities and the extension of commercial leases."[28] Essential ecological information was lacking, as were strategies to communicate information on ecological integrity. Throughout the national parks system, interpretive and public education programs had been slashed beginning in the early 1980s to meet federal government economic priorities for deficit and debt reduction. Meanwhile, Parks

Canada had embarked upon an aggressive marketing strategy to encourage more visitors for longer stays.

Copps reacted defensively, stating that the concerns over Parks Canada's ability to manage the national parks were already being dealt with. As evidence of her commitment, she tabled a new Banff Management Plan the following spring. "Today, we are putting Banff's future back on track," minister Copps declared. The plan incorporated most of the promises she had made upon release of the Banff–Bow Valley Task Force Study. For example, the horse corrals and bison paddocks would be closed, as would the airstrip. Two wildlife overpasses would be built, and a night-time voluntary closure of the Bow Valley Parkway would be implemented to encourage wildlife movement during the spring. The plan stopped short, however, of limiting the number of people visiting the park.

As for the cap on growth of Banff townsite, that proved to be decidedly more difficult to deal with. In June 1997, the mayor and his council passed an extremely controversial resolution to approve an additional 79,000 square metres (850,000 square feet) of commercial development, representing an increase of 25 percent over current levels. This was passed despite an earlier recommendation by a steering committee for only an additional 59,000 square metres (635,000 square feet), and against a backdrop of growing opposition to growth among the town's residents.[29] A month later, minister Copps sternly informed the mayor and council that the federal government would not approve the resulting community plan. Instead, it gave the town a 32,000-square-metre (345,000-square-foot) increase and made the commitment to legislate the boundaries of communities and commercial sections in all affected national parks. This would require them to accept two critical conditions intended to ensure the protection of each park's ecological integrity: "no net negative environmental impact" and "appropriate development and use."[30] Regrettably, these terms were left largely undefined; the best the government could offer was "a test of appropriateness" that included "need to be located in the community," "contribution to a vibrant heritage tourism industry" and, mixed within all the business concerns, "a permissible park activity."

Since the federal government maintains ultimate authority over the national parks and everything within them, the mayor and council were forced to capitulate, and nine months later submitted a revised community plan. A few days later, on June 26, 1998, Minister Copps and Secretary of State Andy Mitchell announced their approval of the plan and reaffirmed their commitment to amending the National Parks Act. "Today is a milestone in the protection of Canada's National Parks," heralded Mitchell. "Our decision arises out of a process started in 1996 with the Banff–Bow Valley Study, and confirms the federal government's larger commitment to one of the greatest national park systems in the world."[31]

The battle for Banff, between the forces of development and the forces of preservation, finally appeared to some to be over, with the latter being declared the victor. "It was a loud and clear 'stop' by the only government with the authority to do so; the only government able to say 'no' to further development of Banff National Park," applauded Catherine Ford, a Southam national columnist, in the *Calgary Herald*. "Canadians who have seen the tourist-trap horrors of Niagara Falls and what development has done to the natural beauty of Vancouver, don't need to be so-called environmentalists to want someone in authority to issue the halt order."[32]

But was the battle really over? Questions still lingered as to why the population of Banff was being allowed to grow to 10,000 and the commercial section by another 32,000 square metres. Leslie Taylor, a former acting superintendent of Banff National Park and the town's mayor for two terms, was very guarded in her assessment. "This sort of battle is never over," she told me, as we sat in her office in the Banff Centre for Mountain Culture. "The forces for development and growth have fallen back. So what we have, at the moment, is only a breather." She was willing to admit that some aspects of the situation were definitely improving, however. "There's been a fundamental shift occurring. A lot of people care about the park, and some important changes are being made." As evidence, she pointed out that the town now has an excellent sewage system; that salt is no longer used on roads, which creates a problem for wildlife; and that Banff has an excellent recycling program.

Mike McIvor, president of the Bow Valley Naturalists and a long-time resident of Banff, was not optimistic. "The battle for Banff will never be won," he asserted. "The pro-growth forces are simply waiting for minister Copps to move on or be moved on . . . I've simply seen too much over the past years to get too excited about the government's recent announcements." I was struck by the intense frustration that burned in his ice blue eyes and etched deep furrows across his weathered brow. "The direction from the minister is very clear, but I think that too many senior managers still don't get it."

As proof, he ran down a list of things that minister Copps said would be done but which Parks Canada had not yet begun to implement or had found ways to get around. The airstrip had been closed, but it was still being maintained rather than restored to wildlife habitat. Draft guidelines for the development and operation of ski areas and outlying commercial areas, such as the lodges and cabins at Johnson Creek or Castle Mountain, were too loose. And then there was the recent approval of an expansion of Château Lake Louise.

Canadian Pacific Hotels had been given approval from Parks Canada for a $45-million expansion of the hotel. The new seven-storey addition would feature a meeting room for 700 people, a 250-person dining area and 80 more rooms. The company wants to boost its business during the slower months by catering to the "incentive travel" market, in which companies reward valued employees, contractors and customers with free trips. Biologists worry that the extra people and development will result in more damage to the surrounding ecosystem and further displacement of large carnivores, such as the grizzly bear.

"Here is an agency [Parks Canada] so accustomed to saying the right thing but not being very good at walking the talk," was

McIvor's final assessment. "They just don't know how to say no, and instead are allowing continual incremental development."

McIvor's critical appraisal of Parks Canada's inconsistent behaviour came back to haunt me several months after the trip to Banff. I had heard of the death of the last wolf in the lower Bow Valley and of carnivor specialist Paul Paquet's intention to sue the organization over it, so I gave Paquet a call to confirm this information. "You've heard correctly," he declared. "The lawsuit will involve the failure of Parks Canada to maintain ecological integrity in Banff. The wolves are just victims of this failure but do represent the 'canary in the gold mine.' Other species are equally in serious trouble." Paquet firmly believes that the failure results from "wilful neglect and dereliction of duty," as required under the National Parks Act, by senior managers, who do not hold park values and have only a superficial understanding of ecology. Paquet asserts that the organization is "philosophically corrupt." "These are people who are more concerned about not pissing off some interest group than about advancing ecological integrity," he raged. "They call this 'social jeopardy.' I call it a violation of sacred trust."

What Paquet wants is nothing less than the removal of a few key senior managers, who he is convinced should be held accountable for the crisis in Banff and the rest of the national parks. Sheila Copps, the minister responsible for the national parks, has personally asked him to hold off on the lawsuit until after the government has received the Panel on Ecological Integrity's report.

His last words were spoken with such incredible emotional intensity that they burned deep into my consciousness. "Somehow, we have got to wake up the Canadian public to the fact that the problems in Banff are not acne. It's cancer, and the park is slowly dying. Something drastic has to be done to save not only this park, but all the parks from overuse and mismanagement."

A light drizzle gave way to a blizzard of wet snow outside my office window as I hung up the phone. In the silence that followed, I struggled to remain hopeful about the future of Banff.

While Parks Canada was taking steps to protect and restore the park's damaged ecosystem, it was clear that much more needed to be done, and quickly, to address the issues of overuse and mismanagement—not only in Banff but throughout the national parks system. The Banff–Bow Valley Task Force said it best. Parks Canada must demonstrate leadership and adopt an approach to management that puts park values ahead of human needs and desires. In addition, visitors and residents within the parks must also share in the responsibility of maintaining ecological integrity by adopting an ecologic ethic that encourages care and respect for wild species and places.

# THREE

# Trouble with the Neighbours

While Parks Canada has the legal authority to control use and development within national park boundaries, it has little power to address threats to ecological integrity arising from adjacent land use. In place of coercion, park staff must rely on good working relationships and influence with neighbouring municipalities, farmers, loggers, miners or land developers. Although there are many excellent examples of such relationships and of co-operative solutions to mutual problems, they are overshadowed by a general attitude of distrust between Parks Canada and local landowners that is found at nearly every national park. As a consequence, the threats to their ecological integrity continue to mount.

Perhaps one of the most instructive case studies within the national park system is Riding Mountain. An ecological island rising about 350 metres above the prairie landscape of southwestern Manitoba, the park clings to a tentative existence in a region that has undergone, and is still undergoing, dramatic change. Over the past few decades, farming, timber harvesting and recreational subdivisions have carved away the surrounding native ecosystems, leaving virtually every metre of the park's boundary sharply defined. Even though it is the fourth largest national park in southern Canada, encompassing about 3,000 square kilometres of boreal forest, aspen parkland and eastern deciduous forest, Riding Mountain is not large enough to protect ecosystems and species from the impacts of activities along its boundaries.

The rate of conversion from wild to domesticated landscape is staggering. The number of cattle within the region surrounding the park increased by 16 percent during the mid-1990s, while cropland in the same region increased by 27.5 percent from 1976 to 1986.[1] With the intensification of agricultural use around the park have come escalating conflicts between wildlife and local farmers. More than $110,000 was paid to farmers by the Manitoba Crop Insurance program in 1994–95 for damage to crops and hay bales by elk and deer, while bears inflicted an additional $13,000 of damage to beehives in 1995–96.[2] As well, irate farmers have been agitating for a control program on the park's beaver for decades. As one crusty old farmer neatly summed it up: "Why should I like the park? It breeds beaver that flood my fields, elk that eat my crops, bears that eat my honey and wolves that eat my cattle. The park is nothing but a damned liability to me."

Of all the species he mentioned, it is the wolf that is in the most serious trouble within Riding Mountain National Park. No single species illustrates the effects of increasing insularization of the park better. Back in the early to mid-seventies, when I worked there as a naturalist, there were seven to ten packs totalling about seventy-five animals; when I visited the park a couple of years ago there were maybe thirty individuals. That's a drop of 60 percent. Biologists and park wardens are very concerned that the wolf population could collapse entirely, causing a major disturbance throughout the entire park ecosystem. Currently, the moose population numbers about 5,000 and elk hover around 4,500—very healthy populations, bordering on becoming too large for the habitat to support. If the wolf were to disappear from Riding Mountain, it is not inconceivable that its favoured prey—the moose and elk—would suddenly increase. This happened once before, with devastating and lasting effects on the park.

Back in 1929, the wolf returned to the Riding Mountain area after more than a hundred years of relentless persecution. At the time, there were about five hundred elk on the mountain; they too had suffered greatly from the effects of settlement in the region. To allow the elk population to recover, park wardens embarked upon an intensive poisoning program to eliminate the recently re-established wolf shortly after the national park was created in the early 1930s. Over the next ten to fifteen years, this simple (and in hindsight inexcusable) strategy was a phenomenal success: by the late 1940s there were more than seventeen thousand elk within the park. Then, just as park managers and their staff were congratulating themselves, the elk began dying from starvation, hundreds at a time. The habitat—the shrubs and plants that they depended on for food—was stripped clean. In desperation, the elk had even risen on their hind legs to nibble the bitter bark of mature aspen, something they do not normally eat. Not even an emergency distribution of hay bales could stop the massive die-off.

It has taken about half a century for the elk and the park to recover. During this time there have also been significant changes in how wildlife populations in parks are managed. So-called predator control programs, which targeted wolves, cougars and other carnivores, were halted in the mid-1960s, and management practices have steadily become more respectful of ecosystem and species dynamics. It is a potent mix of hindsight and state-of-the-art ecological knowledge, therefore, that has focused so much attention on the uncertainty surrounding the wolf's future in Riding Mountain.

One of the people most concerned over its survival is biologist Gloria Goulet. She has been studying the wolf at Riding Mountain for the past eight years, initially while working for Parks Canada as a park interpreter and later on contract to the organization as a researcher. She and I first met in February 1997, while I was on an assignment with *Equinox* gathering research for a feature article on the threats to the park's ecological integrity. "What's happening is pretty scary," she said. "There should be a lot more wolves, because there has been consistently high populations of prey . . . Mange could be a significant factor in the animal's decline," she speculated. "The disease was first observed among the coyotes of the park in 1986 and then detected in wolves in 1992." Mange, a mite infection that occurs periodically in wild canids, causes extreme itchiness that leads to hair loss and skin lesions from scratching. While not life-threatening, the disease can and does contribute to mortality when an infected wolf is subjected to cold weather or poor nutrition. Diseases are natural occurrences within wildlife populations, and in the absence of additional stressors the animals usually recover. But for the moment, the degree to which mange contributed to the wolves' decline remains unclear.

"Establishing the effects of mange is complicated by the fact that the wolves spend part of their time outside the park," Goulet said, "and what goes on [there] is random killing." In Manitoba, the wolf is classified as a big-game species and can be hunted by anyone possessing the proper licence. Hunters do not have to report killing a wolf unless they intend to sell or mount the hide. Farmers and ranchers also have the right to shoot wolves—and often do so when they perceive a threat to their livestock. Information on the number of wolves killed is too spotty to be useful. On top of these killings, the provincial government sets out poison baits as part of its predator control program. With a great deal of detective work, Goulet has established that the park has probably lost an average of twelve wolves a year over the past ten years due to these causes.

"Ultimately, everything comes down to attitudes toward the wolf," she said, "especially among the agricultural community around the park." A recent survey of residents and various interest groups in the Riding Mountain area appears to validate her perception. The survey uncovered a small but strong pocket of hatred directed towards the wolf from among the area landowners, trappers and outfitters. More than 25 percent of the outfitters, 18 percent of the trappers and 12 percent of the local landowners responded that they were not in favour of having wolves in the park. Moreover, when asked if they would try to kill a wolf if they saw one, nearly 40 percent of the outfitters, 32 percent of the trappers and 25 percent of the landowners said they would. What the results indicate is that, for the wolf to survive in Riding Mountain National Park, local landowners and residents have to be brought onside.

That imperative has not been lost on Goulet. Since 1995, she has been presenting educational programs to trappers, outfitters and landowners, as well as to the general public. She has also established a committee of local interest groups to address issues concerning wolf conservation, and created a livestock predation compensation fund. The aim of both actions is to generate greater tolerance—and perhaps understanding—for wolves that roam outside the park. Along with Terry Hoggins, a long-time veteran of the warden service, she has been lobbying the provincial government for the removal of the wolf from the big-game licence, and collecting DNA to test for genetic inbreeding among the wolves. This information is critical to determining if the isolated character of the park is a factor in the population's decline. This is of particular concern since extensive logging threatens to decimate the wildlife corridor between Riding Mountain and Duck Mountain Provincial Park, the closest area for immigrants. It may have been wolves from Duck Mountain that re-inhabited the national park more than fifty years ago.

Says Hoggins: "We are definitely having some success with the trappers. They are doing a 360-degree turnaround, and some landowners are coming onside too. But some old guys just don't want to change. If a wolf comes on their land, it's a dead wolf pretty quick."

Agriculture also poses significant threats to Riding Mountain's elk population. Recently, Manitoba's provincial government made elk ranching legal in an attempt to diversify the agriculture industry. It is a move that wardens fear will have severe biological consequences for Riding Mountain National Park. The province's cash-strapped farmers have great hope for the new industry. The allure is "green velvet," an early stage of antler growth that, when processed into powder for the Asian market, is worth as much as $275 a kilogram, or about $1,500 for a pair of antlers. A princely sum of money can also be made by selling elk. A bred cow may fetch up to $30,000, while a bull in prime condition can sell for $100,000. With potential returns such as these, the elk of Riding Mountain National Park are suddenly drawing a lot of attention.

"The elk found in the park are a unique subspecies, *manitobaensis*," warden Jonah Mitchell told me. "They are highly valuable for the spectacular antlers they produce . . . This elk-ranching thing has gotten out of hand," he continued. "Elk have been lured out of the park to be used for start-up herds, even by provincial government people."

To get the new "industry" rolling, provincial wildlife authorities in the region, under direction from their political bosses, set up a trap very close to the park's eastern boundary and then lured elk out to be trapped and shipped to designated ranchers (according to an article in the *Winnipeg Free Press,* all close friends of the party in power). In just two nights approximately seventy animals were captured, as park wardens later found out from people within the provincial wildlife branch who were angry and ashamed at what had taken place. Much to the chagrin of many of Riding Mountain's wardens, Parks Canada management decided not to confront the Manitoba government over either the abduction or the possible threats of elk ranching to the park's ecological integrity.

"We're very worried about the spread of a black market in live-captured elk taken from the park, the transmission of diseases from domesticated elk back into the wild elk, and interbreeding with other subspecies," Jonah Mitchell said. "All you need are one or two escapees of dubious heritage and you could see the dilution of the wild gene pool."

Elk ranching is not the only adjacent-land-use issue over which Parks Canada has been surprisingly reluctant to tussle with the Manitoba government. Back in the fall of 1994, the provincial government signed an agreement with the multinational forestry company Louisiana-Pacific (L-P), granting the company harvesting rights over an extraordinary 6,000 square kilometres immediately north of Riding Mountain National Park.[3] In an area greater in size than Prince Edward Island, the company will harvest 900,000 cubic metres annually, or about 2 million old-growth aspen trees over a ten-year period to feed its new oriented-strand-board plant near Swan River.[4] In return, L-P will pay the province a paltry 55 cents a tree.[5] During the environmental impact hearings for the granting of the harvesting rights, Parks Canada was noticeably absent, even though the resource extraction activity would have devastating impacts on a vital north–south wildlife corridor that links Riding Mountain to the Duck and Porcupine mountains. Instead, Parks Canada allowed other federal agencies to be the defenders of Riding Mountain's ecological integrity. Forestry Canada charged that the annual allowable cut was too high, while Environment Canada warned that protection of the region's biodiversity was not adequately addressed in the company's proposed management plan.

The many possible causes of Parks Canada's reluctance to address such adjacent land use issues will be dealt with in later chapters. For the moment, let me outline one other adjacent-land-use threat to Riding Mountain National Park.

As mentioned in the preface, I was born and raised on the southern edge of this national park in the early 1950s. At the time, the thick forest, along the boundary near my grandparents' home was dotted with the occasional farm. Today, most of the forests and farms are gone, having been replaced by recreational subdivisions that seem to have sprung up overnight like a fairy ring of mushrooms on one's lawn. This development reflects a desire to live close to nature for at least part of the year, but the sad irony is that the subdivisions are contributing to the further decline of Riding Mountain's ecological integrity.

In addition to impacts associated with contaminated groundwater due to leaky septic fields and the fragmentation or removal of forest cover, the subdivisions create problems for the park's bears, as I found out when I met Pat Rousseau and a couple of young park wardens for coffee a few years ago. Behind a fog of steam from a second or third cup of coffee and the smoke from his cigarette, Rousseau's face was grim, tight and drawn. In his eyes there was a strange brew of sadness and rage. Rousseau is one of the "old-timers" within the warden service at Riding Mountain National Park. He has been there for twelve years, and has put in more than twenty-five years with Parks Canada throughout the West. He is well respected by his peers and by the younger, less experienced wardens for his savvyness and integrity when it comes to caring for the best interests of the park. And that day, his principles were being tested.

"I guess we will have to shoot her," he said in the low, raspy voice of a heavy smoker. "I hate to do it." The night before, Rousseau had trapped a female black bear and her two cubs that had been caught twice before breaking into campers and coolers in the park's main campground. The first time, the wardens hauled the bears twenty kilometres away; they were back in less than eight hours. The second time, they took the bears about as far away as possible, more than sixty kilometres to the west of the townsite; they were back in just two days. "What are we to do?" he asked, his words etched with frustration and anger. "We can't let her continue. Somebody could get badly hurt."

Rousseau's frustration was made all the more intense by his knowledge that the bear's impending death was beyond his control. He felt certain that the bear did not learn her bad habits inside the park. "We've got really good control over garbage, and people are being more careful about leaving food out, but this is not the case outside the park," he grumbled.

The younger wardens sitting with us told of one particular cottage-owner in a subdivision just south of the park's entrance who insisted on leaving garbage to rot in the back of a half-ton until there was enough of a load to warrant him driving to the municipal dump, less than ten kilometres away. It doesn't take much of an imagination to conjure up what garbage smells like when left to boil inside plastic bags under a hot prairie sun. Each tiny rip or hole pecked open by crows and ravens fills the air with an aroma that the bear's hypersensitive nose can easily smell over great distances.[6] Wardens had spoken with the cottage-owner several times, but he persisted in his laziness, in part because he thought it wonderful to watch the female and her cubs feeding in the back of his truck. Whenever there wasn't any garbage there, or whenever she felt like a change of diners, the bear showed up in the campground, crossing over a boundary that she was not even aware of.

"What are we to do?" Rousseau fumed. "We've pretty much done all we can, and now I have to shoot the mother, and at some point I will likely have to shoot the female cub because it's showing all the bad habits learned from the mother."

It's not just wildlife roaming outside the safety of park boundaries that are in trouble; even the native plant communities are showing stress related to adjacent land use. Many of the park's prairies are slowly succumbing to Kentucky bluegrass and smooth brome grass introduced by the livestock grazing that occurred in the park until the late 1960s. In recent years the park has also been invaded by leafy spurge, scentless chamomile and caragana—to mention but a few—which can, as the park's Ecosystem Conservation Plan warns, "move into a habitat and reproduce so aggressively that it may displace some of the original components of the ecosystem."[7] One of the prime sources for the introduction and spread of invasive species is soil disturbance around the park's boundaries, caused by such activities as road building, agriculture and cottage lot development.

Trouble with the neighbours is not unique to Riding Mountain National Park. According to the 1997 *State of the Parks* report, at least half of the thirty-nine national parks are experiencing significant ecological stress due to changes caused by forestry, agriculture, sport hunting and mining. Within the region surrounding Fundy National Park, twenty plant species are thought to have been extirpated; they have not been seen since 1960. They are joined by fourteen species of vertebrates and one species of invertebrates. In their place are now found 153 known exotic species, mostly plants but also including mammals and birds. According to researchers with the University of New Brunswick's faculty of forestry and environmental management, "This comprises 17.5% of the total known number of species in each of the groups."[8] Even more unnerving, they state: "Together, these losses indicate a serious and ongoing decline in the ecological integrity of the ecosystem."[9] The major agent of change within the greater ecosystem in which Fundy is situated is forest harvesting. In the past twenty years, almost a third of the entire ecosystem has been harvested or otherwise disturbed. Within the next twenty this percentage will double, causing even greater change within the greater ecosystem and within Fundy National Park. This grim scenario is being played out in varying degrees at Gros Morne, Cape Breton Highlands, Forillon, La Mauricie, Pukaskwa, St. Lawrence Islands, Riding Mountain, Prince Albert, Banff, Jasper, Kootenay, Waterton, Glacier, Mount Revelstoke, Pacific Rim and Yoho—all threatened by logging on adjacent lands.

As with Riding Mountain National Park, agriculture, in its numerous manifestations from ranching to cash-crop growing, also poses serious challenges to many national parks. At Cape Breton Highlands National Park, park ecologist James Bridgeland told me of his concerns about erosion and pollution from local farms, residences and cottages, which could reduce the water quality of the lower Cheticamp River drainage. But of even greater concern to him was the loss of habitat that follows the clearing of the increasingly rare Acadian forest for rural development. At Forillon, on the very tip of the Gaspé Peninsula, park staff are deeply troubled by the invasion of exotic plant species due to agriculture along the park's border. Even Prince Albert National Park in northern Saskatchewan, once thought to be surrounded by land unsuitable for agriculture, has begun to feel the pressure along its southern boundaries from farmers and ranchers pressed by global economics and encouraged by government subsidies to use more and more marginal lands.

Mining is another major threat arising outside park boundaries. Likely the most high-profile and controversial is the proposed Cheviot project near the eastern boundary of Jasper. Owned by Cardinal River Coals, this mine will cover an area twenty-two kilometres long and one to three kilometres wide, and will feature twenty-six deep open pits at its peak. Although the project will probably create a small and short-lived economic boom for the local communities, biologists and environmentalists have warned that it will have an adverse impact on the national park's environmental integrity. The Jasper Environmental Association labelled the Cheviot mine "a death-trap" for wildlife, particularly the grizzly bear. The development lies smack between the park and some of the best berry-producing habitat in the region, prompting one biologist to pronounce it "one more nail in the coffin of the grizzly." Jeff Anderson, the park ecologist, showed me a map in his office. On it was clearly marked the Cheviot mine, as were five or six other coal deposits that could attract interest. "This is what we are worried about," he said, tapping the map with his pen. "The impacts of the Cheviot mine add to the impacts of forestry, oil and gas exploration, and recreational hunting. Each deals another blow to the grizzly and other wildlife that venture out of the park. If these other deposits are developed, it will get really bad for them." At the moment, the developers and their backers are locked in a court case with environmentalists, who are fighting to have the mine stopped. Meanwhile, mining is implicated in the decline of ecological integrity in fifteen national parks, including Banff, Cape Breton Highlands, Gros Morne, Terra Nova, Kluane and Nahanni.[10]

Increasing urbanization is also taking its toll on the national parks. One of the parks that's really beginning to feel the "human tsunami" break around it is Georgian Bay Islands, a couple of hours' drive north of Toronto. In recent years there has been a boom in construction of vacation, retirement and second homes adjacent to the park. Unfortunately, this sudden influx of people is coming at a cost to one of the area's native species, the endangered Massasauga rattlesnake. "Too many people either hate the snake or are afraid of it," lamented Michel Villeneuve, a warden at the park, as he introduced me to one in a terrarium outside his office. The first thing I noticed was the splint about a third of the way down the creature's spine. "Some idiot took a golf club to it before I could rescue it," he said angrily. "It is so unnecessary. The snake is really quite harmless. It rarely attacks unless provoked. If people could just learn to live with it." In addition to being victims of hostile and lethal attacks, the snake is progressively losing habitat as landowners clear their property of hardy but scrawny Canadian Shield vegetation, cover the rock with topsoil and plant lawns and gardens.

By now it should be apparent that whatever affects ecosystems and species over the broader landscape also affects those inside a national park. For this reason Parks Canada has embraced ecosystem-based management as the preferred approach to this challenge. While previous approaches to park management tended to focus on single species in isolation from other species and the ecosystem in which they were found, ecosystem management requires a holistic perspective that tries to understand the richness and complexity of ecosystems and species as a functioning unity. It can be directed towards one of two ends. Dale Robertson, a former chief of the U.S. Forest Service, says that ecosystem management is to achieve multiple use by blending the needs of people and the environment; while Ed Grumbine, an American conservation biologist, says it seeks to protect the ecological integrity of native ecosystems. The former view is founded on the belief that humans "can continue to manipulate and manage ecosystems to satisfy human needs and desires while protecting ecosystem integrity"; the latter maintains that human use may or may not be permissible, depending on constraints imposed by protecting ecological integrity.[11]

Turning to more pragmatic matters, ecosystem management draws heavily on science. It requires long-term data gathering, experimentation, monitoring and adaptation, backed by highly

educated and skilled personnel. In other words, ecosystem management is not cheap, and recent budget cuts have left Parks
Canada's science program "very, very, thin on the ground," according to Jacques Gérin, chair of the Panel on Ecological Integrity.[12] My
own research confirms this: in nearly every park I have visited, I
found the science programs seriously understaffed and underfunded considering the responsibility that has been placed on them.

The combination of pragmatic and philosophical impediments
to ecosystem management has created a very stressful situation for
many dedicated park staff. "Park staff need to know that they will
be supported with budgets and morale," a former park superintendent told me, "or else they will give up trying to work on these
kinds of problems and restrict themselves to issues inside park
boundaries only."

Michel Villeneuve is one of the dedicated park staff who hasn't
given up on trying to work with local landowners, even though the
organization provides very little support for his work. He spends a
major portion of his time, both on and off the job, trying to encourage greater understanding and tolerance for the Massasauga rattlesnake among the local residents and cottage owners. Just a few
days before my visit to the park, he celebrated a small but significant step toward this goal. He got a phone call from a member of
the local community boasting how he had stopped a couple of
hydro-line workers from killing a snake. This is a guy who had
once bragged to Villeneuve about how many snakes he had killed.

Villeneuve is not alone in understanding the importance of
science and communication beyond park boundaries. Throughout
the national parks system, I have encountered many staff like him
who, despite inadequate budgets and organizational support, are
still managing to find ways to work with local landowners to win
their co-operation in protecting ecological integrity within and
around park boundaries.

The fact remains that, even if Parks Canada weren't handi-
capped by budget cuts and philosophical differences, it would still

have only influence, not control, over adjacent land uses. Ultimate control rests with the landowners themselves, and this presents a very difficult challenge to maintaining the ecological integrity of the parks.

To get a handle on the general level of support for Riding Mountain in the surrounding community, I dropped by the Riding Mountain Guest Ranch south of the park, which is owned and operated by Jim and Candy Irwin. Jim, as I quickly discovered, is no ordinary hospitality sector worker. In addition to being a former cattle rancher and councillor for the local municipality, Irwin holds graduate degrees in wildlife biology and is deeply appreciative of the park and its wildlife. The same cannot be said of most of the people in the area.

"They're deeply suspicious of Parks [Canada] staff," he said, as we strolled into the huge living room of the guest house. "They don't want Parks telling them what to do with their land. That's the whole crux of the problem right there." Many local residents recall the days when they were allowed to graze cattle or cut firewood in the park, and still feel angry about being suddenly shut out when national park policies changed in 1964. They get even more riled when they hear talk of prescribed burns to push back aspen and to restore the fescue grasslands in the park; to them, it is a terrible waste of valuable resources. "What you have is a fundamental difference in philosophies between the two parties," was Irwin's take on the problem. "On the one side of the boundary you have those who want to preserve nature and on the other side you have those who want to domesticate what they can."

Irwin was adamant that something had to be done to keep the two sides talking to each other. I asked him whether Riding Mountain National Park's designation as a biosphere reserve was helping to facilitate this critical dialogue. He responded tentatively, saying that although the designation in 1985 had been a cause for hope, it had yet to fulfil its potential. In fact, there had been one or two occasions when it may have actually contributed to misunderstandings.

"Initially, most local landowners were enthused about the biosphere reserve," Irwin stated. "They saw it as a possible opportunity to finally deal with long-standing problems with beaver, elk and bears.

"Then, at a well-attended meeting in the spring of 1991, the park superintendent and the biosphere reserve committee brought up the idea of a buffer zone around the park. It was like waving a red flag in front of a mad bull," he asserted. "People saw it as another attempt by government to control their lives and property. The unfortunate choice of words alienated a whole lot of people all over again."

An idealized biosphere reserve can be visualized as three concentric rings. The inner ring is the protected core, the next ring is a buffer and the outer ring is the zone of co-operation. While the purpose and nature of the inner core is fairly obvious, there is a lot of confusion about the other two zones. In the buffer, only activities compatible with the protected zone are to occur, while in the zone of co-operation, sustainable resource use dominates. Few biosphere reserves come close to the idealized model in that the buffer zone tends to be absent.

"If they had just stuck to the idea of a zone of co-operation," Irwin concluded as he refilled our teapot in the kitchen, "I don't think they would have stirred up so much anger and resistance."

Having heard Irwin's perspective on the biosphere reserve, the park and the attitudes of the local communities, I decided to visit an old friend, John Whitaker, who is a farmer and the chair of the Riding Mountain National Park biosphere reserve committee. I arrived shortly after noon and found John and his wife, Sharon, along with two neighbours, herding calves through a squeeze chute onto a trailer to be taken off to auction. After the last calf was encouraged onto the trailer and the neighbours departed, the Whitakers invited me up to the house for some lunch.

Once inside, Sharon prepared soup and sandwiches, while John and I settled in their sun-flooded, plant-crowded front room to talk. While admitting that the biosphere reserve committee had made a few mistakes with local landowners, he quickly pointed out all the projects that it had undertaken in the past and was currently initiating, including studies on forest cover change within the park, on long-term ecological change within the region and on attitudes towards the wolf. As for the mistrust between Parks Canada and local landowners, he laid the blame on both parties.

"There's no question that park staff have dropped the ball badly too many times when it comes to talking with people around the park," he stated matter-of-factly. "They haven't seen it as an ecological integrity issue, only an enforcement issue." He went on to say that the local councillors have told him that they rarely see the wardens or other park staff. "And just having coffee with a few friends at the local coffee shop is not enough to get the park's mandate out," he contended.

Whitaker readily admitted that farmers and local politicians are a tough audience at the best of times, and that it was easy for park staff to be put off by their apparent hostility. But he felt this was a mistake. "It's not like you can't reach these people; you can," he declared, although he accepted that ecological arguments are challenging with a hard-nosed farmer concerned about his bottom line. Nevertheless, Whitaker believes that there are more allies within the surrounding community than detractors. And despite his initial criticisms of Parks Canada, he allowed that things were looking better than they had in a great many years, largely because of the increased emphasis on ecosystem management, which was beginning to generate information that could prove useful to farmers and local communities. As examples, he referred back to the studies he had previously mentioned, as well as adding a couple of new ones: one to map land use changes around the park and the other to get a handle on the perennial beaver problems.

Whitaker also had a few choice words to say about the farming community. "Too many local landowners have the attitude 'I can do anything I want with my land and nobody can stop me,'" he observed disappointedly. It's an attitude that has serious implications for the park. "For example, I can pick up hay bales at the end of the season so I don't suck elk out of the park. Or I can be mindful of what I plant and where. Alfalfa is like candy to elk. By changing these things I can avoid having the elk damage my crops." The same kind of thinking, he believes, could be applied by other farmers in the region.

Driving back to Wasagaming, Riding Mountain's service centre, along a gravel road paralleling the park's boundary, I was struck by just how much land was being cleared for more crops, cows or country estates. If the trend continues, with little thought about the impacts on the park's ecosystem and species, the eventual domestication of the park is not unimaginable. The wolves would likely be the first victim, leaving the elk and moose to be managed intensively. A small black bear population would probably be able to hold on, but to what degree native plant communities could do so in the face of increasing invasive species is an open question. The ecosystem conservation plan for Riding Mountain says it best: "We have come to realize lately that the Park itself is too small to be a self-regulating ecosystem. In the long-term, preserving all of the life forms and ecological processes currently found here will require cooperative management of the whole region."[13] The same is true for all national parks.

Almost every kind of land use has the potential to adversely impact the ecological integrity of a neighbouring national park or protected area. And although any one action may seem insignificant, it adds to those of others to create an incremental, cumulative impact that can tip the balance for a species or ecosystem, causing it to slide towards collapse. The activities of farmers, ranchers, clam harvesters, cottagers, loggers, miners, peat-bog harvesters, fishers and townspeople around national park boundaries are contributing to the downward spiral of ecological impoverishment. No national park is big enough or so well protected as to experience no effect from the slow domestication of the surrounding landscape. This flies in the face of popular perception. As the authors of the 1997 *State of the Greater Fundy Ecosystem* report stated:

For over 100 years, our society has set aside national parks and other protected areas in the faith that these areas are healthy functioning ecosystems, representative of wilderness Canada. When the parks were first established, they were enveloped by such expanses as wilderness. Today, Canada's National Parks tend to be surrounded by lands developed for agriculture, forestry or urbanization. These land use changes, coupled with long range transport of pollutants and other large-scale transpositions, challenge the very notion of protected areas. We know that small-sized, highly stressed protected areas are not self-sustaining ecosystems that protect native biodiversity.[14]

Put more simply, our national parks have become islands of wildness in a sea of domestication; but they are too few, too small and too isolated to maintain their ecological integrity and wildness for much longer. The scientists who wrote this report may know this, but how many of the people who own or use land around the national parks know it?

If there is anything that can be learned from the litany of threats arising around the national parks, it is this: everyone who owns or uses land next to a national park has the responsibility, at least, to be a good neighbour. They have this responsibility by virtue of the potentially adverse impacts of their actions. Nothing less is required to avert the slow, inevitable draining away of wildness that is the very spirit of the national parks. The same holds true even for those of us who live hundreds or even thousands of kilometres away.

# FOUR

# The Loons of Keji

In the fading light, Kejimkujik Lake's surface lay like a vast sheet of polished steel around our canoe. Above the distant western shore, dark clouds billowed skyward, foretelling a gathering storm. Their edges were set ablaze by the sun as it slowly receded from our vantage point, turning day into night. A shimmering narrow triangle of gold, with its apex touching our canoe, repeatedly drew my appreciative eye to the deepening hues of red, orange and yellow that bathed the clouds and sky in their warm glow. Occasionally, a faint current of air brushed gently across my cheek and filled my nostrils with the tangy scent of pine. Except for the rustle of our clothing, there was silence. It was as if all Creation was at peace, everything in its place.

Then it began. Out of the growing gloom, the spine-tingling yodel of a loon shattered the evening stillness. Each call bounced off the dark forested shores, creating a cascade of echoes that filled the air with their eerie song. Dianne turned slowly and grinned at me from the bow of the canoe. I could read her expression perfectly in the faint, soft light. It was one of deep inner calm and peacefulness mixed with excitement and wonder. What is it about the call of the loon that has this effect on so many people?

Very few other animal sounds symbolize the spirit of the land, this north country of Canada. Throughout Canadian culture, from literature to advertising, the loon has been closely identified with the wild. A chorus arose from the surrounding bays, touched off by the soloist, and I returned Dianne's smile of contentment.

Even so, a sadness crept over me as I reflected on my discussion earlier that day with Peter Hope, the chief naturalist of Kejimkujik National Park. Di and I had met him as we were docking at Jake's Landing after a quiet paddle up the Mersey River. He had come down to the landing to unload a couple of park canoes. After introductions, I explained that I was in the park to gather information on its ecological health. It was then that he expressed his deep concern about the dramatic decline in the number of breeding pairs and successful fledglings within the park's loon population. Over the past five years, the number of breeding pairs had dropped by more than half, from twenty-two to ten. "This is very serious," he said. "If enough loons do not mate and if enough young do not make it to leave the nest, the loons could disappear from the park." A number of factors could be contributing to the decline of the loon, including the long-range transportation of pollutants and acid rain. Unlike the threats posed by logging around the park, these ecological stresses originate well beyond its boundaries, leaving Hope feeling powerless and frustrated. How can parks staff protect the loons and Kejimkujik's ecosystems from pollution generated hundreds of kilometres to the west in Ontario, Quebec, Michigan and Wisconsin? The simple answer is, they can't—and Hope knows it. The best that they can do is to conduct the necessary research to raise awareness of the issue.

The morning after the loon serenade, I left Dianne at our campsite in the park's only vehicle-accessible campground, on Jeremy's Bay, and drove over to the warden services field station overlooking Grafton Lake. Kejimkujik is a park for the canoe, not the car, truck or RV.[1] It has less than fifteen kilometres of paved roads and less than eight kilometres of secondary roads, which are open depending on the season and environmental protection concerns. But what the park, located in southern Nova Scotia, does offer is 404 square kilometres of some of the best canoeing country imaginable. From Jake's Landing, the park's main canoe launch area, a myriad of lakes and rivers set within a gently undulating landscape covered with maple, ash, birch and pine fans out, providing the canoe enthusiast with trips ranging from a couple of hours to several days in length. The largest body of water is Kejimkujik Lake. Its convoluted shoreline of bays and points encompasses approximately twenty-five square kilometres of water and more than forty islands and islets. Jeremy's Bay, in the northwest corner of the lake, is the largest of the bays.

Grafton Brook enters Kejimkujik Lake from the east. In the late 1930s, the federal fisheries department dammed it just a few hundred metres from the lake's shoreline. The resulting impoundment, which flooded a marshy lowland of cattails and spruce, was named Grafton Lake and was to be used to raise fish from the newly constructed hatchery. When the park was created in 1974, the operation was shut down and the buildings turned over to Parks Canada. Over the next twenty-three years, nature began to slowly reclaim the land; around the edges of the lake, cattails reappeared, followed by seedlings from the surrounding forest. In 1997, after considerable study and research, park staff decided to help nature restore the marshland, in part to provide habitat for the endangered Blandings turtle. They breached the dam and gradually began to drain Grafton Lake.

My reason for driving to the lake was to meet Cliff Drysdale, the park ecologist, to discuss the problems with the loons and other threats to the park. As I pulled up in front of the two-storey research building, he was standing outside, expecting my arrival. After brief introductions, he suggested we talk there rather than in his office. I quickly agreed to the suggestion as it was a beautiful, sunny, warm day and I had not seen very many of these since arriving in Atlantic Canada more than a month earlier. We chose the grassy, shade-dappled slope of the nearby impoundment as the site for our discussion.

"The loons are under stress from a number of threats," he began. "In recent years there has been an explosion of raccoons in the park, mostly around the campground at Jeremy Bay. They are attracted by the garbage and the handouts from the visitors." Unfortunately, these voracious animals also prey on the park's wildlife, including the eggs and chicks of loons. "We are doing our best to stay on top of the garbage problem," he said, "but some visitors just don't seem to get it when we explain that leaving food out or handing food to the raccoons is creating a big problem for the park's wildlife. Maybe they are thinking that feeding one or two raccoons only a couple of times can't really hurt anything, but the trouble is, too many other people are thinking the same thing."

In the park's wilderness areas, canoeists may be contributing to the loon's plight—without knowing it. "We put about 170,000 people through the park each year," said Drysdale, "and there is continual pressure to expand the number of campsites in the back-country. But more people can mean more stress on the loons. Some birds take flight when approached too closely; others frantically try to swim away. In either case, the loons burn up vital energy or are unintentionally diverted from important tasks such as tending eggs or chicks."

While Drysdale was talking, I reflected on a conversation that Dianne had overheard the night before. She had gone to the pay phone in the campground only to find it in use by a man who was talking excitedly with someone in Toronto. The caller had just returned from a week-long canoe trip through the park, and one of the highlights had been paddling along for an hour and a half close behind a pair of loons, which had kept up a cacophony of yodels and wails. When I mentioned this incident to Drysdale, he replied, "That's exactly what I mean. The fellow probably didn't realize that those were distress calls. The loons were trying to tell him and his friends to back off. While they were chasing the loons, the unguarded nest may have been plundered by a raccoon or fox." The solution to this problem, he felt, was more education of park visitors. "Basically, most backcountry users are pretty conscientious and would likely change their behaviour if they knew about the harm they may be doing to the loons," he stated.

The most difficult stress on the loons, however, was one that Drysdale was powerless to affect: the insidious poisoning of Kejimkujik's lakes by long-range transportation of pollutants. Each year, industry in the United States generates approximately 11 billion tons of toxic waste.[2] That's a staggering forty-one tons of hazardous waste for every American. Despite numerous industry and government assurances to the contrary, these poisons still escape into the environment each year. Almost forty years ago, Rachel Carson sounded the alarm on their sinister effects, drawing our attention to the decline in reproductive success among birds of prey found with too-high levels of DDT in their tissue and blood. Perhaps for the first time, we began to see what could happen to us if we continued to pump it into the air and water. Our governments passed laws to control the production and use of DDT, and less of it began showing up in eagles, falcons and osprey. But we have continued creating even more complex and lethal mixtures each year in the stubborn belief that they are an unfortunate by-product of a healthy economy. Meanwhile, the loons of Kejimkujik National Park are among those species paying the price for human irresponsibility toward the planet.

For the past few years, a team of researchers have been studying the effects of the long-range transportation of mercury on the loons that frequent Kejimkujik Lake. They chose this heavy metal because of its tendency to accumulate in the tissues of organisms and to become more concentrated as one organism consumes another up the food chain—a process called *biomagnification*. The researchers ran tests on samples taken from the air, precipitation, water, fish tissue and the blood of loons. What the tests revealed was that the loons of the park have blood mercury levels higher than at other North American sites used for comparison. Furthermore, they discovered that the fish upon which the loon preyed had mercury concentrations in excess of levels known to cause reproductive impairment in the birds. Unfortunately, more research is necessary to determine how much of the mercury in Kejimkujik Lake occurs naturally and how much is carried on the winds and in the rain from as far away as southern Ontario or the northeastern United States. Nevertheless, a few simple conclusions can be drawn from the research. "There is sufficient evidence," say the researchers, "that mercury poses a real threat to ecosystem health, human health and biodiversity." It also makes sense to do what we can to reduce, and possibly eliminate, the amount of mercury and other toxics we put into the environment. If we do not, then we run the real risk of losing the loons from Keji, and probably from other places as well. Every year, fewer and fewer will be heard, until only the silence bears witness to their disappearance.

Other national parks too are suffering from the deadly effects of toxins. The Banff–Bow Valley is also subjected to contamination by long-range transportation of pollutants to such an extent that the headwaters of the Bow River watershed, high in the Canadian Rockies, have been found to be laced with a wide range of toxic chemicals.[3] Indeed, owing to their worldwide production and to the fact that the earth is a closed system, toxins are increasingly turning up in the ecosystems and species of all the national parks, even those in the far north.

In the evening after my meeting with Drysdale, clouds rolled across the moon and stars, blotting out their silvery glow and casting the forest surrounding our campsite into pitch blackness. Soon the patter of raindrops could be heard on the tarps we had strung overhead to protect our fire, picnic table and chairs. In moments, our ears were assailed by a loud drumming above us and by the forlorn call of a loon bobbing somewhere in the dismal gloom of Jeremy's Bay. Even it seemed to be unhappy with the change in the weather. The tarp quickly began to sag under the of pooling water, which threatened to snap the lines holding the tarp in place. Anxiously, I pushed the tarp up to dump the water. For a while

I managed to keep pace, but then, with a clap of thunder and a flash of lightning, the heavens opened up.

Before I could readily grasp what was happening, pegs and ropes went flying and the tarp began dropping toward the fire. Di and I dove simultaneously to intercept it, nearly colliding in mid-air. Standing under the tarp, to keep it out of the fire, we found ourselves being asphyxiated by the smoke that billowed around our faces. Choking and gasping, we peered out toward the tent to assess our options. The tent was barely visible, and what could be seen was not heartening. A river of water flowed past us directly under our tent. For a brief moment we debated sleeping in the car, but then decided to take our chances in the tent. We threw what we could under the tarp and dashed to the tent. A few seconds spent fumbling with zippers ensured that we were thoroughly soaked before climbing in on top of our sleeping bags, which we were grateful to discover were still pretty dry thanks to the air mattress underneath them. Exhausted, we stripped off our wet clothes, slipped into the warmth of the bags and dropped off to sleep.

While the rain was a nuisance, causing us some minor inconvenience, for the loons of Keji it has become something much more serious. Not only did each water droplet carry traces of heavy metals or PCBs, but also sufficient amounts of sulphates and nitrates to be considered acidic. Like the threat posed by airborne pollutants, the acid rain that falls in Kejimkujik arises from human activity far to the west, in southern Ontario and the northeastern United States. Research confirms that acid rain can have a negative impact on aquatic ecosystems, even at relatively low levels of atmospheric deposition. Just as it corrodes the stone and metalworks of our cities, so it destroys sensitive ecosystems, first killing off the smallest life forms at the base of the food chain and then moving up to cause fish populations to collapse, followed by their predators, such as the loon. Scientists have also discovered that highly acidic waters render female fish, frogs and salamanders incapable of producing eggs or of producing enough eggs that hatch.[4] This slow process of sterilization is now believed to be affecting the loons of Kejimkujik in the same way. In addition, under acidic conditions, the chemical bonds that keep heavy metals locked in the soil are broken, releasing these trace elements into streams, rivers, lakes and marshes, where they accumulate and become highly toxic, especially when the aquatic system is already receiving excessive amounts of heavy metals and other pollutants carried on air currents from thousands of kilometres away.

The loons of Kejimkujik National Park are not the only victims of acid rain. Some scientists believe that it has likely contributed to the disappearance of the wild Atlantic salmon within the region.[5] It is also attacking the forests throughout Atlantic Canada. In Cape Breton Highlands National Park, near the end of a trail, we came upon an interpretive sign explaining the impacts of acid rain on the forests of the region and urging visitors to write to their elected representatives to urge speedy passage of laws to control pollution. The degree of forthrightness on the issue surprised us; rarely do you encounter such overt advocacy in the national parks—an indication of just how serious the problem of acid rain is. What the sign left unsaid was what changes individuals could make in their own lives to help alleviate the problem.

The morning after the deluge, Di and I surveyed the wreckage that had been our idyllic campsite. Around the picnic table and firepit lay soaked and mud-spattered clothes and equipment that we hadn't had time to toss under the balled-up tarp the night before. For a moment we stood staring sullenly at the mess, then we both started laughing. Everywhere we had been throughout Atlantic Canada over the past four weeks, we had been hit with downpours that even the locals assured us were highly unusual. In Kouchibouguac National Park, a sudden intense shower struck the campground, leaving Dianne, who was returning from the pay phone, soaked to the skin and sending me scrambling to cover our tent with the fly. In Terra Nova, the Trans-Canada Highway turned into a river of sorts, as a horrendous squall blew in, dumping tonnes of water everywhere. Park staff were called out to a fatal accident caused by a vehicle hydroplaning on the pools of water that lay camouflaged on the slick asphalt. Rounding the southernmost tip of the Avalon Peninsula a couple of days before catching the ferry from Argentia to North Sydney, a violent storm caught us on a wide-open stretch of highway. The car rocked violently from time to time as the wind gusted to 110 kilometres per hour. The wipers failed miserably to keep pace with the driving rain, robbing us of sight much beyond the window. At Cape Breton National Park, one of our suppers was abruptly ended by a cloudburst that had crept in seemingly out of nowhere under the darkness of the early evening. And now, here at Kejimkujik, yet another remarkable climatic event.

Could there be a pattern here? Or were they just random, coincidental events? The questions commanded my thoughts in the campsite as I picked up and began drying off the white-gas lantern. Maybe. I knew that there was solid scientific evidence showing a pattern emerging at the planetary level. In his thought-provoking book *Discordant Harmonies*, Daniel Botkin, a biology professor at the University of California, presents four graphs in which the earth's temperature over the time scales of 1,500, 30,000, 150,000 and 1 million years is plotted. At first, the impression gained looking back over the past 1 million years is, as Botkin says, "periods of little variation and periods of great variation, times of apparent cycles and times without cycles." In fact, if Botkin's graphs had gone back billions of years closer to the big bang that gave birth to the planet, we would see that the average temperature has always fluctuated yet remained within a narrow range conducive to life. If one looks closer, however, a subtle but unmistakable trend emerges: for most of the time the planet's temperature was significantly colder than it has been only recently. Even more disturbing, the rate of warming appears to be rapidly increasing. Today's global temperature hovers very near the most extreme that earth has experienced in the past 1 million years. A slight increase of just two more degrees Centigrade is all that is needed to push the global climate beyond this previous record.[6] Global climate has already warmed by .5 to .6 degrees Centigrade in the past hundred years.[7]

Even more disconcerting is the prediction that the average global temperature could rise over the next century by 1 to 3.5 degrees Centigrade. With the rise in temperature comes more erratic weather patterns, featuring increasingly extreme events such as hurricanes, droughts or downpours.

Why should this concern Canadians? Because of the way the planetary systems work, this seemingly insignificant variation could translate into an increase of five to ten degrees Centigrade for some regions of Canada.[8] A global warming of this magnitude would have dramatic impacts on the country's ecosystems and species, as well as on the quality of life and livelihood of virtually every Canadian. Listen to what one of the country's most respected plant ecologists has to say on this matter. "The predicted rate of global warming for the next 50 years magnified northward in continental Canada, is greater than Canada's biomes experienced during deglaciation or indeed during the last million years," wrote Stan Rowe in a brief background paper for Parks Canada. "Only the most adaptable plants, especially those with small mobile seeds, will be able to shift northward." Black spruce may invade the tundra, dense stands of the boreal forest will probably give way to either grasslands or deciduous forests, depending on the relative moisture present, and the prairies will likely become deserts. In Central Canada, birch could dwindle from sight as they are forced to shift north onto the less productive soils of the Precambrian Shield. "In the mountains where biomes occupy vertical zones," warns Rowe, "a warming trend will tend to drive each vegetation belt upward, placing the uppermost (tundra and subalpine) at risk of being squeezed off the island-like tops which of course lack contact with any escape terrain." Across the country, from east to west and from south to north, species will be confronted with a few stark options: rapidly adapt, migrate, cope with mounting stress or simply become extinct.

In Ontario's Algonquin Provincial Park, grey jay nesting sites have been empty for the past three years, and researchers speculate that global warming may be the cause.[9] Other indicators of ecological stress caused by global warming are the inhibited break-down of forest litter and less production of humus and other soil matter; the promotion of exotic and weed species; the spread of grasses; and an increase in insects and diseases that, according to Rowe, "take advantage of organisms under stress."[10] Meanwhile, glaciers melt at unprecedented rates and the weather becomes more unstable, with extreme fluctuations. Nineteen ninety-eight was the warmest year on record, as were six other years in the 1990s.[11] During the same time period there have been floods and droughts across Canada, and, of course, there was the ice storm that crippled Ottawa, Montreal and the surrounding regions.

The implications of global warming are immense. To fulfil Parks Canada's mandate of preserving representative examples of Canada's natural heritage under such conditions, Stan Rowe recommends the establishment of more national parks that are large, topographically diverse, surrounded by environmentally sensitive land uses and sited near the northern limits of the country's biomes. With dark humour, he has suggested that "[w]ith greater foresight all of Canada's parks should have been much larger and laid-out with a lengthy north-south dimension similar to the national mountain parks of Alberta but starting at 49 degrees latitude and running right to the pole!"[12] With the last two years being the hottest on record, global warming has also been implicated in the inability of polar bears to complete their routine migrations at Wapusk National Park in northern Manitoba owing to the melting of ice pans.

Is Rowe overreacting to global warming? A few scientists probably think so, but they are in the minority. The weight of evidence clearly indicates that there is something amiss with the earth's climate and that it is becoming worse. "I think it is still bleak," says Michael Whiticar, a biogeochemist at the University of Victoria, who worries that the public has grown apathetic to the threat. "The hardest challenge is not to keep forcing the issue down their throats," he says, "but to create a groundswell of appreciation that things change slowly."[13] The challenge is made more difficult by the tendency among people to look only at what is happening locally. There is also the problem, mentioned in the first chapter, that we simply do not register slow, imperceptible change, despite the fact that it is occurring too fast for us and the rest of life on earth to adapt to. In accord with Rowe, Whiticar believes that "we have to grow up as a civilization" and start making some critical changes in our attitudes and behaviours toward the environment.

What kind of changes? Well, we know that life on earth is sustained by an envelope of gases that regulate the amount of solar heat that is trapped or dissipated. Known as the greenhouse effect, this natural phenomenon maintains the planet's temperature in a range that averages out around fifteen degrees Centigrade. Without these gases—of water vapour, carbon dioxide, methane and nitrous oxide—the average temperature would probably plummet to minus eighteen degrees Centigrade, or worse.[14] At that point, as a report on climate change by Environment Canada puts it, "Life as we know it would be impossible."[15] The same can be said if too much of these gases builds up, causing the temperature to soar.

This leads us to the second thing we know. Since the Industrial Revolution, human activity has been rapidly adding more greenhouse gases to the atmosphere. Environment Canada scientists estimate that "[c]urrent concentrations of carbon dioxide are 30% above pre-industrial levels" and that about half of this growth has come in the last thirty years.[16] Each year, the burning of fossil fuels around the world generates five to five and a half billion tonnes of carbon dioxide, while deforestation adds another one and a half billion.[17] That's more than a tonne for every man, woman and child on the planet. Canadians hold the dubious distinction of being the highest per capita contributors of greenhouse gases in the world, with about 80 percent of our share coming from the burning of coal, oil and gas.

Knowing these two things alone should encourage more precautionary measures. Certainly our current minister of the environment, David Anderson, thinks so. In a recent speech to the

Alliance for Responsible Environmental Alternatives, he warned: "One of the most dangerous attitudes towards climate change is that because there is still scientific uncertainty about climate change, we should not begin any major measures. This attitude is dangerous because it appeals to our human instinct to procrastinate and put off difficult choices and wraps it up in the mantle of scientific respectability."[18] With that warning, he reaffirmed the federal government's 1997 commitment to reduce greenhouse gas emissions 6 percent below 1990 levels and to achieve this target between 2008 and 2012:

> To meet this target, given the projected growth in our economy and population, we will have to reduce our greenhouse gas emissions by about 25 percent below "business as usual" projected levels by 2010 . . . We realize that these targets cannot be reached without significant changes to the way our economy functions and to our way of life as individuals. But the scope of these challenges must not prevent us, or even delay us, from taking action now.[19]

Around the time of making these statements, Anderson publicly retreated from other comments in which he suggested taxing large, gas-guzzling sport-utility vehicles, which represent the fastest-growing sector of the automobile industry. Instead of using a stick to bring about change, he favoured a carrot. "I think what you have to look at is the incentives," he pointed out. "What about an improved public transit system in major cities—how can we encourage people to stop having the single-occupant vehicle at rush hour, for in some cases, hours on end, spewing out pollutants and moving just a few hundred metres down the road."[20] When asked whether this meant the federal government would put money into the development and upgrading of public transit systems, Anderson ducked the issue, saying it was more a question of doing things differently.

Anderson's evasiveness might have had something to do with the federal government's promise the previous month to spend upward of $5 billion on upgrading Canada's highways."[21] Whatever the reasons, the federal government's resolve on climate change has been called into question by the Canadian Climate Change Network, representing over a hundred environmental organizations. Noting that since 1990 the number of private vehicles in Canada has risen by 9 percent and the amount of greenhouse gas from those vehicles has increased by 12 percent, the Network lambasted the government. "The federal government promised to stabilize greenhouse gas emissions in 1990," they argued. "Since then Canada's emissions have risen by 17 percent and are expected to rise by 24 percent by 2008."[22] The group called upon the government to divert investment in roads and highways into such actions as supporting the development of alternative forms of transportation and renewable energy sources, and encouraging the renovation of commercial, industrial and residential buildings to higher energy efficiency. Many of their ideas Anderson has identified as critical priorities; it remains to be seen how far he wins the necessary support of the business community and ordinary Canadians. Government cannot achieve greenhouse gas emission targets by itself, no matter how many laws and regulations it passes. Ultimate success depends on the willingness of business, communities and individuals to undertake drastic changes.

After picking up our gear, cleaning it and packing it into the car, Di and I went for one more paddle before leaving Kejimkujik National Park. The air was fresh, clear and charged in the wake of the previous night's storm. Along the banks of the Mersey River, hints of the advancing season were evident in the splashes of red, ochre, yellow and gold appearing among the maples. A stiff breeze greeted us as we swung our canoe around the last meander of the river before entering Kejimkujik Lake. Ahead, among the reeds, bobbed a pair of loons. As we struggled by, one let loose with a short burst of song, and then they both dove out of sight, leaving us guessing where they would re-emerge.

We take for granted that they will return to the surface, just as we do that they will return to the lakes of our national parks each year. It is as if we think the parks are somehow impervious to such large-scale changes as global warming, acid rain and long-range transportation of pollutants, not to mention ozone depletion and smog. Or maybe we just don't understand how serious the problem is. Whatever the reason, it is plain that we are pushing the planet's ecosystems and species to the "red line" and running the risk of causing their eventual collapse—even in those few places where we have said we will provide them with the highest level of protection.

# FIVE

# Parks Canada Inc.

As if the threats within, around and beyond their boundaries weren't bad enough, the national parks must also cope with "an internal process of renewal" that is nothing less than a re-entrenchment of the old "parks as profit centres" myth. Spurred by a series of major budget cuts that began in the mid-1980s, the senior management of Parks Canada has aggressively adopted "an entrepreneurial approach" focused on running the national parks like a business. They have actively pursued new ways of generating revenue, developing "sponsorships and partnerships" with the private sector, experimenting with "alternative service delivery" mechanisms and "downsizing" staff through early departure or early retirement incentives. Through it all, the federal government and senior bureaucrats have steadfastly assured the Canadian public that protecting the ecological integrity of the national parks would not be compromised by any measures to cut costs or generate revenue. However, the evidence suggests that we shouldn't be lulled into a false sense of security by these promises.

Take the golf course in Cape Breton Highlands National Park as an example. As pointed out in Chapter 2, the golf course has long been associated with significant ecological impact to the lower Clyburn watershed. So why did Parks Canada make the decision to upgrade it, instead of decommissioning it and restoring the area to wildlife habitat? When I asked park staff this question, they just smiled knowingly and suggested that I talk with the superintendent first.

I doubt that I shall ever forget this discussion. After being ushered into his office, I sat at a round wooden table in front of an imposing stone fireplace. My eyes fell on a shiny new golf ball wedged between the rocks and a bronzed plaque hanging just above it, expressing the gratitude of the local golf and country club for the superintendent's assistance in upgrading the park's course. I stared in disbelief.

After a quick telephone call, the superintendent rose from behind his desk and joined me at the table. For the next hour, in speech laced with terms such as "park products," "customer service," "revenue targets" and "business opportunities," he answered my question. First, I had to understand that the park now had to generate approximately $1.7 million a year to offset the impact of budget cuts. Of this, the refurbished golf course was projected to bring in about $700,000. Second, the golf course played a crucial role in the region's economy by attracting tourists. As for the ecological impacts, these, he assured me, could be mitigated. I left his office stunned. Despite his assurances, it was plain that revenue and profits were treated as ultimately more important than protecting the park's ecological integrity.

Throughout the national park system, there are too many examples like this. In Forillon National Park, staff were anxious to show me something that greatly angered them. We bounced down a rough road, slowly passing people hiking in and out of Cap-Gaspé. Then we came upon a string of trailers and someone directing traffic. "What is this?" I asked my hosts. They grinned and drove on a little farther. Soon we stopped, and there below was a movie set consisting of a house, outbuildings and a garden ringed by trucks, lighting booms and smaller trailers. I was told that the set was for an $11-million television series that was set in the late 1600s and was about a cod fisherman and his family and their struggle with a dishonest fish-buyer. The park was chosen for the location as it offered a pristine backdrop, but it played no role in the story itself; however, in exchange for providing the site, Parks Canada would receive $30,000.

Permits for development were given from somewhere up the chain of command within the organization. Trees were cut, trails were widened and surfaced to act as service roads, and native vegetation was removed. Then somebody in a position of authority realized that an environmental impact assessment had not been done, as required by national parks policy. Hastily an assessment was ordered and prepared. Then, to add insult to injury, further site modifications were approved after the fact. All for a relatively paltry sum.

At Gros Morne National Park, I discovered that the operator who runs tour boats on Western Brook Pond was being squeezed to turn over more revenue to the park. In exchange, he was permitted to incrementally increase the size of his concession building and run more tours. The net result is added pressure on an ecologically vulnerable aquatic ecosystem.

Why has Parks Canada put business ahead of protecting ecological integrity? Partly it is a function of changes in societal and political values over the past fifteen years or so. In 1984, Brian Mulroney and the Conservatives swept into power with an unprecedented majority. His promise was clear and simple: to get the country's deficit and debt under control while leaving the country's social programs intact. Pierre Trudeau's Liberal government had left a fiscal legacy of a $38.5-billion deficit and a national debt of more than $200 billion.[1] Mulroney saw only two choices: raise taxes or introduce program cuts. He chose a combination of the two: program cuts together with the introduction of user fees. Soon, critics were decrying the gutting of Crown corporations such as the CBC, Via Rail and Air Canada. Within the government itself there were across-the-board budget cuts and below-inflation salary increases for employees. Nothing was sacred—not even the national parks.

Even as they were gearing up to celebrate the centennial of Canada's national parks system in 1985, Parks Canada was reeling from several body blows delivered by the Hon. Suzanne Blais-Grenier, minister of the Department of Environment.[2] An enthusiastic champion of the ruling party's ideology of running government like a business, she had immediately begun cutting "fiscal fat" from the department. Shortly after assuming power, the Conservative government had set a target of eliminating 1,500 public service positions by the spring of 1985; over one-quarter of these were to be in the Department of Environment.[3] Blais-Grenier lost no time in cutting the staff and budget of Parks Canada, reducing the latter by $30 million. In addition, she eliminated guided hikes and walks because they were not "cost-efficient"[4] while increasing park entrance fees and introducing new user fees. She openly favoured business interests, especially those represented by the Alberta caucus of MPS, who were pushing for more development in the four mountain parks of Banff, Jasper, Yoho and Kootenay. However, when she publicly entertained the idea of reopening the national parks to timber harvesting and mining, all hell broke lose. Her comment caused so much public outrage that she was soon replaced by Tom McMillan, the former minister of tourism.

While McMillan quickly distanced himself from the policies of his predecessor, he did not attempt to reverse them. Instead, he gave assurances that he would do what he could to protect the national parks for as long as he was the minister responsible for them. His "maiden speech" before the Canadian Assembly on National Parks in the fall of 1985 drew three standing ovations from a crowd convinced that Blais-Grenier's "reign of terror" was over. "I'm an environmentalist, and I am proud of it," he declared, before promising to secure South Moresby as a national park, to create Northern Ellesmere National Park and to ensure that no industrial development occurred in any national park. And in quick succession, McMillan began to make good on his promises. He created a special task force to come up with innovative ways for establishing and funding new parks; negotiated and signed an agreement for the creation of Ellesmere Island National Park; settled differences with the province of British Columbia over boundaries and compensation for Pacific Rim National Park; and rejected a proposed management plan for the four mountain parks on the grounds that it was "unduly development-oriented."[5] Of even greater significance was his perspective on the age-old clash between use and preservation. "Protection is to be given priority," he stated, while proclaiming a "new bias" in how the national parks were to be managed. Furthermore, he asserted that government "must protect more vigorously the wilderness character of our national parks" and announced his intent to update the National Parks Act in keeping with this shift in priority.[6]

True to his word, and backed by a concerted effort on the part of many of the country's most influential conservation groups—Canadian Parks and Wilderness Society, World Wildlife Fund, Canadian Nature Federation and others—McMillan was able to successfully shepherd a bill to amend the National Parks Act through the labyrinth of bureaucratic and political decision making. In the fall of 1988 the bill was declared the will of the people and made law. With regard to the goal of management, the new law stated:

> Maintenance of ecological integrity through the protection of
> natural resources shall be the first priority when considering park
> zoning and visitor use in a management plan.

The coalition of environmental organizations, who had had a major influence on the wording of the amendments, was jubilant. Preservation now had primacy over play and profit. There would be no more questioning or debate over which came first; the matter was settled. Or so a great many people within the environmental community thought.

Although McMillan was a strong defender of national parks, he was not able to protect Parks Canada from further budget cuts. By the late 1980s the situation had become so bad that there was a projected shortfall of nearly $75 million to restore aging park infrastructure.[7] Without enough money to maintain normal park operations or to acquire new parks, Parks Canada negotiated a revenue-sharing agreement with the Treasury Board of Canada that allowed them to retain some of the revenues the national parks were now generating. Largely as a result of increases in park entrance fees and numbers of visitors, total revenue had risen from $20 million to $35 million. But the pressures to become even more businesslike continued to build.

In a scathing attack on the federal government's mismanagement of the country's economy, author D'Arcy Jenish alleges that, contrary to perception, Mulroney and the Conservative Party practised "business as usual." Cuts to programs were inconsequential and ineffective, while government spending surged forward, fuelled by new income from "user pay" services previously provided by tax dollars. "Total federal spending went up every year the Tories were in office, rising from $110 billion in 1984–85 to almost $160 billion by the time they were defeated in October 1993," he claims.

> But the deficit and the national debt remain the most telling
> evidence of Mulroney's failure to reduce the size and cost of
> government. The Tories inherited a deficit of $38.5 billion from
> Trudeau. They never managed to get the shortfall below $28 billion.
> And they left Chrétien's Liberals with a record deficit exceeding $40
> billion. The debt was approaching $210 billion when Mulroney
> became prime minister. It was surging toward $500 billion when he
> resigned in June 1993.[8]

The Tories were able to pull this off, in part, because they were "astute students of recent Canadian electoral politics" and knew that "asking the voters to make sacrifices and accept some suffering was no way to win at the polls."[9] However, as the old saw goes: "You can fool some of the people some of the time, but you can't fool all of the people all of the time." At some point, illusion collides with reality and the truth is found out. On this, Jenish says: "Long before the Conservatives' defeat in October 1993, it had become evident to most observers, even those on the right, the Tories had failed to make any meaningful improvement in the country's finances and frequently failed to meet their own deficit projections."[10] On top of this, their deficit-reduction strategy managed to anger just about everyone, no matter what colour their political stripe.

The 1993 election resulted in a major reconfiguration of the country's traditionally staid political landscape. Canadians were so eager to get rid of Mulroney and the Conservatives that the party was left decimated at the polls, managing to win only two seats. The New Democratic Party, representing the country's social democratic tradition, was also nearly wiped out. In their place, two new parties emerged out of deep-seated frustrations festering within the country. The anger of the West found expression in the Reform Party, while the disillusionment of Quebeckers spawned the Bloc Québécois. But Canadians were not prepared to cast all tradition to the wind, and chose to put the Liberals back in power, this time led by Jean Chrétien, a former cabinet minister responsible for the national parks under Trudeau.

Confronted with a runaway national debt growing at $85,000 a minute, and keenly aware of the public's increasingly grumpy mood, Chrétien and his colleagues first attempted to address the crisis through a program of "economic renewal and revitalization," which focused on creating jobs and reducing the deficit from $40 billion to $25 billion over three years.[11] Within eight months it became apparent that they were going to miss their targets if deeper cutbacks weren't made. On February 27, 1995, Paul Martin, the minister of finance, presented the Liberals' second budget to the House of Commons. Unlike its predecessor, this one contained definite measures "aimed at saving the federal government $29 billion, of which $25.3 billion would come from spending cuts, over the following three years."[12] In September of the same year, while speaking at an international conference of bankers, Martin assured everyone that the Liberals were "under no illusions about the magnitude of the challenge" before them and were determined to redefine the role of government.

When the Conservative government fell in 1993, hopes rose for a kinder, more generous approach to the funding of national parks. After all, while sitting as the Official Opposition, Jean Chrétien and his Liberal colleagues had been extremely critical of the "Tories' willingness to sacrifice environmental promises on the altar of cost-cutting, to reduce the deficit."[13] During the election campaign Chrétien had repeatedly stated that protection of the environment would be a top priority for his government because to do so was in the best long-term interests of the country. However, no sooner had the nameplates on Parliament Hill been switched than the Liberals began to backtrack on their promises. If they were going to make good on promises of improving the country's economy, then the government would have to make substantial cuts to environmental and social programs.[14]

Mindful of two recent surveys which revealed that Canadians held the national parks system as the third most important icon of national identity after the flag and national anthem, and that most Canadians viewed the primary purpose of the national park system to be "the protector of natural resources, not a promoter of recreation opportunities,"[15] the government ordered a series of comprehensive operational reviews of Parks Canada, aimed at reducing costs and generating more revenue from the parks.[16] Sensing that very significant cuts were on the way, senior management within Parks Canada began preparing a plan for the organization's response. In February 1995, when the hammer fell, striking Parks Canada with a devastating cut of 24 percent, or about $98 million, to be spread over five years, the organization was ready with a national parks business plan.

In a document designed to familiarize staff with the business plan, senior bureaucrats first assured them of the primary organizational goal. "We want to be the best we can be at protecting and presenting our natural and cultural heritage. We are serious about

this," they said—before pointing out that, in fact, protecting ecological integrity was only one of three key accountabilities. The
other two were "service to our clients" and "wise and efficient use
of public funds."[17] The plan itself stressed that the only way that
all three accountabilities could be fulfilled was through "adopting
an entrepreneurial approach" that would enable Parks Canada to
reduce its reliance on tax dollars and "increase its revenues significantly."[18] In fact, it aimed to double revenues, from $35 million to
$70 million. To achieve this goal, the plan set out cost-cutting and
revenue-generating strategies. Over the next three years, day-to-
day operating costs were to be reduced by 17 percent—or more.
Camping was to become "fully cost recovered." Repairs and
replacement of facilities and equipment were to be cut by 10 percent, while the funding available for providing facilities in new
parks would drop by 23 percent. There was a silver lining in this
black cloud: "This means that agreements for new national parks
will no longer fund developments within park boundaries that
have caused problems in the past," observed Kevin McNamee,
wildlands director of the Canadian Nature Federation, who then
added, "Hopefully, as federal funds shrink, the building of more
park facilities in environmentally sensitive areas will stop, and
repairs to facilities and roads that are no longer required will not
take place."[19] Of even greater importance was the promise that
financial support for protecting ecosystems and cultural assets
would remain stable and would double for the establishment of
new parks and historical sites.

Revenue would be generated through marketing and promotion
aimed at attracting more visitors for longer stays over more of the
year; and by implementing new and higher fees, pursuing partnerships and sponsorships with the private sector, and developing
"alternative service delivery," which would turn selected park services over to businesses to operate. The business plan also reaffirmed the intent of the government and senior bureaucrats to
redefine Parks Canada as a "special operating agency." Similar to a
Crown corporation, this entity would permit greater flexibility in

generating and retaining revenue, but would still receive base funding from government appropriations. Under this new structure, the national parks were to be managed as "business units," each with its own unique objectives for investing, streamlining and revenue generation. Welcome to the brave new world of park values.

"We will retain revenues and re-invest them into public services, freeing our appropriations for the protection of the natural and cultural heritage, provision of essential information and education services, and creation of new parks and sites," the senior bureaucrats declared, while reassuring the six hundred to eight hundred employees who would be affected by the plan that the Department of Canadian Heritage was "committed to a caring, supportive and respectful transition."[20]

Within Parks Canada, the business plan and intent to become a separate operating agency were met with eager receptivity by some, with seething resistance by others. At a workshop in Jasper National Park held to familiarize staff with the new concept of entrepreneurially driven national parks, the consultant leading the workshop took a $100 bill from her purse, snapped it and told her stunned audience that this was what it was about. Staff turned to the senior manager present, hoping for assurances that this wasn't true. Instead, he chose to remain silent. One distraught warden stumbled out of the workshop in disbelief and seriously contemplated turning in her badge. Surely this could not be the organization she believed in so deeply? Suddenly, Parks Canada was dominated by a bean-counter mind-set in which what seemed to matter most was the fiscal bottom line.

Details of the business plan didn't become public until the spring of the following year. That's when Michael Valpy, a columnist with *The Globe and Mail*, got wind of it and sounded the alarm. "Familiarize yourself with the terms 'separate service agency,' 'alternative service delivery' and 'employee takeover,'" he urged. "In bits and pieces over the past few months, the national government has been constructing the machinery to privatize and entrepreneurially transform many of its operations. Parks Canada has been designated a test model."[21] Hot on his heels, the National Component of the Public Service Alliance of Canada, the union representing most of Parks Canada's front-line employees, came out with all guns blazing, charging that the government was about to "off-load" critical functions of Parks Canada, which would result in less protection and care for the national parks. By October, even some Conservatives had joined the growing chorus of protest. In an article in *The Vancouver Sun*, Pat Carney, a B.C. senator and former cabinet minister in Mulroney's government, challenged, "Are we inadvertently prostituting Canada's financially stressed parks system, under the guise of privatization?"[22]

Some of the opposition was aimed at the new and increased "personal use fees." Their introduction was premised on the basic principle that "tax dollars pay for the cost of *having* and protecting national parks and national historic sites; those who derive additional benefit will pay to *use* them."[23] The principle and the specific proposal for user fees were tested through a public consultation process that involved no fewer than 24,000 people, who generally gave their approval to the idea. Nevertheless, as soon as the fees began going up, so did the voices of protest. Noting that the cost of an annual pass to the national parks had jumped from $35 to $70, a Reform Party MP fumed: "This land of Canada belongs to each and every Canadian. It is our birthright and our legacy. It must be available to persons of all socio-economic groups to experience." The suggestion that Parks Canada might price the national-park experience out of the range of less well-off citizens has some validity. Several visitor service managers, mostly in Atlantic Canada, told me that the personal use fees were pushing up the socio-economic profile of the typical park visitor.

The intention to aggressively solicit sponsorships from big business or to partner it in the operation of park facilities or services also sparked sharp allegations that the government was privatizing the national parks. "At this point in time, as government works to find new partners, how far are they willing to turn to the private sector?" worried Kevin McNamee of the Canadian Nature

Federation in the summer of 1996. "We don't know what will be untouchable."[24]

The strongest and loudest opposition was directed at "alternative service delivery" and "employee takeovers." As the former term suggests, the objective was for the government to find alternative ways of providing services to the public, while the latter term refers to what was planned to be the primary form of service delivery in the national parks. Under the employee takeovers (ETO's), staff in "non-core" activities, such as painters, electricians and general maintenance workers, were to be laid off, but would then be given the opportunity to bid for their old jobs on a contract basis. However, since there would be fewer jobs to bid on, not everyone laid off would have work when the dust settled. The winners would get less money and fewer benefits as Parks Canada clawed back on budgets for operations and maintenance. To top it off, those who did not bid could also find themselves without a job, creating a hellish dilemma. What was an employee to do?

The National Component of the Public Service Alliance attacked the ETO's as a "dismantling" of the national parks. "It is the privatization of the parks," said Doug Chalk, president of the National Component. "The quality and standards in the parks will be pushed to the limit and eventually will have to be dropped."[25] In all, two thousand of Parks Canada's five thousand–strong workforce would be affected by the ETO's.

Internally, it quickly became apparent that ETO's were tearing the organization apart, particularly in Western Canada, where they were being pushed most aggressively. Morale plummeted as affected staff were pitted against each other and against managers and wardens, who seemed buffered from the harshest effects of the bottom-line mentality. At Riding Mountain National Park, a proposal from some employees to take over maintenance of the main campground, gardens and garbage collection in the townsite generated resentment and suspicion among staff, who were fighting the ETO's and saw them as having "sold out." In Kluane, affected workers in maintenance and clerical services were angry at the wardens, whose jobs were considered "core" and were therefore protected. In most cases, employees remained respectful of each other but became increasingly hostile toward senior management. Of the several hundred proposals received, fewer than ten were approved. Due to the growing backlash, the program was scuttled within a year. In its wake, the ETO experiment left a profound level of demoralization that has still to be addressed.

The budget cuts forced or encouraged park managers to not only generate revenue but also to cut funding to programs critical to the maintenance of ecological integrity, despite reassurances that this wouldn't happen. In Calgary, I met with a wildlife biologist with Parks Canada who was facing the prospect of losing his job. He told me very candidly: "Senior management has knocked the stuffing out of our science programs. Too many of these people have very little science background. Consequently, the organization is only paying lip service to ecosystem management." While in Kouchibouguac National Park, I discovered that the ecosystem science program had been cut by $20,000 to shunt funds to the restoration of a barn at the Anne of Green Gables National Historic Site at Prince Edward Island National Park, meanwhile several new picnic shelters in Kouch were constructed at more than $30,000 a piece. Time and again, as I have travelled through the national parks system, I have heard the same refrain from Parks Canada biologists: "We are seriously underfunded and understaffed. If the organization is truly committed to ecosystem science, then it has to come up with more dollars for the program. Otherwise, it isn't walking the talk." But if these people complain or protest, they run the risk of having their career "limited." "We're supposed to carry out ecosystem science, but when we argue that we don't have the resources to adequately do so, we are dismissed as whiners or troublemakers," said a frustrated park biologist in southern Ontario. Even more irritating, park biologists frequently find themselves "outgunned" by scientists who are bankrolled by the proponents of developments inside and adjacent to the national parks.

As hard as the ecosystem sciences have been hit in the drive to turn the national parks into profit centres, the blows are light compared to those suffered by the interpretive and public education programs. Throughout the national parks system, these programs are hanging by a very thin thread. In fact, when I visited Jasper National Park in the winter of 1997, I discovered that they had been axed completely the year before; only very recently have they been reinstated, albeit at a greatly reduced level.

In Atlantic Canada, I recall arriving at a meeting with an acting chief interpreter and finding her in tears. She had a public event that day, but some equipment she needed had not been delivered, so at the last minute she was having to develop a new approach. While not a major crisis in itself, the failed delivery compounded an already over-the-top stress level caused by too few staff trying to do too much with too little. She not only acted as a manager but also provided supervision for interpretive and visitor service staff at her park, as well as at several national historic sites in the region, while also being called upon to deliver programs. At another park, the acting chief interpreter shared with me an intense feeling of isolation from others in the same profession within the organization, since system-wide conferences and seminars have become a thing of the past. Everywhere, the interpretive programs are also suffering a decline in attendance due to an imposed policy of cost recovery, which means that visitors now have to pay for guided hikes or evening programs. In Banff National Park, for example, the price for guided hikes in 1996 was $6 for adults, $4.50 for seniors and $3 for youths between the ages of six and sixteen (children under six could attend free). Throughout the system, interpreters scramble to come up with "revenue-generating" special events, like paddles in a voyageur-style canoe, but with too few staff to go around, events with a more substantive educational content are cut back. The few thousand dollars that might be generated over a season from these events comes at a very high hidden cost.

"It seems that senior managers just keep tugging the rug out from under us," vented several interpreters in a western national park. "They keep taking away more while demanding more from us. We managed to make $19,000 by busting everyone's back this year, but what good has it done us? There's got to be more than this to what makes for a good interpretive program. Is anybody paying attention to what's happening to us?"

The answer is yes. Damage to the interpretive programs within the national parks did not escape the eye of the Auditor General of Canada. "Information and interpretation are identified in Parks Canada policies as 'principal means of achieving its protection and presentation objectives,'" the Auditor General stated in a recent report on Parks Canada. "In our opinion, Parks Canada could do more to communicate information that would help it explain and protect the ecological features of national parks."[26] Underscoring the point, the report went on, "Given the potential for benefiting ecological integrity, Parks Canada should strengthen public education programs to better communicate ecological information to park visitors and Canadians in general."[27]

An independent internal review conducted in 1997 reaffirmed the concerns of the Auditor General, revealing that "[t]here has been a loss of focus and drifting in educational activities; there has been a significant decrease in resources committed to heritage presentation; there has been a dissipation in energies devoted to educational programming; there has been slippage in the consistency on programming; there has been substantive organizational re-structuring; there has been a decrease in quality and professionalism."[28] Senior bureaucrats within Parks Canada grudgingly agreed with the Auditor General and the independent review, and promised to renew heritage presentation, as interpretation and public education were now called. They followed up by establishing heritage presentation as a priority in the draft legislation to create Parks Canada as a separate service agency. Senior managers also met interpretive staff from across the country to draft a renewed vision and objectives for interpretive and education programs. However, at the time of writing, there has been no real improvement on the ground.

I remember a discussion I had with the director of national park operations for Western Canada several years ago, before the regional office in which he worked was gutted. "People perceive cost cutting and revenue generating as driving the organization," he protested. "They're not. However, we must have a stable revenue regime. It's a matter of survival. Without it we cannot fulfill our mandate . . . I realize it may be discriminatory against some parts of society to charge for services in the national parks," he continued. "But relative to other forms of entertainment, a visit to a national park is still a good deal. People will pay seventy bucks to see a Calgary Flames hockey game, but they will scream like hell about paying the same to get into a park. But really, what's the problem with charging for services or pursuing sponsorships with the private sector? The national parks are not much different than hockey. Both are quintessentially Canadian, and yet we readily accept sponsorship of hockey; why not parks too?"

But there is a fundamental difference between running the national parks as a business and operating them as a public trust. I got a finer appreciation of this distinction in the summer of 1996, when the controversy was erupting over the increase in user fees, the employee takeovers and the pursuit of corporate sponsorships. I had driven to Qualicum Beach to get the perspective of Jim Christakos, a former Parks Canada senior manager, who had recently retired from the organization. It was a balmy summer day and, after offering me a cold beer, he ushered me out onto the front deck overlooking the sparkling ocean below with the shimmering mountains of the mainland in the distance.

"There is no way that the national parks can be made to double the amount of revenue they generate, from $35 million to $70 million, without eroding ecological integrity," he began. "The two conflict—always have and always will." He made it clear that he wasn't opposed to the idea of managing parks in the most fiscally responsible manner; however, the primary purpose of parks, as opposed to businesses, is not to make money. "The national parks are a public trust, which protect and present something we know instinctively to be intrinsically priceless. They should not be treated like products to be bought and sold in the free market. There is a limit to how many compatible services there are that can be made into income-generators. After that you must look to the 'Disney' approach to open new markets. These will come at a steep price to national park values."

The problem, we agreed, was that the pressures to run Parks Canada like a business were immense. Indeed, they were a direct manifestation of the federal government's unreserved embrace of the idea. Furthermore, the government maintained that it was only doing what the public wanted it to do: reducing the country's deficit and debt.

"The national parks must be adequately funded," Christakos concluded. "But the only way this will happen is if there is a groundswell of public support for the national parks."

# SIX

# Office Politics

In the previous chapter, I argued that Parks Canada is contributing to the decline of ecological integrity through inconsistencies in management caused partly by the pressure to run the national parks as a business. However, I am equally certain that the inconsistencies are also a function of political interference, interdepartmental rivalry and organizational dysfunction—much like those lampooned in the popular "Dilbert" comic strip. Office politics, from the ministerial to the field level, not only result in decisions that adversely impact the national parks, but they also have a devastating effect on morale. A great many employees within Parks Canada are deeply committed to protecting the wildness of the national parks. They have been, and continue to be, frustrated, angered and saddened by the mistreatment of the parks and themselves.

One of the most recent and most distasteful examples of political interference involves the Greenwich Dunes, near Prince Edward Island National Park. In early February 1998, the minister of Canadian Heritage, Sheila Copps, and P.E.I.'s premier, Pat Binns, signed an agreement to transfer the dunes from provincial Crown land to the Government of Canada, to be added to the sixty-one-year-old national park. At the time of their transfer, the dunes were managed under the provincial Natural Areas

Protections Act, and were little used. Only a rough, rutted road offered vehicle access to the edge of the area. Except for the occasional transgression by people on ATV's, the dune ecosystems were largely free from human impact.

The transfer of the dunes, contained in three parcels of land amounting to 365 hectares (about 900 acres), to the national parks system was cheered enthusiastically by local environmental groups, who had been lobbying the respective governments for several years to have the dunes better protected. In her speech announcing the transfer, Copps seemed sympathetic to their concerns. "I am delighted that we are adding these unique sections of land to Prince Edward Island National Park," she said. "The Greenwich Peninsula offers natural features which cannot be found anywhere else in North America."[1] Her speech was followed by one from Lawrence MacAulay, minister of Labour and the member of Parliament for Cardigan, the riding that encompasses the Greenwich Peninsula. MacAulay emphasized a very different set of priorities. "An expanded national park will bring with it sustainable economic benefits," he crowed. "Through a park advisory board, Parks Canada will ensure the concerns of Islanders are considered in planning and managing the park lands."[2] He then took immense delight in announcing a $1.3-million development plan to prepare the dunes to receive upward of 100,000 visitors annually after their official opening in the early summer of 2000. His vision for the fragile dune system deeply worried environmental groups.

Near the end of 1998, MacAulay, now Solicitor General, and Andy Mitchell, the secretary of state for Parks, proudly released an approved development plan for the Greenwich Dunes. MacAulay said:

Parks Canada conducted Island-wide public consultations in the spring to solicit comments on the future of these park lands. With the support and effective engagement of the local community in this process, I am delighted to announce that the development concept has been reviewed and endorsed by the Greenwich Peninsula Advisory Board. As a proud Canadian, and Islander, it is particularly gratifying for me to be involved in developing this site in a sensitive and responsive manner, which will preserve these lands for centuries to come.[3]

He did not mention that his brother headed up the advisory board.

A couple of months after the announcement, two directors of Earth Action visited the dunes. One of them, Sharon Labchuk, said of their visit:

We were horrified to see a ten-foot clear-cut swath had been cut around the perimeter of the park, damaging and fragmenting wildlife habitat. A pathway, excavated to a depth of about 8 inches and filled with gravel, now goes over the top of four out of six identified archeological sites, in contravention of the Archeological Sites Protection Act, which prohibits any excavation or alteration.[4]

A hastily constructed trail was already collapsing over the side of one of the dunes and onto the beach below. They also found survey stakes marking out a parking area to accommodate ninety cars and ten buses, toilets, showers and food concessions. "It is now clear that our sense of security and hope has been ill-advised," lamented Dr. Irene Novaczek, the other director. "Islanders who care about Greenwich and who believe that this province should have at least this one small area protected from mass tourism and commercialization need to wake up and take note of what has been going on."[5] They immediately began turning up the heat on MacAulay and Dave Lipton, the field unit superintendent for Prince Edward Island.

In October 1999, the controversy came to a full boil when it became known that MacAulay was now backing a $3.5-million proposal for the construction of an interpretive centre and forty-room "eco-lodge" on land within easy walking distance of the dunes. With his encouragement, Parks Canada had joined with the provincial government in purchasing the 50-hectare (123-acre) site for an estimated $800,000. The interpretive centre and so-called "eco-lodge" are just the first stage of a development that could eventually grow to include time-shared condos, shops, restaurants and tourism-related businesses.

MacAulay does not see any contradiction between his avowed commitment to the protection of the dunes and his enthusiasm to see them developed. Answering critics who accused him of being on a mission to exploit the fragile ecosystem for votes and economic gain, he bristled, saying they were right about one thing: "I am on a mission for economic development. However, I am also responsible for the protection of this very important national jewel."[6] Supported by Lipton, he firmly argued that the circle can be squared through something called "sustainable tourism," which would revolve around educating people before and during their visit about how to reduce their impact on the dunes.

In theory, it sounds good. But there is a real credibility problem here. Lipton has recently admitted on CBC radio that P.E.I. National Park is already experiencing impacts from too many visitors. "Our biggest challenge," he said, "is basically visitor and tourism facilities that are putting external pressures on us, and accommodating larger numbers of visitors to the national park itself."[7] Later, referring to the national parks as a "sustainable resource," he stated that increasing visitation meant that more services had to be provided. The Confederation Bridge, in only three years, has caused a 60 percent increase in visitation to the Island and, according to Lipton, a 25 percent jump at P.E.I National Park.[8] "And we've actually reached threshold limits in terms of managing the visitor population that enters the park," he confessed, further emphasizing his point by calling the park "maxed out."[9] Then there is the development company APM, which has publicly declared that it wants to maximize "the opportunity for visitors to experience the purity and nobility" of the Greenwich Dunes. The choice of words made critics cringe and cynics sneer. The history of maximum sustainable use of forests, fish or wildlife in Canada has shown it for what it is: a sure path to overexploitation and collapse, a passage from economic boom to ecological bust. Maximum sustainable tourism is no different.

Regrettably, MacAulay is not the first, nor is it likely he will be the last, politician—federal or provincial—to use the power of public office to influence national park management decisions. The tendency to promote and encourage development in and around parks to gain favour in one's riding (and with the general populace) is obviously very strong, judging by how frequently it occurs and how far back it goes. More than one park superintendent has told me of being pressured to bend the National Parks Act and Policy or to keep quiet on development and resource activities near park boundaries to keep some elected official happy. During the mid-1980s, Conservative members of Parliament from Alberta threatened to sink the amending of the National Parks Act being put forward by Tom McMillan unless he allowed more development within the mountain parks of Yoho, Banff, Kootenay and Jasper.

Damaging office politics also occurs at the senior bureaucratic level. Over the past fifteen years, Parks Canada has been through a couple of bewildering shuffles between envious and hostile departments. First there was the amalgamation with the Department of Environment in the mid-1980s, which should have been a marriage made in heaven; instead it was one from hell. Under the guise of integration, and goaded by the popularity of its newest acquisition, senior bureaucrats within the department reduced Parks Canada's staffing and budgets.[10] In the early 1990s, just as Parks Canada staff thought that their situation couldn't get any worse, their organization was placed in the completely new Department of Canadian Heritage, an eclectic umbrella for citizenship, official languages, multiculturalism, sport, the Canada Council and the CBC. Suddenly, Parks Canada staff found themselves reporting to managers who had very little understanding of and commitment to national parks, and having to spend more time at ribbon-cutting ceremonies, sod turnings or cheque presentations and less time caring for the parks. Not surprisingly, morale within

Parks Canada nosedived as the organization was led further from its mandate of maintaining ecological integrity.

The situation had deteriorated so much by the mid-1990s that the Second Century Club, consisting of former Parks Canada employees, many of whom were middle to senior managers, sent a letter to Suzanne Hurtubise, deputy minister of the Department of Canadian Heritage, asking that something be done immediately to reverse "the decline in the health and effectiveness" of the organization. The president of the club wrote:

> In the past, organizational changes resulting from integration within new departmental structures largely took place at the corporate level, with the foundation element, namely the park/site level especially, remaining unchanged. The principal reason for my concerns lies in the fact that this foundation level has now been impacted in a significant way, resulting in loss of efficiency and effectiveness with accompanying lack in client focus. This is to a great extent the result of a serious decline of staff morale to the point where pride in the organization is at an all-time low.

Of particular concern to the club was the elimination of key management positions from some parks in Western Canada. At Riding Mountain National Park, where the superintendent and the chief park warden—who together represent more than seventy years of experience and wisdom—were pressured into taking early retirement, park staff were left reeling from the devastating blow. If the organization cared so little for people of this calibre, how would it treat ordinary park staff? As one long-time warden bitterly remarked shortly after their departure: "You lose so much knowledge when you get rid of good people like that, and all you are left with is more and more new people who don't have the history. Many of them are also seasonal, so who's to say they will even be around long enough to gain the knowledge of the park."

Anger and frustration over the issue drove the park's ecologist to take drastic action. Sitting at his computer, he composed an e-mail in which he poured out all his pent-up emotion. Then, with a simple keystroke, the message was sent to every employee with a computer in Parks Canada. "You can imagine what was going through my mind," he told me. "I suddenly realized that there was no stopping what I had done and that my career with the organization may have just come to an end." He had good reason to think this. In his e-mail, he decried the forced and embarrassing end of some of Parks Canada's finest superintendents and chief park wardens, which he blamed on a "network of control-hungry, self-serving bureaucrats who live in hierarchies and who care more about power and personal status than they do about national parks." He went on: "When we lose people like those, we also lose integrity, the integrity that comes with experience, and wisdom, and a strong dedication to the system of national parks spanning this country. Integration with other Heritage Canada components has muddled our mission and compromised our conviction."

Pushing back his chair, he picked up his coffee mug with shaking hands and went to get himself a fortifier. As he walked down the corridor, a chorus of calls began to echo throughout Riding Mountain's administration building. "People were calling out my name from every office and saying, 'What have you done?'" he said with a pleased grin. "And when I got back to my computer, my e-mail basket was filling rapidly. I had obviously touched a hot spot." The avalanche of debate almost crashed Parks Canada's server, until Sheila Copps sent out an e-mail of her own, saying that a special electronic bulletin board had been created for the debate so as not to tie up the organization's computer system. Whether it was intended to or not, the e-mail message from the minister herself squelched any further discussion; staff may have felt that anything they said might come back to haunt them. As for the park ecologist, all he got was a warning. It seemed to him that senior management were anxious to bury the incident rather than do anything that might further agitate staff.

A couple of months after the superintendents in Western Canada were axed, Prime Minister Jean Chrétien made a surprise visit to Prince Albert National Park. Upon arrival, he asked to meet with the park superintendent. Chrétien's jaw dropped in disbelief when he was told that the position had been eliminated and the superintendent had been let go. He promptly ordered the positions re-established and filled. However, it was already too late; the damage had been done.

The noted Manitoba ecologist Jack Dubois was working at Riding Mountain National Park on a special assignment at the time, and what he saw left him disheartened and angry. "It's been quite a rough ride for the past few years," he told me. "There isn't an area where senior managers haven't run roughshod over employee morale." As a consequence, he saw employees who were so worried about their jobs that they had less time and energy to care for the park. "Parks Canada is a very old-fashioned, autocratic system, in which fear is rampant," he concluded.

A chief park warden from one of the northern national parks agreed with Dubois's assessment and added his own unique twist on the damage done by the recent string of reorganizations. We were sitting in an outdoor bar, enjoying a beer and getting to know each other after meeting at a conference. On a paper napkin, he drew a replica of a "Far Side" cartoon that a speaker had used. The cartoon showed a snake in a large chair, watching television. It was in the process of swallowing a pig when the phone rang. In a thought cloud above the snake's head appeared the single word, "Damn!" "You know who the snake is?" asked the warden. "The Department of Environment. You know who the pig is? Parks Canada." By now, we were both in stitches. Laughing and gasping for air, he asked, "And you know who is on the other end of the line, don't you? Department of Canadian Heritage, of course."

The brief moment of humour quickly faded when our discussion turned to the reorganization of Parks Canada into a separate service agency within the Department of Canadian Heritage. Announced as part of the 1996 budget, the new status for Parks Canada was intended to provide a policy environment less prone to tampering by departmental directives or agendas, and greater flexibility in generating and retaining revenues.[11] On the upside, the warden thought it could be an opportunity for the organization to regain its focus on maintaining ecological integrity; on the downside, the agency status might simply mean more staff and program cuts in a continued drive to run parks like a business. After weighing the two sides, the best he could say was that he was very suspicious but guardedly optimistic.

A few months later, in Moncton, New Brunswick, I got my times mixed up and inadvertently sat in on a meeting chaired by Tom Lee, the assistant deputy minister of Parks Canada, and Andy Mitchell, the secretary of state for the national parks. They were in town to brief staff within the Atlantic Region on progress toward becoming a special operating agency. After Lee had explained the reasons for Parks Canada becoming an agency, he said he wanted to hear and discuss staff concerns. There were a few minutes of anxious silence, then someone asked the question probably foremost in everyone's mind: "Will there be any more cuts?" Mitchell replied: "The genesis of the agency was not to seek further staff reductions. However, I can't say what a future government may or may not do. For the time being, you will just have to trust us on this." Instantly, people tensed and the air in the room became charged. Sensing he had crossed a line, Mitchell hastily added, "You will trust this process of becoming an agency as we earn it from you."

This was too much for another employee, who said with barely restrained emotion: "I've been hearing a lot about trust lately—that there is nothing to fear. But how far can employees be asked to trust given the recent past of staff cuts and changes in direction?"

An employee sitting beside me added that morale at his historic site was very low, to which Lee responded: "What can we do to help? If people are feeling like that, they should be helped." The employee immediately shot back: "It wasn't long ago that we were pushed into a room to accept employee takeovers from you. What is the basis for trust?" Lee and Mitchell exchanged a sideways glance and then the former repeated, "We know that we will have to work very hard to regain your trust."

Fresh in everyone's mind were similar comments made just a year before by the minister of Canadian Heritage, Sheila Copps. In a speech to other park ministers from across Canada, she stated:

> We have a dual obligation here: to meet our financial requirements, and to meet our conservation and protection goals. It's a tricky balance, but a balance that Canadians demand we maintain. Is it going to be difficult? Of course. I am not going to tell you, or any Parks Canada employee, that we can do both without a lot of stress, and strain, and change. I am not going to talk in terms of "rightsizing" or "reengineering," that only masks the pain that's going to be felt. Real cuts are happening, and real human beings are being affected—that's the plain spoken truth.[12]

She then made a commitment that Parks Canada employees would have input into the implementation of the cuts and resulting changes. "We need to hear from our employees—the people who *made* it the best park system in the world," Copps asserted. "Our parks deserve the most careful thought we can give. Our employees deserve an orderly and thoughtful approach to the challenges that lie ahead."[13] The words were good, but they didn't match reality. Staff felt powerless to effect change in a process that seemed disorderly and ruthless.

One of the saddest cases of demoralization I encountered involved Bernie Lieff. Here was a middle manager who was held in extremely high regard by other park staff and park advocates for his personal integrity and commitment to national parks. I had met with Lieff a few weeks before the Moncton meeting, while passing through Calgary. As I had been warned, his battle with cancer was taking a heavy toll on his energy and spirit, but so were the reorganizations and budget cuts. "We had one of the most dedicated organizations in government," he said in tones heavy with regret. "People believed in the cause, but they have been so badly screwed lately. The disrespectful treatment of elders—long-time employees—sends a very bad message down the line. The subsequent lack of trust is deep. It will probably take ten or more years to rebuild." As I shook his hand, the pain and hurt in his eyes was terrible to see. He passed away a couple of months later.

The concern that the real motivation behind the new agency was to run parks more profitably also came up at the Moncton meeting. Responding to this concern, Mitchell said: "We didn't establish parks on their ability to pay for themselves. We're not a business. We just want to operate in a more businesslike manner." He stated that the government was committed to provide 75 percent of Parks Canada's budget from tax dollars; the new agency would have to generate the rest.

In the spring of 1998, when the government introduced the legislation to establish Parks Canada as a special operating agency, it was a move generally supported by the environmental community, who had also been alarmed by the loss of mission under the Department of Canadian Heritage. "Parks Canada itself is not mentioned in the National Parks Act and really doesn't have much of a legislative mandate," said Kevin McNamee, director of wildland conservation for the Canadian Nature Federation.[14] However, he also expressed some concerns about the new agency, in particular that it could open the door to more privatization of the parks and that too much power was concentrated in the hands of its chief executive officer.

The secretary of state for parks, Andy Mitchell, once again defended the new agency. "I want to be crystal clear, this is not the privatization of Parks Canada," he protested. "We believe strongly in a public stewardship of our special places. This entity is a public entity. It is going to provide that public stewardship and be very accountable."[15]

The act to establish the Parks Canada Agency came into effect on December 3, 1998, with many of the concerns still prevalent. The new law gives the chief executive officer (CEO), now elevated to a rank equivalent to deputy minister from that of an assistant deputy minister, complete control over the organization. However, there are some checks to this power. The CEO must comply with direction given by the minister responsible for the national parks, which continues to be Sheila Copps, the minister for the Department of Canadian Heritage. Furthermore, the minister will convene, at least once every two years, a round table of external experts to assess and advise on the performance of the agency.

The concerns over the agency's purpose also remain. Nowhere in the legislation is the maintenance of ecological integrity stated as Parks Canada's mandate. It gets only a brief mention in the act's preamble, which is not considered to be legally binding. The overwhelming impression is precisely what many people feared: the act compels the new agency to operate like a business. On the bright side, since the new agency status was first proposed, there have been positive signs that the organization is beginning to regain control over its own destiny, rather than being tossed around by other agendas within the Department of Canadian Heritage. A joint union and management steering committee has agreed upon a set of values and principles to resolve long-standing grievances. Doug Chalk, the president of the National Component of the Public Service Alliance of Canada, is optimistic on this front. "The values and principles mark a real change at the top. They are sincerely trying to rebuild, but it will probably take quite a while before the effects are felt at the field level," he said in a recent telephone conversation. However, other things—critical things, deep within Parks Canada's culture—have not changed, which suggests that Chalk's optimism may be premature.

Office politics arising from organizational culture remains the single biggest challenge for Parks Canada in its path to alignment with the mandate of ecological integrity. Ideally, culture is understood to be all those things that hold a group of people together, whether a company, bureaucracy or country. It is what bolsters common identity, and it emerges out of such things as how an organization or group is structured, how it makes decisions and what values guide it. Like many large organizations, whether in the public or private sector, Parks Canada is intensely hierarchical, to the point that there is little real communication between its various sections. Wardens do what wardens do, interpreters do what interpreters do, maintenance crews do what maintenance crews do—all without much effort to break out of their own little "stovepipes" and share information. Communication between senior management and the rest of the organization is evident, but it is dysfunctional in at least two ways: from the top down, it is predominately used as an instrument of control, with subordinates being expected to obey directives without questioning; from the bottom up, it is filtered to ensure that potentially "career-limiting" information is not passed along to superiors. As a chief park warden commented to me as we left a meeting of the Panel on Ecological Integrity a few months ago, "There is a huge amount of denial within the organization. People are so afraid to speak the truth." During the meeting, one of the panel members asked the delegation of Parks Canada managers why they had encountered significant levels of frustration and stress within the organization. Without thinking, one of the managers piped up, "Because we don't walk the talk!" When asked for examples, he suddenly realized what he had said and quietly replied that he couldn't. Everyone in the room knew, however, that he *would* not rather than *could* not offer examples. Nobody wants to be the bearer of bad news that might anger or embarrass senior management, out of fear for the consequences.

The organization is also male-dominated. It tends to encourage people to remain outwardly stoic in the face of loss or pain and not to ask for help, no matter what they may be feeling. The insensitive treatment and loss of highly respected staff from the "family" of Parks Canada continues to haunt many of those who remain like the pain that persists in the body long after the loss of a limb. People are not like parts of a machine, which can be popped in or out without consequences to the organization as a whole. In fact, leading management thinking conceives of organizations more as living organisms than as machines. In the words of two highly respected management consultants:

Caught now in the Communications Age, we have stretched the models of the Industrial Age to the limits of implosion. It is time to replace our mechanistic view of business with a more organic one, and to endow the recently discovered biological nature of our corporations with a new spirituality that recognizes the sanctity of individual human life and has compassion for individuals.[16]

In other words, organizations must begin to "reconnect with the people that comprise them."[17] This is even more critical as the dark side of the Communications Age and a bottom-line fixation sweep over organizations, aggravating "individual isolation" and "a loss of genuine human contact." Long-term, meaningful success, the two consultants argue, ultimately depends on the development of new social contracts in which organizations demonstrate a commitment to the total well-being of their employees.

The combined effect of all of the above is the suppression of learning within Parks Canada, which runs counter to good ecosystem management and the maintenance of ecological integrity. As conservation biologist Ed Grumbine points out, "Resource agencies have been structured not so much to be responsive to new learning, but to maintain control over resources, information and people."[18] An organizational culture that fosters learning is crucial because ecosystem management and ecological integrity require new thinking about nature, biological diversity and humanity's place in the grand scheme of things. A key feature of this new thinking is that it is systems-based. "We know at a subliminal level that it is the whole that is important," say Katherine Jope and Joseph Dunstan, two researchers with the U.S. National Park Service. "Yet, in seeking to learn about nature, we divide landscapes into discrete compartments of soil, water, vegetation, geology, and slope, and then attempt to reconstruct the ecosystem based on what we have learned about each piece."[19] They maintain that "[e]xamining every ecosystem process individually will tell us little about how an entire ecosystem works. We can only hope to understand ecosystems—and conserve them—by adopting an ecological world view based on a systems perspective."[20]

Grumbine distinguishes the ecological world view by contrasting it with the traditional resource management world view. The latter focuses on "resources," that is, products that can be extracted from nature and used to satisfy human desires and needs, whereas the former concerns itself with the protection of "sources"—the ecosystems and biological diversity that produce the resources. Systems thinking, as implied by Jope and Dunstan, conceives of nature as existing in "nested hierarchies"—much like those Russian wooden dolls that are housed one inside the other—with cells within tissues, tissues within organs, organs within species, species within populations, populations within ecosystems and ecosystems within the planetary "eco" sphere. Each level of organization is seen as discrete, and yet exists interdependently with the parts it is made of and with the next larger whole of which it is a part.

One of the most critical areas adversely affected by internal office politics is the development and application of science to support ecosystem management decision-making (the other area, interpretation and public education, was discussed earlier). No less an authority than the Auditor General of Canada has heavily criticized Parks Canada for this failing. In a scathing 1996 audit of the systems and processes in place to maintain ecological integrity, the Auditor General warned that ecosystem conservation plans throughout the park system were either out of date or incomplete; that there were poor linkages between science and management concerns; and that management plans tended to emphasize social and economic concerns over ecological ones. The Auditor General admonished the organization:

> Parks Canada has not systematically collected scientific data on natural resources and monitored changes in their condition over time for all the national parks. Without this critical information, Parks Canada will have difficulty assessing the condition and trend

of natural resources in these national parks, including species at risk. This increases the risk that Parks Canada will be unable to protect ecological integrity in these parks.[21]

The Banff–Bow Valley Study said much the same thing, as I suspect will the Panel on Ecological Integrity.

Part of the problem is that the dominant culture of Parks Canada does not consider itself science based; instead, it is much more operations based. The tendency is to place a low priority on ecological research and a higher priority on the provision of facilities for the benefit and safety of visitors. This inherent bias is reflected in the fact that out of some three thousand employees, only fourteen have Ph.D.s and forty or so have masters degrees in either the natural or social sciences. Even more disturbing, there is very little understanding of ecological principles among the organization's senior management. As a consequence, ecological science is rarely represented in the park management decision-making process. If ecological integrity or ecosystem management does come up in these forums, they are generally treated as one of many goals to be achieved by the national parks. As a field unit superintendent in Atlantic Canada once said to me: "Well, you see, there are many, many interests that must be thought of, and there are all these values that parks represent: recreational, spiritual and even economic. It's like a big matrix that has to be managed. Also, we must keep in mind that national parks are not strict nature preserves." The real mandate of the national parks, he maintained, was to achieve a careful mix between visitor use and protection of resources. When I countered that both the National Parks Act and Policy stated that the maintenance of ecological integrity was to be the first priority in park management, he disagreed, saying that the act and policy only made it one goal to be achieved among many others.

I left his office depressed. I had encountered too many examples of this kind of thinking throughout Parks Canada. No wonder that among the majority of staff who are fiercely dedicated to ecological integrity, park management is often seen as the biggest threat. As one park warden bitterly put it, "I used to believe that my personal values and the values of the organization were one and the same, but I was deluded." What his comment reveals is that beneath all the problems within Parks Canada, whether the result of politicians and bureaucrats, reorganizations or budget cuts, there is a philosophical split that is arguably even more damaging to dedicated staff and to the national parks themselves.

# SEVEN

# Walking the Talk

Nowhere are Parks Canada's inconsistencies more blatant than over questions concerning "the mandate." While the amending of the National Parks Act in 1988 and the revising of the National Parks Policy in 1994 are widely perceived internally as having established the mandate to maintain ecological integrity, there is still a great deal of controversy over the primary purpose of the national parks and of the agency itself. The issue is a loaded one, touching on deeply held values, beliefs and perceptions about the world and the place of humans in it. Uncovering and debating these things can be, and often is, an intense experience filled with pain and passion, because the process cuts to the heart of personal and collective identity. Nevertheless, the debate is essential to restoring the health of Parks Canada and the national parks.

"The fact of the matter is that the organization is deeply fractured," said a chief park warden as we strolled along a dirt road through a pine forest. "Basically, there are two camps vying for control, with a whole bunch of people in the middle unsure of which to join." It was a warm spring day in the Rockies, and a bright sun hung almost directly overhead in a pale blue sky. Along the twin ruts we followed, snow was melting and puddles of water had collected in shallow depressions, compelling us to intersperse our sedate saunter with moments of frenzied hopscotch as we negotiated tricky patches of slush, mud and ice. We had set out to look for bighorn sheep on some of the bare slopes south of the administration building and to get well away to have a candid discussion.

Stopping by a large, old and twisted pine, we swept our binoculars over the tawny grass-covered flank of a low mountain that ran parallel to the road. "As I see it," he said, continuing the conversation while keeping his gaze directed at the mountain, "On one side are those who hold an anthropocentric world view while on the other side are those who believe in an ecocentric world view. These are two fundamentally different ways of seeing things, and unfortunately, the former are still in control. They refuse to embrace the mandate of maintaining ecological integrity."

I lowered my binoculars and gave a soft grunt of agreement. I had heard a similar analysis on numerous occasions from other Parks Canada staff throughout the system. With no sheep in sight, he slipped his binoculars into a pocket of his windbreaker and asked if I was familiar with the writings of Stan Rowe. I replied that I was. "Then," he said enthusiastically, "you understand what I'm driving at!" "You bet," I replied, thinking back to Rowe's delightful book of essays entitled *Home Place*, in which he argues that there are basically two sets of values behind the preservation of wild species and places: the first is based on their utility in meeting some human need or desire; the second is symbolic, based on an appreciation for the inherent worth of nature's wildness. Parks as resources, as things to be used, versus parks as sources, sacred places to be protected—the conflict has existed since the birth of the national parks 115 years ago, but it has become increasingly more intense and stressful over the past four decades.

When one looks back over the history of Canada's national parks, three overlapping but nevertheless fairly distinct eras emerge. The first, wherein parks served multiple purposes or uses, began in the 1880s and lasted approximately until the 1960s. The second era was one in which parks had only two purposes: they were to be "maintained and made use of" and to be protected, "so as to leave them unimpaired for the enjoyment of future Canadians."[1] Frequently referred to as the Dual Mandate era, it began in the early 1910s, achieved supremacy as the dominant park management philosophy in the 1950s, began to weaken in the 1960s and 1970s, but received reinforcement and support in the 1980s and 1990s as national parks increasingly were seen as potential profit centres. In the third, the primary purpose for national parks is to maintain the ecological integrity of a representative sample of Canada's landscapes, ecosystems and species. Use is secondary, and is only permitted within limits that err on the side of conserving biological diversity. This era began in the early 1960s and has been steadily gaining strength, despite some major setbacks, to the point that it may soon eclipse the former era—something that couldn't happen too soon for my companion. We started making our way back to his truck while discussing the evolution of the national parks' mandate.

The year was 1883, and it was a crisp November day when a construction foreman with the Canadian Pacific Railway, along with one of his workers, set off by handcar to inspect the newly laid rail line that now penetrated the Rocky Mountains. Near Sulphur Mountain, they disembarked to explore its lower slopes. Crossing the Bow River, they stumbled upon something that would change the course of history for the region and the country: a stream of hot water flowed into the river. Following it back to its source, the two men found a cavern. Peering through a hole in the roof, they saw a hot spring bubbling out of the rocks below. Instantly, they realized that they had discovered something both remarkable and potentially profitable. Wishing to secure the natural feature for themselves, they built a small cabin next to the springs and applied for squatters' rights.

Word soon spread, and it wasn't long before the federal government of Sir John A. Macdonald became interested in the springs. William Pearce, superintendent of mines with the Department of the Interior, was sent out to inspect the springs. He returned, extolling their beauty and the spectacular mountain setting. He urged the government to act quickly to reserve the land around them, as there were tremendous economic gains to be made if the springs were developed for tourism. Strapped for cash after building the transcontinental railway, Macdonald and his government seized the opportunity, and in November 1885 created a 26-square-kilometre reserve around the springs. Immediately, work began on roads and facilities to service the reserve.

Over the next ten years, several more reserves were established throughout the Canadian Rockies; these would eventually become Waterton Lakes, Yoho, Glacier and Revelstoke national parks. In each, the management regime was essentially the same: develop them for tourism while allowing pre-existing resource extraction activities to continue. Coal mines operated in Yoho and Banff, while a small camp sprang up around a possible oil well in Waterton Lakes. A sawmill on the shore of Middle Waterton Lake processed trees harvested within the fledgling park to provide lumber for the construction of early park buildings and facilities. In his reports back to Ottawa, the first superintendent of Rocky Mountain Park (now known as Banff) boasted proudly of the numbers of visitors and of the amount of timber harvested and coal mined. Parks served multiple purposes, and that was considered to be good and proper management.

This isn't to say that there was no concern for the protection of wildlife; there was some. Shortly after establishing the Banff reserve, the government sent W.F. Whitcher, a former commissioner of fisheries, to investigate the condition of the reserve's wildlife. His research quickly determined that many of the native species were severely reduced or no longer found within the local area, largely because of uncontrolled hunting, especially to supply meat for the lumber and mining camps and for the growing tourist trade. He immediately recommended stricter controls on "hunting, shooting, trapping and fishing,"[2] which were soon incorporated into the Rocky Mountains Park Act. However, Whitcher also urged that all predators be eliminated to maintain healthy populations of more valuable animals. This recommendation was faithfully followed by park wardens for the next three-quarters of a century, until more enlightened understanding of ecology put an end to the ill-conceived practice. The act governed "the care, preservation and management of the park and of the water-courses, lakes, trees and shrubbery, minerals, curiosities and other matters therein contained" as well as "the preservation and protection of game and fish, or of wild birds generally."[3] Unfortunately, the act came at a time when the political will to enforce wildlife protection was weak. The dominant perception of Canada was of a vast, limitless frontier overflowing with wildlife.

But the times were a-changing. By the turn of the century, the decline and disappearance of wildlife throughout the west had reached a crisis point. The bison, grizzly bears and wolf had been exterminated, and herds of elk and antelope had become a rare sight across the Prairies. On the verdant West Coast, old-growth forests were being laid to waste by logging companies who wreaked havoc while taking only the biggest and best.

In 1906, Prime Minister Wilfred Laurier convened a special conference to address the destructive forest practices. His special guest and keynote speaker was Gifford Pinchot, chief of the U.S. Forest Service and leading advocate of a new land management approach that he called "conservation." "I have no interest in a forest that is not of use," he proudly declared. "If our forests are to stand unused there, and all we get from them is the knowledge that we have them, then, as far as I am concerned, they disappear from my field of interest. I care nothing about them whatever. But use is the end of forest preservation, and the highest use."[4] In a paper published after the conference, Pinchot explained:

There has been a fundamental misconception that conservation means nothing but the husbanding of resources for future generations. There could be no more serious mistake. Conservation does mean provision for the future, but it means also and first of all the recognition of the right of the present generation to the fullest necessary use of all the resources this country is so abundantly blessed with.[5]

The fullest necessary use meant "multiple use" directed toward the "maximum sustained yield" of products to provide "the greatest good for the greatest number over the longest time." For Pinchot, conservation rested on two simple premises: "The first duty of the human race is to control the earth it lives upon. The earth and its resources belong of right to its people."[6]

As the new doctrine swept across North America like a prairie wildfire, the Canadian government passed the Dominion Forest Reserves and Parks Act in 1911. The act established a series of forest reserves throughout the west in which conservation or "wise" use would be the order of the day. Of greater long-term significance, the legislation consolidated the numerous park reserves into a unified system and created a Dominion Parks Branch to manage it. It was the first organization of its kind in the world.

To head the new branch, the government appointed thirty-six-year-old James B. Harkin, who would serve as its leader for the next twenty-five years. Like most of his contemporaries, he was greatly influenced by Pinchot's ethic of conservation. At the same time, he was just as much influenced by Pinchot's arch-rival John Muir, founder of the Sierra Club, who espoused a radically different view of nature and of conservation. Once, upon observing an alligator, Muir remarked:

Doubtless these creatures are happy and fill the place assigned to them by the great Creator of us all. Fierce and cruel they appear to us, but beautiful in the eyes of God. How narrow we selfish, conceited creatures are in our sympathies! how blind to the rights of all of the rest of creation! . . . The world we are told was made for man. A presumption that is totally unsupported by the facts. Nature's object in making animals and plants might possibly be first of all the happiness of each one of them, not the creation of all for the happiness of one. Why ought man to value himself as more than an infinitely small composing unit of the one great unit of creation?[7]

Not surprisingly, Muir's ethic of conservation centred on the preservation of wild places and species for their own inherent worth and for the enjoyment of people through appreciative, non-consumptive activities such as hiking and nature study. In and through Harkin, these two fundamentally different views of nature gave birth to the Dual Mandate era in the management of Canada's national parks.

Harkin strongly believed that the national parks were "holy places" created by nature "in accordance with some divine law of harmony of her own," where "wonder, reverence and the feeling that one is nearer the mystery of things" were inspired.[8] As such, they were to be protected because "[m]an can maim, disfigure, and weaken Nature, but once he has destroyed original conditions, he can never replace them."[9] In accord with Muir's ideas, protection was necessary to maintain wildness and to provide humanity with a crucial opportunity. "People sometimes accuse me of being a mystic about the influences of the mountains. Perhaps I am," Harkin once wrote. "I devoutly believe that there are emanations from them, intangible but very real, which elevate the mind and purify the spirit."[10] Through "wholesome, outdoor recreation," people could "escape the pressures and tensions of modern life" and reconnect with nature. Accordingly, those in charge of national parks were bound by duty "to make them freely accessible by road and trail, to permit, under regulation, for the provision of accommodation, refreshments, and other needs."[11]

"Use without abuse" became Harkin's motto, similar to Pinchot but with one important exception: uses that degraded or destroyed the national parks, such as mining and logging, were not compatible with protection of wildlife and provision of outdoor recreation, so they were to be phased out. To ensure that this dual mandate was upheld in a time when multiple use was the dominant land management practice, Harkin had his vision incorporated into the first National Parks Act, which was passed in 1930. The general purpose clause of the act stated: "The Parks are hereby dedicated to the people of Canada for their benefit, education and enjoyment . . . and shall be maintained and made use of so as to leave them unimpaired for the enjoyment of future generations."[12]

In addition to being a visionary, Harkin was also a hard-nosed pragmatist. "We have, therefore, to stand very closely ourselves by the economic view in order to secure the whole-hearted interest of the people of Canada in the conservation of forests and the wild life that may be accommodated therein," he acknowledged. "We have to show that we are aiming at something more than the luxury of watching wild life at play."[13] What was this something more? Economic return. As he boasted: "What revenue this country will obtain when thousands of autos are traversing the parks."[14] In adopting this line of reasoning, Harkin was able to prove that the "highest and best use" of the national parks was not resource extraction but preservation and play.

The strategy proved extremely successful, securing greater and greater budgets, enabling Harkin to undertake ambitious road-building projects such as the Banff–Jasper Highway, and providing an array of recreational facilities including picnic sites, campgrounds, tennis courts, lawn bowling greens and golf courses. The construction provided much-needed employment and economic advancement for local people like my grandfather, who helped build the golf course in Riding Mountain National Park. However, it was an approach with attendant dangers. As Harkin warned:

[T]he more the parks are used the more difficult it is to prevent abuse. There are increased demands for more and more roads, cheaper forms of amusement, commercial exploitations, and the danger is that if these demands are acceded to, the parks may lose the very thing that distinguished them from the outside world. The battle for the establishment of national parks is long since over but the battle to keep them inviolate is never won.[15]

Harkin retired in 1936, leaving a legacy of sixteen national parks, a dedicated and professional park management organization, and a vision of parks as serving two missions: one social, the other ecological. Parks were for people to play in, understanding that this meant forms of recreation that reconnected people with nature; and parks were to protect and preserve wildness, that "emanation" which so moved him to feelings of mysticism and which he sensed was the essence of the difference between what was found inside and outside their boundaries. So, unlike the philosophy that had guided national park management through the first quarter-century, which held that parks were for tourism, resource exploitation and profit, Harkin saw these two things for what they were: a means to a higher end, not a goal to be pursued at risk to the integrity of nature or to the experience of reconnection. To ensure this, he knew that they had to be strictly controlled.

Very little happened over the next decade. The war in Europe directed budgets and human energy into supplying the troops. Only one national park was established during this time—Prince Edward Island—and it had been set in motion by Harkin before his retirement. With workers and dollars scarce, development within the parks also came to a near standstill.

As the Second World War came to an end, Canadians turned their war-hardened industrial might to an old battle with the vast wilderness that still dominated much of the land. Armed with bigger and more powerful machines and tools, produced en masse by an unleashed industrial economy, they began to attack and ravage the landscape as if berserk. Mountains, prairies, lakes and seas were wastefully plundered for their resources: lumber, minerals, hydroelectricity, fish or wildlife. Multiple use deteriorated rapidly into multiple abuse. Not even the national parks were inviolate.

Despite his best efforts, Harkin had not succeeded in having all resource extraction activities stopped within the parks, owing to pre-existing, legally recognized rights, although he had managed to keep them under fairly tight control. In the postwar boom, however, mining, logging and dam-building interests sensed that the time for expansion was upon them. Kicking Horse Forest Products held cutting rights to a number of timber berths that had existed before the creation of Glacier National Park, and in the mid-1950s they announced their intent to log the Beaver River Valley.[16] Timber berths also existed within Yoho, Banff, Mount Revelstoke, Waterton, Wood Buffalo, Riding Mountain and Terra Nova parks. Elsewhere, mining companies pushed for greater access to the parks. Just a few years previously, the federal government had removed an area from Cape Breton Highlands National Park to allow mineral development to proceed. Two years later, another chunk was deleted, this time for hydroelectric development.[17] At the same time, the Canadian Cement Company was seeking permission to quarry limestone in Jasper National Park.[18] To the south, Kootenay National Park rang with the sound of pickaxes and shovels as miners extracted lead, zinc, talc and ochre from its landscape.

Even as they were being ravaged by resource extraction, the national parks were also beginning to show signs of being loved to death. Between 1945 and 1955, the Canadian economy, fuelled by the rapid liquidation of the country's natural capital, surged forward at unprecedented rates. Economic output grew by an average of 5.3 percent per year, the gross national product nearly quadrupled and unemployment hovered around 2.5 percent.[19] After enduring a decade-long depression followed by the hardship and horrors of the Second World War, Canadians were ready to have some fun. With job prospects and wages good, retailers, suppliers and producers began to encourage consumption by allowing consumers to pay over time. Credit, in turn, spurred on the acquisition of previously unattainable items, such as fridges, stoves, television sets, boats and cottages. Indeed, a brand-new station wagon became the hot status symbol, and more often than not it was seen, packed with kids, pets and camping equipment, heading for the national parks.

Recreation and tourism in the national parks skyrocketed, setting a new record of more than 5.5 million visitors in 1960. The sudden surge in popularity washed over the entire park system. For a time in the latter half of the 1950s, Riding Mountain became the second most popular park after Banff. Instead of imposing limits on growth, managers within the National Parks Branch did the exact opposite, promoting another flurry of development to accommodate it. Harkin probably spun in his grave. Here was his organization aiding and abetting the destruction of Canada's national parks—partly due to political interference, partly due to the rise in consumerist values within Canadian society and, more sadly, partly because of a loss of vision about what the national parks truly represented. His dual mandate of appropriate use and careful protection was being corrupted into the old management philosophy that emphasized profits and tourism while disregarding or paying lip service to preservation.

Perhaps it was the distraught ghost of Harkin that prompted the frustrated outburst of Alvin Hamilton, the minister responsible for the national parks, before the House of Commons in 1960. "How can a minister stand against the pressures of commercial interests who want to use the parks for mining, forestry, for every kind of honky-tonk device known to man, unless the people who love these parks are prepared to band together and support the minister by getting the facts out across the country," he exclaimed angrily. But his exhortation appeared to fall on deaf ears—both political and public. Except for a few minor blemishes, the parks still looked great, especially when viewed through the rapidly expanding economic bubble that engulfed a growing proportion of Canadian society.

However, not everyone was blinded to what was happening in and around the national parks. In 1962, Fred Bodsworth, on assignment to *Maclean's* magazine, sounded a shrill alarm. Summing up a tour of the national parks the summer before, he bluntly stated:

I found commercialization, political meddling, and a disregard for traditional park aims and ideals eating like a cancer into our national park system. I found a reluctance to remove or correct what are admitted to have been park management blunders of the past for fear of rousing angry protests from local businessmen and politicians. I found a rankling discontent and frustration in many of the park officials themselves. They see a splendid park system deteriorating because national parks are wide open to political pressures and patronage, abuses that the lower echelon officials are powerless to combat. And it is in this lower echelon that the most dedicated parks defenders are to be found . . . I heard cautious hints that there are worried officials within the Parks Branch itself who would welcome a royal commission investigation where they could make charges that would have them instantly fired if they made them now.[20]

Even more scathing, Bodsworth alleged that the government and senior parks management were trying to cover up the crisis "behind a facade of eloquent words and public announce- ments . . . The truth is that what the parks brass say it is doing in the national parks and what it is actually doing are two quite different things."[21]

The exposé came at a critical time. As in the United States, the early to mid-1960s marked the dawning of Canada's wilderness and wildlife preservation movement. Although very much relegated to the fringes of society, the cause was attracting a growing number of people, in no small part due to writers like Bodsworth who were outraged by what they saw happening to the environment. On February 8, 1963, a small group of representatives from a variety of Ontario-based conservation organizations came together to form a national organization with one purpose in mind: to push for greater protection of the national and provincial parks. From this meeting arose the National and Provincial Parks Association (NPPAC), later renamed the Canadian Parks and Wilderness Society.

At the time, there was only the vague wording of the National Parks Act of 1930 to guide the use and management of the parks, and although it stressed in rather vague terms that use and protection were both important, the former greatly overshadowed the latter. Sensing a mounting backlash over its mismanagement of the national parks, the government directed senior bureaucrats within the parks branch to develop a clear statement of policy that would henceforth guide decision making throughout the system. In the fall of 1964, Canada's first National Parks Policy was released to the public, and while clear on some issues, it was riddled with ambiguities on others. Much to the delight of parks supporters, the policy made clear that activities such as forestry, mining, haying or grazing were no longer acceptable within the national parks; the multiple-use philosophy of parks was finally dead. Now, attention focused squarely on the dual mandate, and the question was: what would be primary, use or protection? On the one hand the policy stated that "maintaining and preserving the parks for future generations" was a "basic part of the branch's obligation" and that the purpose of the national parks was "to preserve, for all time, outstanding natural areas and features as a national heritage."[22] On the other hand, it also said that the national parks were a special kind of "resource" of which the "best and highest resource use" was recreation, and that they were created and protected for this purpose.[23] On the surface, all the policy appeared to do was to reaffirm the status quo: neither came first; it was a question of balancing the two. However, the NPPAC and other park supporters could claim a small victory in that the importance of protection was publicly stated and emphasized, even if there was very little change on the ground. For all the talk of balance, recreation and tourism still dominated.

The election of the Liberals under the leadership of Pierre Elliott Trudeau in 1968 stirred hope for real change. After all, here was a prime minister who was an avid canoeist and outdoorsman, and who understood the importance of wild places. In addition, he appointed as minister of Northern Affairs his close friend Jean Chrétien, who boasted that he would create ten new national parks within five years (a promise he made good on). But flickers of hope soon gave way to flames of outrage as the NPPAC found itself battling the new government over a proposal to permit the massive expansion of Village Lake Louise. The NPPAC first appealed to the minister to reject the proposal on the grounds that it would cause severe ecological damage, thereby compromising the protection role of national parks. Chrétien dismissed their appeal, reminding them that the parks were not strict nature reserves and that tourism was entirely compatible with parks. Disillusioned but not beaten, the NPPAC took their case to the streets, holding rallies and marches as part of an intense campaign to get Canadians to speak up and oppose the development.

The response was stunning. Of the 2,500 people who submitted written briefs and letters, and of the more than 900 who attended public hearings on the proposal, the overwhelming majority strongly opposed it.[24] At one point prior to the hearings, opposition ran at an estimated 70 percent of the letters and briefs received by the government.[25] Confronted by a widespread lack of public support for the Village Lake Louise proposal, Chrétien blinked, then caved in—but not without issuing a stern warning that the national parks "should be accessible to those Canadians who have neither the health, the advantage of location, the physical stamina, the time or the money to explore the vast roadless wilderness zones," and that "the deliberate denial of access to essential services for those using the park should not be considered as an acceptable control device."[26]

Despite the tough talk, Chrétien and his senior bureaucrats could not deny the public demand for greater protection of the national parks. And so, in 1979, the National Parks Policy was revised once again. From now on, the primary purpose of the national parks would be "to protect for all time those places where there are significant examples of Canada's natural and cultural heritage" while also encouraging "public understanding, appreciation and enjoyment" in ways that left them unimpaired."[27] The policy also introduced the term "ecological integrity" for the first time and stated that it would be a prerequisite to use.

While the revised and strengthened policy was a cause for cel-ebration by the National and Provincial Parks Association and other park supporters, inside Parks Canada it drew mixed reviews. At the time, I was finishing my last year as a park interpreter at Riding Mountain National Park before taking a position with the Manitoba Parks Branch. I was also a member of NPPAC, as were many other Parks Canada employees, and for us too it was a vic-tory, representing a much-needed deterrent to management deci-sions that contributed to the erosion of national park values. However, to those who believed that parks were primarily resources to be developed and used for recreation and tourism, the policy was a frustrating setback. The net effect was to aggravate the internal split over Parks Canada's core values.

The continent-shifting tectonics of change showed no signs of letting up. Throughout the 1980s, the loss of biological diversity came to be seen as one of the most serious global environmental problems. The World Commission on the Environment and Development urged governments to establish this issue as a "first priority" on their political agendas. Among scientists, the new field of conservation biology emerged, aimed solely at maintaining and restoring the planet's species and ecosystems. Under pressure to demonstrate leadership and to give greater protection to the country's wilderness and wildlife, the Canadian government responded, in part, by amending the National Parks Act in 1988 to make the maintenance of ecological integrity the first priority in management. This event marks a decisive turning point in the struggle between the anthropocentrists and the ecocentrists within Parks Canada. To the latter, it appeared that the issue had been resolved once and for all: from now on there could be no mistak-ing the primary purpose of the national parks.

"We really believed that the organization would see the light and get solidly behind the new mandate," the chief park warden said to me as we kicked mud off our boots before climbing into his truck, our discussion of Parks Canada's mandate nearing an end.

"But instead, the anthropocentric forces just dug in deeper and have been reinforced by government policy to run the national parks like a business. For those of us desperately wanting change, it's been deeply frustrating. Now the organization is even more divided than ever."

As he was putting the key in the ignition, he stopped and added: "The problem is that it is an uneven struggle between the two groups. Those who believe that parks are first and foremost resources clearly still hold the most power." When I asked him how this power imbalance was played out within the management of the national parks, he immediately launched into a long list of grievances. "We are actively discouraged from engaging in advocacy for ecological integrity, especially when it comes to adjacent-land-use issues," he fumed.

"The incredibly frustrating aspect of this issue," the warden lamented as we pulled up in front of the administration building, "is that those of us who are committed to the mandate are put on the defensive whenever we bring up ecological integrity concerns. We are subjected to endless cross-examinations and micro-management, and demands for more information. It seems management decisions are dominated by a tendency to compromise in favour of incremental use, rather than adopting the precautionary principle from conservation biology which says that the lack of scientific evidence should not be taken as an excuse to forge ahead with accommodating greater human use. When will things change?"

This was a complaint I had heard many times before. Just a few weeks earlier, I had talked with a superintendent of a western park who had left the system because of the lack of support for him and his staff when they took strong stances on these types of issues. "The reason I quit," he said angrily, "was that senior management doesn't have the guts to make strong decisions. Whenever we stood up for park values and caused some forest company grief, they would complain to their elected representative. First thing we knew, the message would come down from above, 'What the hell are you doing?' instead of asking 'How can we help?' It doesn't take long before you stop speaking out." At that point, he argued, frustrated staff find other ways to get things done, like leaking memos or reports to the media or environmental groups. I could certainly verify this latter point, having received a flood of confidential e-mails and documents over the course of writing this book.

I recalled one of those confidential e-mails in which a Parks Canada employee attacked the organization's new mandate: "Ecological integrity is nothing but a bunch of pious verbiage without placing people in the context. Parks only exist in a human world, they are a human concept, and we are not an altruistic species despite what some zealots might say." The cutting edge of his remark is the accusation that ecocentrists who are committed to ecological integrity want to exclude people from the parks and that parks only exist because people want to use them. No use, no parks.

When I told my companion about the e-mail, he winced and said: "Ouch, that really hurts. Nothing could be further from the truth. We don't want to see people excluded. In fact, many of us believe that parks can serve a vital role in reconnecting modern society with nature. But clearly there have to be tighter limits on the use of parks and on the environment generally. Only a fool would argue that the current path of the human species is sustainable.

"As for the idea that parks are a human concept, that is true, but it misses the point. What we are most concerned about is protecting the wildness that remains in these special places. If we can't do it here, where will we do it?"

The lack of congruency between personal values and organizational ones is very hard on a great many employees of Parks Canada. They are angered and saddened by their organization's inability to walk its own talk. During the spring of 1998, an anonymous pamphlet bearing the large bold question "Fed Up?" suddenly began to circulate among park staff. It announced the creation of a new group: Parks Canada Employees for Ethical Service to Parks. The language was damning:

Commercial development approvals continue to be rubber stamped despite recommendations of Parks Canada staff, while outside public interest groups who protest continue to be marginalized or vilified by some Parks Canada managers. Too many good Parks Canada staff have chosen to resign or take early retirement rather than endure continued frustration and shame . . .

The vast majority of Parks Canada employees work professionally and ethically to provide wise and principled public service. Even so, we all share the shame when Parks Canada fails in its duties to present and future generations. Our pride and morale suffer and our public credibility is eroded when Parks Canada engages in closed-door deals and smooth rationalizing of decisions that work against the public interest and compromise the integrity of the national treasures we have been entrusted with.[28]

The "time for change has come," its ghost authors proclaimed, and employees were invited to join the new group by writing to a post office box in Calgary or sending an e-mail to a "hotmail" address.

I sent an e-mail to the group, offering whatever assistance I could, and received a reply from someone called "The Ghost of Harkin." Indicating that I had spoken with some of their founding members, the Ghost said they wanted to remain nameless for the time being "because we don't know how our initiative will be received by the brass. We will only go public when we have enough members to spread the consequences!" At the time, they had 27 employees signed up and were shooting for a critical protective mass of 150. Unfortunately, they didn't achieve their goal, and in my last communiqué with the Ghost it mourned the lost opportunity and said it was returning to its grave, perhaps to be revived again.

The quiet revolution fizzled for a couple of reasons. In his first contact with me, the Ghost identified one of the biggest barriers. "Some people are very nervous and feel they are 'being set up' because they received this [invitation] anonymously. That alone tells you how much paranoia and distrust certain senior managers have created!" His last message to me said that because the minister of Canadian Heritage had taken a strong stance against further development in the national parks, and because the new agency offered the possibility of a fresh start, employees were wanting to take a "wait-and-see" approach before doing anything that might have damaging consequences to their careers.

The status quo remains nonetheless entrenched, and Parks Canada continues to stumble from one embarrassing situation to another. The need for a major cultural transformation within Parks Canada has never been stronger, and an ethical service group could be just the catalyst to help make it happen. Ecological integrity must be seen for what it really is: not just a passing fancy, but the lens through which all decisions affecting the national parks must pass; not just the job of a park ecologist or designated warden, but of everyone, from the maintenance worker digging ditches to the CEO and his executive making system-wide policies.

Even this will not be enough. Ecological integrity must be embraced by the Canadian public, because no matter how good Parks Canada becomes, its best can only have a marginal impact on the threats to the national parks.

# EIGHT

# Oh, Canada

The folks at Parks Canada are not the only ones confused about the purpose of the national parks. The majority of Canadians are equally confused, probably even more so. While we endorse the idea that they are for protection first and foremost, we continue to use and abuse them in thousands of small ways. A 1993 Angus Reid survey confirmed that most Canadians believe the primary purpose of the parks is the protection of wildlife and of ecologically sensitive areas. The majority also agreed that Parks Canada's top priority should be managing visitors and minimizing their impacts, rather than attracting more visitors or providing more services.

How then do we explain our actions that negatively impact park ecosystems and species? How do we rationalize the ever-increasing levels of visitation and the concomitant rise in demand for services such as hotels, restaurants, shops, picnic sites, campgrounds and trails? And how do we explain the construction of recreational subdivisions adjacent to the parks, which, along with intensifying mining, logging, farming and other resource extraction activities, threaten to drown these tiny islands of wildness in a vast and spreading ocean of domestication? Do we simply not understand that all the toxic materials produced by our industries, vehicles and machines follow that old folk saying, "whatever goes up must come down"? That whatever we put into the air and water comes back to harm us and the people and things we love? A cynic would probably say that Canadians are just as negligent as the citizens of any other country when it comes to environment protection.

"A big part of the problem is that most Canadians simply do not perceive a problem," Monte Hummel, president of World Wildlife Fund Canada, told me a couple of years ago. He also pointed out that, on top of this lack of awareness and understanding about the nature of the crisis, the public seems to have blind faith that Parks Canada is doing a good job of managing the parks. According to the 1993 Angus Reid survey, Parks Canada has more credibility on issues pertaining to the environment than "scientists, academics, environmental groups, the media or Provincial or Federal Departments of the Environment."[1] This finding is very significant, since it suggests that we are likely to trust Parks Canada's statements on matters of environmental impacts caused by development. If they say that something isn't seriously affecting the ecological health of the park, most of us believe them. As indicated in the previous chapters, however, there are good grounds for skepticism. "As a result of the inability to detect the slow ecological deterioration of the parks and an uncritical trust in Parks Canada, most Canadians remain unaware of the serious crisis occurring within the national parks," Hummel observed, "and much less of how their individual choices contribute to it."

There is no question that ignorance, arising from not being able to see change and to understand its effects, contributes to the inconsistencies in Canadian attitudes towards parks and wildlife. As environmental educators have noted, over the past twenty to thirty years North Americans have become much more concerned about environmental issues, but they remain woefully lacking in knowledge about their contribution to the problems.[2] As a consequence, they will sign petitions and join peaceful rallies while at the same time continuing to pollute and degrade the environment in thousands of ways. Indeed, the argument could easily be made that North Americans are ecologically illiterate, as are most of our species.

I've given this idea of ignorance a lot of thought over the years, and I recall doing so after my discussion with Hummel. After leaving his office in the World Wildlife Fund's headquarters near downtown Toronto, I picked up Dianne from a nearby restaurant and drove south on Mt. Pleasant Road toward the Queen Elizabeth Way, which would take us back to our friend's place in Mississauga. By the time we hit Jarvis Street, it was clogged with late afternoon rush-hour traffic. Forced to proceed at a snail's pace, I took the opportunity to study the mounting gridlock with great interest. Much of the traffic consisted of large, gas-guzzling, four-by-four sport-utility vehicles, which I suspected were rarely, if ever, taken out of the urban landscape, and only carried one or two occupants. Their tired, anxious faces betrayed the accumulated stress of another workday, and the wear and tear of the daily commute between the city centre and the outlying suburbs.

As I slid our little 1981 Mazda into the creeping lanes of traffic backed up on the QEW, Dianne, perceptive as usual, asked what had me so preoccupied. "The ignorance of the human race," I replied absently. "What do you mean," she probed. "Well, look at us," I said, with a brief wave of my hand at the surrounding vehicles. "Do you think we know how much of an impact we are having on the planetary ecosystem? Why do we downplay the significance of our actions in the big scheme of things? It would be tempting to say this is just 'human nature,' that it is somehow 'hard-wired' into our genes, but I don't believe it is. It seems pretty clear to me that ignorance can only partly explain it. Human consciousness must also play a role."

From the beginnings of human consciousness, people have held two fundamentally different views of nature. Prehistoric peoples generally believed that the earth was invested with supernatural powers that would either reward or punish them, depending on their observance of strict codes of conduct and the use of prayers, rituals and magic.[3] Equally important, they experienced themselves as being fully embedded in nature. There was little, if any, sense of separation; nature was deeply integrated into personal and group identity. Hence, what happened to nature also happened to them. If they mistreated nature, it would punish them. If they treated it well, nature would reward them. Survival depended as much on the readiness of the animal or plant to give up its life as it did on the skills of the hunter-gatherer. To maintain balance and show respect, parts of the kill were offered back to the supernatural forces in a spirit of reciprocity. Wild animals also served as totems, that is, as reminders of an individual's or group's true ancestry. As a result, says Paul Shepard, a professor of human ecology, "[o]ur species once did (and in some small groups still does) live in stable harmony with the natural environment."[4]

On the other hand, there is compelling archeological evidence going back as far as 100,000 years which reveals that Stone Age hunters exterminated many large species. More recently, between 50,000 and 10,000 years ago, humans have been implicated in the extinction of large numbers of species in the British Isles, Middle East and Australia. Over roughly the same period of time in North America, as many as one hundred species of mammals and birds may have been wiped out by the newly arrived two-legged immigrants to the "new continent."[5] Referred to as the "Pleistocene Overkill," this worldwide phenomenon is thought to have resulted from a period of rapid change, during which the creation of new tools and weapons allowed humans to become so much more efficient at hunting that their prey were unable to develop new coping strategies quickly enough.[6] In other words, cultural evolution outstripped biological evolution. Naturalist and former professor of environmental studies John Livingston theorizes that early humans very quickly realized their dominance over many other creatures. He concludes:

There appears to be nothing genetic in the tradition of self-confidence which so quickly evolved into arrogance. Like other primates, man is very low on the "instinctual" scale, and has to learn almost everything he does. The cultural transmission from generation to generation of refinements in tool-making techniques, of improved cooperative hunting methods, and of evolving social conventions of all kinds, was the essential underpinning of the conceptual man/nature dichotomy long before there was *Homo sapiens*, and quite probably before there was *Homo*.[7]

While the early hunter-gatherers recognized themselves as different from other creatures, as evidenced by early cave paintings, they also accepted that they were inseparable from nature at a very profound and personal level. However, the link between humans and nature weakened as the agricultural revolution kicked in. Aided by advancing technology, which made it possible to cultivate and harvest crops, humans gave up nomadic ways of life for more sedentary forms. Soon villages, towns and cities began popping up almost overnight, relatively speaking. The supernatural forces of the cosmos were recast as gods and goddesses, the most common and enduring being the earth mother.

To the ancient peoples of the Mediterranean region, the earth was a living organism of feminine gender and was to be treated with a mix of fear, awe and respect. To the early Greeks she was known as the Great Goddess or the Universal Mother, and represented the great creative principle that underpinned all phenomena, as well as the unification of all attributes of divinity. Later she was renamed Gaea and was believed to have given birth not only to the universe and all other gods, but also to all living creatures, including the human race.

Even as Gaea was being celebrated and revered, the Greek landscape was being laid to waste. More than two thousand years ago, Plato recorded his concern, noting that the destruction of the forests and erosion of soils was akin to a body being consumed by disease.

Unlike the hunter-gatherers, who depended on nature for their survival, the agriculturists and the early city dwellers saw the wild primarily as a threat. Meanwhile, some of their best minds were engaged with questions that would irrevocably change the course of Western thought and history. Were there "natural laws" that, if understood, would give the human race more control over nature? they asked. Aristotle firmly believed there were. True reality, he argued, was the perceptible world of concrete objects, not the world of myths or ideas. Objects, or "substances," were separate and distinct from each other, and stood in contrast to "qualities," such as goodness or beauty, which he viewed as mere abstractions. Looking outward, he conceived of nature as a "Great Chain of Being," which began with the notion of an Absolute Being as the first cause of the universe, and then descended through humans, animals and plants to the earth. Among all living things, humans were unique by virtue of possessing an intellect that, with cultivation, could experience the Divine or Absolute Being.

"Weren't Aristotle's ideas incorporated into Christianity in the early Middle Ages?" Dianne inquired as we approached the turnoff to Mississauga.

"Yes," I replied, checking over my shoulder before making a lane change to exit the QEW. "It was Thomas Aquinas who came across the writings of Aristotle and fused them with his Roman Catholic faith." Religious dogma broke the Great Chain of Being into three distinct entities. God, humans and the rest of Creation. Humans were to serve God and Creation was to serve humans.[8]

"And this was when rituals that celebrated and revered nature were branded as pagan and the worshippers persecuted to the point of being put to death," she added.

"Yes," I concurred, "and tracts of land not yet brought under human control and made to fulfill 'God's will' were denounced as 'wilderness,' areas of waste and desolation."

"Yet isn't it interesting that Jesus wandered in the wilderness for forty days and forty nights before receiving spiritual enlightenment," Dianne mused, partly to herself.

In 1543, a slim volume entitled *De Revolutionibus Orbium Coelestium* shook religious dogma to the core and turned the entire Western view of the world on its head. Its author, Nicolaus Copernicus, who died in the same year, theorized that, contrary to what the Church maintained, the earth did not appear to be at the centre of the universe. So marked the beginning of the Age of Enlightenment and its precocious offspring, the Scientific Revolution, which would further deepen the widening gulf between humanity and the rest of Creation.

In the late sixteenth century Francis Bacon published a series of essays in which he proclaimed that it was humanity's divine right to use knowledge to gain power over nature as a means of attaining material and spiritual progress. Nature was to be placed on the rack of objective observation and forced to reveal her secrets through skilful experimentation.

René Descartes established a firmer philosophical foundation for the emerging field of study called science by suggesting that to doubt everything was a necessary first step to truth. The only thing that could not be doubted was one's own doubting; hence his famous conclusion, *Cogito, ergo sum*—I think, therefore I am. Through a disciplined critical rationality, the essential hierarchy and structure of nature would be discovered. As a devout Christian, he continued to embrace the idea of God, who was the common source for both human reason and objective reality. The basis of this rationality was inherently dualistic; that is to say, all phenomena could be classed as either this or that: reason–faith, mind–body, fact–value, human–non-human, and so on. Only humans possessed subjective awareness, purpose or spirit. As for nature, it was viewed as a great machine, much like the clocks and printing presses of Descartes's day. As such, it consisted of parts that fit together, that were replaceable and that were readily comprehensible and therefore predictable. Subsequent philosophers of science, economics and biology built their theories on these core ideas.

This cold, dispassionate view of nature provoked an angry reaction among those who still held to a more organic or divinely ordered universe. These poets and philosophers challenged not only the fundamental beliefs of science but also the very process of formulating those beliefs. Wordsworth and Blake saw the rise of science, with its narrow acceptance of what was "real," as fundamentally dehumanizing. For them, nature, and especially wilderness, was the source from which the human spirit sprang, and it was not meant to be dissected by the unseeing and uncaring eye of science. Listen to the protest of Blake in his poem "The Tyger":

Tyger! Tyger! burning bright
In the forests of the night,
What immortal hand or eye
Could frame thy fearful symmetry?[9]

Or how about Wordsworth's "The World is Too Much with Us," in which he rages:

The world is too much with us; late and soon,
Getting and spending, we lay waste our powers;
Little we see in Nature that is ours;
We have given our hearts away, a sordid boon!
This Sea that bares her bosom to the moon,
The winds that will be howling at all hours,
And are up-gathered now like sleeping flowers,
For this, for everything, we are out of tune;
It moves us not.—Great God! I'd rather be
A Pagan suckled in a creed outworn; . . .[10]

Their perspective, sometimes referred to as the Counter-Enlightenment or Romanticism, spread to North America and flourished for a brief period during the nineteenth century in the writings of trancendentalists Ralph Waldo Emerson, Walt Whitman and Henry David Thoreau. But the protests were not enough to stem the rising tide of science and technology and their combined impact on the "new world."

Not long ago, I had a discussion with the venerable historian and prolific author Pierre Berton. He was in Victoria promoting his recent book, *Seacoasts*, which celebrates the beauty of Canada's coasts and the spirit of those Canadians who live in close association with them, and yet brims with outrage and sadness over the destruction of these once bountiful ecosystems. "I was shocked by what my research showed," Berton exclaimed. "We're lousing them up!" When I asked for his thoughts about why this is happening, he explained: "This is a country where history and geography are inextricably mixed. The geography has shaped the history, and the history has shaped the geography. I mean, what is this country? The thing about this country is that it is a vast frontier, a wilderness."

There is no doubt about that statement: Canada's size and natural attributes are mind-boggling. It is the second largest country in the world. If laid overtop of Europe, it would stretch from the west coast of Ireland to the Ural Mountains of eastern Asia. Between its eighty-eight degrees of longitude and forty-two degrees of latitude can be found nearly 10 percent of the world's forests and about as much of the world's fresh water. Indeed, Canada may have more lake area than any other country in the world, with more than 565 lakes over 100 square kilometres in size. It ranks third after Russia and Brazil in its share of the world's forests and fresh water. Perhaps the most defining feature of the land is the Canadian Shield, a great dome of Precambrian granite that spans almost half of the country, from the Strait of Belle Isle by the St. Lawrence River to the mouth of the Mackenzie River in the Northwest Territories. Said W.L. Morton, another highly respected historian, of its influence: "The Canadian, or Precambrian Shield is as central in Canadian history as it is to Canadian geography, and to all understanding of Canada."[11] To underscore the point, he drew this comparison: "The heartland of the United States is one of the earth's most fertile regions, that of Canada one of earth's most ancient wildernesses and one of nature's grimmest challenges to man and all his works."[12]

Bruce Litteljohn and Jon Pearce, two instructors at Upper Canada College, produced a seminal anthology on this theme back in 1973, entitled *Marked by the Wild*. In it, they contend that "[o]ur history, our painting, and our literature are all fundamental elements of our collective memory and imagination—of Canadian culture and identity. All have been deeply influenced by the wilderness and proclaim direct experience of it as part of our rightful heritage . . . It remains important as an idea and symbol, abstraction and inspiration—an integral element of our cultural geography."[13] Having said this, the editors were quick to point out that our relationship with the wild has been acutely ambivalent; sometimes we see it as an adversary, other times we approach it with something akin to love. Poet and novelist Margaret Atwood is more blunt in her assessment of this relationship: "The central symbol for Canada . . . is undoubtedly Survival, la Survivance. What you might call 'grim' survival as opposed to 'bare' survival."[14] Given that the country has more rocks, trees and lakes than people, she says it is not surprising that images of nature are commonplace. However, what is of interest is that, added up, "they depict a Nature that is often dead and unanswering or actively hostile to man; or seen in its gentler spring and summer aspects, unreal."[15] Even in these more benign seasons, one may be engulfed by hordes of mosquitoes and biting flies which can quickly dispel any notions of paradise on earth.

"Early explorers such as David Thompson, Samuel Hearne or Alexander Mackenzie perceived Canada's great northern frontier with minds deeply influenced by the Age of Enlightenment and by the Scientific Revolution," Berton continued. "As such, they viewed the land as hostile and unforgiving."

Not surprisingly, this became the prevalent attitude towards nature among the pioneers and settlers who followed the early explorers. Nature was something to be fought against. As Atwood asserts: "The war against Nature assumed that Nature was hostile to begin with; man could fight and lose, or he could fight and win.

If he won he would be rewarded: he could conquer and enslave Nature, and in practical terms, exploit her resources."[16] A casual read of Canadian literature, she maintains, will reveal a dominant theme of "death by nature," usually by drowning or freezing. It didn't take long for the tide to turn, however.

With the ever-increasing advancement of science and technology and economic growth, the vast wilderness that was Canada began to shrink. Along the East and West coasts, up the St. Lawrence Valley and fanning out from the shores of the Great Lakes, forests were "creamed" of the best trees, or cut, burned and plowed under to make way for fields, crops and livestock. Across the Canadian Shield and the Prairies, many wildlife species were trapped, poisoned or shot to, or over, the brink of extinction. This was sometimes a matter of greed, other times of malice. Neither bison nor grizzly bear, both once plentiful from Manitoba west, survived beyond the mid-nineteenth century.

Even as the forests, swamps, birds, fish and animals were disappearing, a few lone voices called out for the wilderness. One of the most eloquent was Grey Owl. In the opening to his 1936 book *Tales of an Empty Cabin*, he wrote:

> Man, that is civilized man, has commonly considered himself the lord of creation, and has been prone to assume that everything existing on this planet was put there for his special convenience, and that all animals (to say nothing of the "subject" races of his own kind) were placed on earth to be his servants. The Wilderness should now no longer be considered as a playground for vandals, or a rich treasure trove to be ruthlessly exploited for the personal gain of the few—to be grabbed off by whoever happens to get there first. Man should enter the woods, not with any conquistador obsession or mighty hunter complex, neither in a spirit of braggadocio, but rather with the awe, and not a little of the veneration, of one who steps within the portals of some vast and ancient edifice of wondrous architecture.[17]

Although his lectures drew sellout crowds in Eastern Canada and England, and he was employed by the fledgling National Parks Branch as its first naturalist to promote wildlife conservation, Grey Owl's warnings and plea went largely unheeded by the Canadian public and their elected representatives.

A lot of water has flowed through the turbines of progress since Grey Owl's day. Over the past sixty-plus years, Canada has grown to an incredible degree of wealth. By 1994, Canadians were the second richest people in the world, after their American neighbours, and we are the second most environmentally unfriendly nation in the world, again after the United States as measured by our generation of greenhouse gases, industrial and household garbage, and hazardous wastes. Meanwhile, publicly driven budget cutbacks are rapidly eroding environmental protection measures. The federal government doesn't collect data on many of the toxic substances released into the environment, nor does it have a strategy in place to reduce pesticide use. Indeed, only Canada and the poorest countries of Eastern Europe don't keep track of pesticide sales[18]. The health risks alone should be incentive enough to try to remedy this situation.

The historical record of our country is abyssmal. Since Confederation, Canada has lost 65 percent of the Maritime tidal marshes, 70 percent of the Great Lakes–Superior Basin wetlands and 70 percent of the Fraser River delta wetlands. The Acadian forest of Atlantic Canada, the Carolinian forests of Ontario and the short-grass prairie of Western Canada have all been reduced to tiny vulnerable remnants, barely capable of sustaining the species that depend on these unique ecosystems. Currently, there are seventy-two species designated as threatened and another seventy-three listed as endangered.

"Survival is certainly the story of the Canadian experience, but we've taken it too far," Berton thundered in concluding our discussion. "Ye Gods! We are destroying the geography and forgetting our history—both the mistakes we've made and the importance of the wilderness to our national identity and character. In forgetting, we forfeit the opportunity to learn."

Back in Mississauga, that night after supper, I went for a walk in the suburban neighbourhood around our friend's home. I needed some solitude in which to reflect on my earlier discussions with Monte Hummel and Dianne. The experience of living in a vast urban landscape was overwhelming and profoundly disturbed me; I was relieved to know that we would soon head home to Victoria. The stop-and-go traffic that afternoon had given me ample opportunity to take in the surrounding city. In every direction, as far as I could see, it sprawled to the distant horizon. During the day, a brown smudge hung over it. From the tops of the overpasses, I saw row upon row of houses, all looking terrifyingly similar, lining the grid-like streets. What nature existed did so in tiny pockets, either as carefully manicured parks or as weed-choked vacant lots. How could the residents of this megalopolis feel any attachment to the wild? I wondered as I strolled along the empty and quiet streets. What would it take to motivate them to shake off ignorance and an outmoded way of seeing the world? An eco-catastrophe? My thoughts became gloomier with each passing block.

We have known about the mounting environmental crisis at least since the 1960s. At first glance, the pattern doesn't look hopeful. With each new crisis, whether it be climate change, species extinction or acid rain, the response is much the same: lots of hand wringing and calls for action, which typically result in a few minor changes, followed by a settling back into business pretty much as usual until the next crisis. The cycle repeats endlessly, perpetuating the downward spiral of the planetary ecosystems toward the yawning abyss of collapse. As I was crossing a playing field, the grim futility of it all hit me like a blast of icy wind cutting to the core of my being. On the verge of tears, I slumped into a child's swing and gazed up at the weird pinkish-grey night sky. Only a few stars were strong enough to overpower the harsh light cast back at them from the defiant city. Their presence, although faint, reminded me of the diamond-studded night skies that still existed over most of the country, and I drew strength from this knowledge. Eventually, I rose from the swing and resumed walking and mulling things over.

The pattern was more complex and hopeful than my fears had initially allowed. As the environmental crisis has escalated, so too has the frequency and intensity of our alarm. This pattern has recently been validated by an Environics poll, which found that one in two Canadians were "very concerned" about wildlife and wildlife habitat.[19] In Ontario, British Columbia and Atlantic Canada, the ratio rose to six out of every ten people. Not since the early 1990s has concern for the environment been so high. "These findings are particularly remarkable, given current high levels of economic concern in [British Columbia and Atlantic Canada]," says Environics research director Angus McAllister. "This recent upsurge flies in the face of conventional wisdom which says that environmental concern only rises during periods of economic boom."[20] The survey also found nearly all Canadians agreed that nature was essential to human survival and that it had very important spiritual qualities.

As I circled back toward the warmth of my friend's house, I derived further encouragement from the knowledge that a growing proportion of Canadians were taking personal responsibility for the environmental crisis and making significant changes. In 1994, 80 percent of us recycled paper, glass, metal cans and plastics, and 60 percent purchased paper towels or toilet paper made from recycled paper.[21] A 1998 federal government study revealed that slightly more than a quarter of a million Canadians engaged in activities aimed at providing habitat for wildlife on their property and in their region. However, it is equally clear that many Canadians, increasingly aware that they are up against some very big and complex problems, are already beginning to show signs of stalling. "Canadians are feeling a growing sense of helplessness with regard to environmental issues, which are increasingly perceived as global in nature," says McAllister. "While most have incorporated activities like recycling, water filters, sunscreen and green consumerism [purchasing environmentally friendly products] into their day-to-day lives, a majority feel these activities are insufficient to deal with problems like species extinction and global warming."[22]

Out of a sense of "stuckness" over what can be accomplished through individual action, Canadians are turning to governments and, to a slightly lesser degree, to the private sector to do more. For example, a recent survey found nearly 80 percent of Canadians believe that the federal government should pass stricter laws to protect endangered species, even if it means limiting resource extraction activities such as forestry or mining. And suddenly, after nearly ten years of playing deaf on environmental issues, the federal government is listening. David Anderson, my local member of Parliament, who has a proven track record as a conservationist, was recently appointed as minister of environment, and he has made climate change and endangered species his top priorities.

While he has yet to find a sure footing on the first priority, he has taken tentative steps on the latter. Currently, Anderson is shepherding a new Species at Risk bill through the minefield of parliamentary debate. If it becomes law, it will give his department increased powers to protect vitally important habitats. The federal government will have the right to "prosecute landowners, impose heavy fines of up to $500,000 and perhaps confiscate their habitat lands if they deliberately or recklessly engage in the 'outright destruction' of critical lakes, woodlands, swamps or forests."[23] Before using this big stick, Ottawa will try to obtain landowner co-operation by offering an enticing carrot, consisting of compensation to offset economic losses and cash incentives to encourage the adoption of measures to improve habitat or recover an at-risk species.

While the proposed legislation represents a potentially powerful tool in the urgent work of protecting endangered species, critics stress it doesn't go far enough. At the same time, there is a mounting backlash to it in Alberta, Quebec and Atlantic Canada. Only time will tell whether the necessary political and public commitment will be there in time to save endangered species.

Crossing a six-lane street behind my friend's house, Monte Hummel's last words came back to haunt me again. Ignorance could probably explain many of the inconsistencies Canadians demonstrate towards the environment generally and the national parks specifically. However, so could a number of other things, like the history and geography of our country. "To many Canadians and international visitors, the country still appears to be one vast wilderness, but this is not the case," he had said during our discussion. "Just beyond the forest's margin lie clear-cuts, strip mines and hydroelectric reservoirs. What wilderness remains will be gone in less than a decade if current rates of resource extraction continue." And given the rampant materialism and consumerism that our society embraces, the prospects for maintaining what wildness remains outside the national parks and protected areas don't look promising—and neither do the prospects inside the parks' boundaries. The problem is overlaid with the sinister ideology of individualism, which emphasizes rights over responsibilities. We are becoming caught up in the fight for narrow self-interest and caring less about the common good. Our field of concern is collapsing into an egotistical paranoia perpetuated by a constant bombardment from businesses and their promoters that we don't have enough or what we do have is not good enough. When confronted with the environmental damage accumulating rapidly from our individual choices, we cross our fingers and say our prayers to the gods of science and technology to bail us out.

Stepping through the gate into the backyard, I stopped beside an apple tree and stared up at its bare limbs. A quote from Henry David Thoreau came to mind: "There are a thousand hacking at the branches of evil to one who is striking at the root." So what is the root of all evils? I asked myself rhetorically. It had to be the largely unexamined, deeply held values, beliefs and assumptions that inform our interactions with the world around us. As Stan Rowe has argued: "As long as we see ourselves as the centre of creation we will rationalize our proclivities to use, waste and destroy whatever parts of the world our technology qualifies as 'resources.'

To be at home on the planet and welcome here, humanity must understand and appreciate the primacy of that home, the Eden we have never left, and the wild that is its emblem."[24] What he, and others like him, are calling for is a major realignment of perspective: nothing short of a cultural transformation in the way we relate to the wild and our national parks. This transformation needs to happen within both Canadian society and Parks Canada if the wild is to be maintained in the national parks.

A sharp, bitter wind sliced through my coat, sending a shiver through my body. It was time to go in, which is where the change had to start: from the inside.

# NINE

# Love is All There Is

When I was a little boy, I had a fascination with the Vikings and dreamed of one day visiting L'Anse aux Meadows, their first settlement in North America. Forty years passed before I was able to fulfil that dream, and to my delight it was even more special than I had imagined. Surrounding a tiny cove at the extreme tip of Newfoundland's Northern Peninsula, the area once occupied by the settlement has been designated a national historic site and a world heritage site in recognition of its cultural significance to Canadians and the global community. While there is a fine interpretive centre with many informative exhibits, I was most compelled by the reconstructed sod buildings that rise like giant green loaves of bread out of the windswept heath. On the day of our visit, interpreters in period costume bustled about cooking meals, sharpening crude tools and weapons, or sewing clothes with bone and sinew. I was in heaven. For a few magical moments I was teleported back in time to 1066, when the Vikings landed here and named the region "Vinland" in honour of its natural beauty and abundance.

After wandering through the buildings and conversing with some of the interpreters about the site, Di and I strolled back to the interpretive centre. We struck up a conversation with the senior interpreter. I soon discovered that he had been born and raised in the little village nearby and that, like his grandfather and father, he had been a cod fisherman, until the bottom fell out of that fishery, plunging him, his community and many others along the Rock's coast into turmoil and confusion. "I've seen many changes in my day," he said ruefully. I guessed he was in his late forties. "When I was a kid, we played on the mounds that were the remnants of the Viking settlement. The streams near them ran thick with fish every year. Today they are all gone." He could remember when someone from "away" brought monofilament nets to the village. "Up till then, my grandfather and father had been using cotton nets, which the fish could see, and so many would escape," he explained. "But they couldn't see the new nylon nets and so the men caught so many fish each time they went out that they almost sunk their boats. In fact, some did swamp." The really heavy plundering of the cod stocks, however, came from large off-shore trawlers that scooped up the fish by the tens of thousands. By 1992, the cod had become so badly depleted that the federal government was forced to put a moratorium on the fishery. So much for the Viking "paradise on earth."

A few nights later, Di and I were sitting by the fire at our campsite in Gros Morne National Park's Berry Hill campground when Gerald, the night watchman, dropped by for a chat. We had become casual friends with this gregarious old-timer and so I felt comfortable asking him for his thoughts on the collapse of the cod fishery. "My grandfather and father always said there would be lots of fish and trees. Now look what has happened," he said bitterly. "Too many people took too many fish, and now we are doing the same with the forests. Soon they, too, will be all gone." After he had left and Di had gone to bed, I sat and gazed into the dying embers, reflecting on the parallels with a similar crisis taking shape back in my home province of British Columbia with the salmon. It occurred to me that as long as we humans continue to see ourselves as separate from the wild and superior to it, we will drive it to extinction. To save the wild, to keep it alive in this world anywhere, will take a dramatic change on our part—or more precisely, a change of mind and heart.

Reason or emotion, fact or value, physical or spiritual—the dualistic legacy of Aristotelian/Cartesian logic forces us to perceive reality as either this or that. How long will we persist in seeing economic development and environmental protection, use and preservation, people and the planet, as conflicting opposites? We have been steeped for so long in this kind of thinking that we may even doubt that there is an alternative reality, in which apparent opposites are seen for what they really are: two sides of the same coin. But there is another way of perceiving reality that allows things to be different from each other and yet also acknowledges that they are part of a greater whole. Many other cultures and mystics have known this for a long time.

Seven years ago I had the good fortune to attend a remarkable gathering of scholars from around the world. They had been drawn together by the Centre for Studies in Religion and Society at the University of Victoria to grapple with global problems arising from overpopulation and overconsumption. What was unique about the symposium was that they were scholars of religion. As the centre's director, Harold Coward, stated in his welcoming comments, the role of religion is rarely mentioned in discussions of environmental issues and, if it is, usually only in disparaging terms. Yet religion can have a profound and positive impact on the attitudes and behaviours of people towards the environment. It can provide much-needed insight on ways to resolve the either-or dilemmas that lie at the heart of the global environmental crisis.

"Aboriginal spirituality was more than a ritual," declared Daisy Sewid-Smith, a member of the Kwakiutl Laich-Kwil-Tach First Nation, whose traditional territory encompassed a good portion of the mid-coast of British Columbia, including much of northern Vancouver Island. "It was a daily encounter with what we call the 'supernatural' and through this encounter an individual is changed from within."[1]

Contrary to the traditional Western idea of the material world and spiritual world being separate, the Kwakiutl Laich-Kwil-Tach believe they were "only divided by a thin veil and one only had to walk through it."[2] This was achieved by means of such rituals as fasting or vision quests. Daily they would bathe and rub themselves with hemlock boughs four times, and then meditate on the inherent interconnectedness of reality and on their proper place in the order of the cosmos. "These practices may seem foolish to modern man, but these daily acknowledgments seemed to remind the Kwakiutl that they were not the only important species on this planet," she said. "It also helped to remind them one must live within certain boundaries, otherwise there would be consequences." Moments later, she added insightfully and wryly, "Man is the only species on this planet that seems to need laws to keep him within his own boundaries."[3]

Among the indigenous peoples of the world there is a common tendency to link the idea of the supernatural with that of the world around them being inhabited by spirits. Things like mountains, rivers, trees, birds or animals possessed "a consciousness, reason, and volition, no less intense and complete than a human being's."[4] Even the earth itself is considered a living organism. As for their own existence, these people hold that they are a part of the land and that the land is a part of them. Such a belief structure encouraged them to be respectful and caring in their relationship with the Creator's world. Writing in the *Journal of Environmental Ethics*, Annie Booth and Harvey Jacobs state:

> In the Native American system, there is no idea that nature is somewhere over there while man is over there, nor that there is a great hierarchical ladder of being on which ground and trees occupy a very low rung, animals a slightly higher one, and man a very high one indeed—especially "civilized" man. All are seen to [be] brothers or relatives . . . all are offspring of the Great Mystery, children of our mother, and necessary parts of an ordered, balanced and living whole.[5]

Probably more difficult for many non-Aboriginal people to accept is the idea that identity as an individual is inseparable from identity with all beings and ultimately with Creation itself. Not surprisingly, then, protection of the environment was at the pinnacle of importance within traditional Kwakiutl Laich-Kwil-Tach spirituality.

Strong parallels can be found elsewhere in the world, as the next speaker, Elisheva Kaufman, an environmental educator from the eastern United States, made abundantly clear. According to her, the early Hebrews also held that the earth was a living organism. She paraphrased the medieval Jewish philosopher Maimonides as saying:

> We must consider the entire globe as one individual being which is endowed with life, motion, and soul, not, as some persons maintain, inanimate matter like the component elements of fire or earth, but an animate, organized and intellectual being capable of comprehension and response.[6]

Maimonides also had a fair bit to say about the notion that the earth and all living things on it were created for the sake of humanity, an idea he found preposterous:

> [T]he universe does not exist for Man's sake, but each being exists for its own sake; not for any other purpose. No part of Creation exists for the sake of another part—but each part is an expression of the order of the Universe, of God's wisdom, and fulfills the intention of the Creator.[7]

Taken all together, early Hebraic teachings counsel taking personal responsibility for living in accord with Creation.

Hinduism offers similar insights, as was revealed by Klaus Klostermaier, head of the Department of Religion at the University of Manitoba. "It is a world view which fosters a holistic, universalist and reverential thinking, in contrast to the absence of reverence for things higher than pleasure and profit which has much to do

with the degradation of life in the so-called advanced countries,"
he argued. "Humans are to meet nature with reverence as something divine, and doing harm to nature is equivalent to sacrilege."[8]
Later he added, "nature is a means of salvation, a marvel in and by
itself, the basis of everything."[9] As with Aboriginal spirituality and
Judaism, the proper relationship with nature is one of respect and
self-control.

Like Hinduism, Buddhism advocates "non-harm" of other
beings, and for one very fundamental reason: "Rather than being
isolated and independent entities, Buddhism sees all beings as interconnected with one another in a great web of interdependence,"
contended Rita Gross, a scholar and practitioner of this gentle way
of life. The interdependence goes well beyond the usual ecological
understanding. According to her, Buddhists affirm that "all beings
have at some time been our mothers and we theirs."[10] Because of
this interdependence, Buddhists strive to follow the Middle Path or
Middle Way, which harmonizes individual needs with those of the
greater good. The outward expression, and the central practice, of
the Middle Way is loving-kindness or compassion.

Nawal Ammar, a professor of criminal justice studies and a
Muslim, spoke next, offering an interpretation drawn from Islam's
sacred texts. "In the Qur'an the protection of nature is based on
the principle that God created the various components of the universe, and that all these components are ordered, have purpose
and function," she stated. "It is assumed that humans are
immersed in a Divine environment, but are only unaware of the
reality due to their own forgetfulness and negligence."[11] Ammar
also noted that the Qur'an holds that all forms of life emerged from
a common origin; as such, there is ultimately no distinction
between the human and the non-human world. However, the
former are set slightly apart from the latter in that humans
"accepted the earth in trust from God" and were bound by an ethic
stipulating that nature was not to be damaged, abused or distorted
in any way and that it was only to be used in a kind, balanced,
non-excessive manner.[12]

So, what of Christianity? Perhaps no other religion has been so implicated in the degradation of the planet. Catherine Keller, a professor of theology, chose to focus her remarks on the issue of overpopulation. Nevertheless, she too found numerous references within the religion to humanity's critical challenge to "know oneself as a creature inextricably created in interdependency with all other denizens of creation."[13] Matthew Fox, a Dominican priest and theologian, has found much the same thing. Writing in his book *A Spirituality Named Compassion*, he claims that interdependence is fundamental: "that I am not only I but we are one another."[14] And by "we," he means all living creatures and even the planet.

A number of key points emerge from this cursory overview of religion in relation to the environment. First, nature is seen to be endowed with intrinsic value; that is, it is worthy or important in and of itself. Second, humans exist interdependently with nature. Indeed, they are often viewed as two aspects of a greater whole or unity, sometimes called God, the Creator or some other similar term. Third, humans have a moral obligation to live in harmony with nature. Fourth, although reality is experienced as opposites, such as humans/nature or material/spiritual, these opposites are complementary rather than conflicting; they are aspects of a greater unity.

I attended another conference in 1999, to celebrate the thirty-fifth anniversary of the Canadian Parks and Wilderness Society. The banquet speaker was Harvey Locke, the organization's former president and now vice-president of conservation. A gifted and eloquent speaker, Locke rarely suffers from a loss of words or courage, yet he readily admitted upon taking the podium that the topic of his speech made him feel nervous. What was the topic? Wilderness and spirituality. "We need to restore a sense of the sacred to Creation if we are to save it," he commenced. "We must reach out to those who have religious and spiritual impulses, and strive with them to protect the full diversity of life on earth." He hastily added: "This is a scary thing to say to a room full of highly educated people, skilled in rational and analytical thought." He also acknowledged that many of the world's religions are associated with environmental degradation. Nevertheless, he said, "I think that instead of focusing on what is wrong with one tradition or another, we must look at what these traditions could bring to the protection of the earth.

"What we have in common is a deep and abiding concern for the earth," he continued. "Whether we call it God's Creation, or Napi's work, or whether we see it the other way around—that nature itself is our Creator—we share a sense that nature is sacred and worthy of protection. We are here because we feel a deep and awesome connection to Creation," Locke elaborated; "because we know in our cores that we would be immeasurably poorer if we could not feel nature's power and receive it in our hearts and in our pores. And we feel a deep reciprocal duty to protect Her."

He pointed out that a growing number of religious groups shared the same sense of duty to nature, using the example of a group of evangelical Christians who stopped the Republicans from gutting the Endangered Species Act and national parks by arguing that it was a sin to destroy God's work. "As the American example shows, there is a fertile and yet largely unexplored confluence of values between organized religion and we who love nature," said Locke, while noting that religious and environmental groups in the United States and British Columbia were beginning to explore ways of working together. "We must take active steps to engage with all communities of faith and all spiritually oriented people if we are to succeed in our quest to save nature."

No sooner had he finished his speech than the room exploded into thunderous applause. Clearly he had touched a deep and receptive chord. Although Locke had been anxious about how his speech would be received by the rationalists in the audience, he needn't have been. Over the past hundred years or so, there has been a slow and tentative convergence occurring between religion and its arch-rival, science. Cracks in the old Newtonian/Cartesian world view started to appear at the end of the nineteenth century and the beginning of the twentieth, spurred on by discoveries in physics, principally relativity theory and quantum mechanics.

Labelled the "new physics" by some, these fields attacked the very basis on which the old physics had been constructed. Newton's laws only worked in the "middle zone" of reality, lying between the macrocosm and the microcosm. Instead of atoms being the hard, solid particles they were thought to be, closer inspection revealed that they were more space than solid, and what solid bits did exist in turn could best be described as "packets of energy." Atoms, it seemed, were both something and nothing, depending on how they were being examined. Light, meanwhile, was found to be both a wave and a particle; which one was observed depended on experimental design. Even more revolutionary, when an atom was split into two subatomic particles of opposite charges and the charge on one was reversed, the other simultaneously reversed its charge. How could this be, when for all intents and purposes the two particles were separated by a microcosmic universe?

Another field turning modern science on its ear is general systems theory. Pioneered by biologists in the 1920s, this theory maintains that the whole is always different than the sum of its parts. Says physicist Fritjof Capra in his book *The Web of Life*: "According to the systems view, the essential properties of an organism, or living system, are properties of the whole, which none of the parts have. They arise from the interactions and relationships among the parts. These properties are destroyed when the system is dissected, either physically or theoretically, into isolated elements."[15] In other words, the mechanistic, reductionist approach, which breaks reality down into parts and then attempts to understand the whole from the parts, is woefully narrow and inadequate for a complete understanding of organisms and their relationships with other organisms and the environment.

Systems theory also demands that we be able to shift our focus back and forth between various levels of organization. As I have explained elsewhere in this book, systems exist as nested hierarchies, much like the wooden Russian doll that pops apart to reveal a still smaller doll inside. Within living systems, cells form tissues, tissues form organs, organs form organisms and organisms form communities. Each thing is really nothing more than a discernible pattern that emerges from the level below it and then dissolves into the level above it. Part becomes whole and whole becomes part—a phenomenon called "interpenetration." For this reason, systems thinkers are more interested in relationships than in entities. They are especially fascinated by complex ones that exhibit chaotic behaviour and yet create order.

"Where chaos begins, classical science stops," boldly declared the highly respected science writer James Gleick in the foreword to *Chaos*, his fascinating book on this topic.[16] Think of water cascading over a ledge, curling smoke rising from a snuffed candle or a flag fluttering in the wind. What makes these things so challenging for Newtonian physics is that they cannot be described by a straight linear equation, where direct one-to-one relationships are used to predict behaviour and outcomes. This approach has worked for many problems, like the prediction of the return of Halley's comet, but it does so by assuming that very small differences can be ignored: a meteor striking the third moon of Jupiter would not affect the rotation of Earth. But when a scientist attempting to model global weather patterns forgot to add a couple of decimal points into the base equation, the outcome was startling, especially given that the difference was a mere one-thousandth. At first the computer behaved as usual, generating a familiar cyclic pattern, but then it began to cascade into more and more erratic behaviour. In seeking to understand why, the scientist discovered the tiny error. The phenomenon was labelled "the Butterfly Effect" to metaphorically capture the idea that a butterfly flapping its wings in China could set off a chain of effects that produce thunderstorms in Canada. In other words, systems, whether living or not, are what chaos theorists refer to as "sensitive-dependent on initial conditions."

The revolutionary aspect of chaos was not the discovery that tiny differences can trigger dramatic, erratic behaviour. No, it was something much more provocative. When the scientist sat back and contemplated the computer printout, a pattern emerged from the apparent randomness. Careful and complex mathematical equations pointed towards the presence of some force or tendency that subsequently became known as "the strange attractor." In its presence, systems exhibit both stability and instability, order and chaos—not order *or* chaos, but order and chaos together. Like the two sides of a coin, neither can exist without the other.

In addition to giving birth to systems theory, biology in the early twentieth century also begat ecology, a science that some have called subversive because of its implications for accepted ways of perceiving and acting towards the environment. The word "ecology" was first used in 1866 by a German biologist. Its Greek root, *oikos*, means household, suggesting "the study of the relationships that interlink all members of the Earth Household."[17] In 1909 the word "environment" made its first appearance and quickly came to be the accepted term for the outer world in which an organism existed. In keeping with biological models, groups of organisms were called "superorganisms" for a brief period of time; however, because they were viewed, at the time, as mystical connotations, it was replaced by the term "ecosystem."

More than just new words were contributed by the new science of ecology to systems thinking; it also introduced the innovative concepts of community and network. As Capra explains it:

> By viewing an ecological community as an assemblage of organisms, bound into a functional whole by their mutual relationships, ecologists facilitated the change of focus from organisms to communities and back, applying the same kinds of concepts to different systems levels. Today we know that most organisms are not only members of ecological communities but are also complex ecosystems themselves, containing a host of smaller organisms that have considerable autonomy and yet are integrated harmoniously into the functioning of the whole.[18]

An ecosystem can, therefore, be viewed as communities of organisms linked in complex patterns or networks. When one considers the bacteria in our guts or the microscopic mites in our eyebrows, the human body can be seen more as an ecosystem than as a discrete entity.

> The view of living systems as networks provides a novel perspective on the so-called hierarchies of nature. Since living systems at all levels are networks, we must visualize the web of life as living systems (networks) interacting in network fashion with other systems (networks).[19]

Where the lines of relationship cross, there is found an organism or a community that, when examined more closely, becomes yet another network, and on and on it goes.

> In other words, the web of life consists of networks within networks. At each scale, under closer scrutiny, the nodes of the network reveal themselves as smaller networks. We tend to arrange those systems, all nesting within larger systems, in a hierarchical scheme by placing the larger systems above the smaller ones in a pyramid fashion. But this is a human projection. In nature there are no "above" or "below," there are no hierarchies. There are only networks nesting within other networks.[20]

As the ancient religious mystics intuitively understood so well, everything is truly interconnected—a profound insight that has huge ramifications for parks and protected areas.

This fundamental precept of ecology is the essence of its subversiveness. If we were to fully accept its implications, we would be forced to move beyond making minor adjustments, such as recycling or low-flow shower heads, to engage in a critical questioning of the largely unexamined belief structure that perpetuates our unsustainable habits, such as the overconsumption of metals, fossil fuels or water. Such is the contention of the deep ecology movement that sprang from the mind of a feisty Norwegian philosopher, Arne Naess, in the early 1980s.

Years ago, I had the immense pleasure of serving as his host for a day while he was in Victoria to give some lectures at the university. While hiking in a provincial park close to the city, he explained the difference between deep ecology and what he called "shallow" ecology. "Take your car as an example," he said. "The fuel it burns is non-renewable and highly polluting. Replacing fossil fuels with cleaner-burning hydrogen would be a good thing, but it doesn't go far enough. It doesn't address all the other problems, such as the millions of derelict vehicles that are junked each year; the oils, acids and other toxic substances that they leak into the environment; or the valuable space that is taken up by roads and parking lots. Most of all, it doesn't confront the underlying world view that perpetuates the escalating consumption of materials from nature." The deep ecology movement, on the other hand, is built on the idea that a radical change in how we view ourselves as a species and our relationship with the planet is urgently needed.

"Deep ecology revolves around two central norms: self-realization and ecocentric equality," Naess continued. "The first asks that we reject the modern Western notion of the self as an isolated ego and instead work to realize the 'self-in-Self,' where the latter refers to organic wholeness, ground of being or divine unity." I had come across a similar idea in the writings of Neil Evernden, a professor of environmental studies at York University, who had developed the idea of "fields of care" to replace that of "isolated ego"; in other words, the sense of self can, and often does, extend beyond what we usually take to be our selves. "The idea that an organism regards parts of its environment as belonging to its field of self seems strange only when we begin with the assumption that visual boundaries are more real than experiential boundaries," he says.[21] We do not "really experience the boundary of the self as the epidermis of the body, but rather as a gradient of involvement in the world."[22] I could easily relate to what Evernden and Naess were saying. Frequently, when immersed in wilderness, I experience a dissolution of my ego, and with the release comes an expansive sense of unity or wholeness with my surroundings. In these moments I am one with the forest, mountains or prairies. They and I become interpenetrated. If I experience the world beyond my skin as part of me, then would I not want what's best for both it and myself?

Ecocentric equality, or the idea that "all things in the biosphere have an equal right to live and blossom and to reach their own individual forms of unfolding and self-realization," logically follows from the first norm.[23] "Ecocentric equality rests upon the realization that all life forms and the ecosystems that support them have inherent worth," asserted Naess. "By this I mean that they have value or importance in and of themselves, quite apart from what we humans may think of them." The effect of these two norms is to shift humanity from "conqueror of the land-community to plain member and citizen of it," in the words of the American conservationist Aldo Leopold.[24] Respect and care become the defining principles for our relationship with other species and the planet as a whole.

So what's missing? Religion and science are telling us that everything is interconnected and interpenetrating, and deep ecology provides a set of principles to guide us in the realization of this basic insight. Yet we blunder on, living as if nature, especially wild nature, didn't matter. Why is this? Stan Rowe offers a couple of reasons. "Two related ideas could bring a more balanced perspective to land use, in Canada and everywhere in the world," he says. "One is a concept, the other an attitude, and the land is hurting because of their absence. The missing *concept* is the ecological one of *landscapes-as-ecosystems*, literally 'home systems,' within which organisms, including people, exist."[25] By this he means that we experience ourselves and all forms of life as fully embodied by the land rather than perceiving ourselves as somehow separate from it. "The missing *attitude*," he says, "is sympathy with and care for the land and water ecosystems that support life." Elsewhere he is even more direct, stating: "Love of the land, love of place, love of our endangered Living Spaces, is the grass-roots cure for the sin of species narcissism."[26]

Rowe is not alone in his belief that love is the answer; historian Theodore Roszak is equally convinced of its importance. "If ecological wisdom cannot be made as engaging as the reshaping of continents, the harvesting of the seas, the exploration of space, if it cannot compete with the material gratifications of industrial growth, it will run a poor second to those who appeal to stronger emotions," he asserts, before asking rhetorically: "Is there an alternative to scare tactics and guilt trips that will lend ecological necessity both intelligence and passion?"[27] His answer: "It is the concern that arises from shared identity: two lives that become one. Where that identity is experienced deeply, we call it love. More coolly and distantly felt, it is called compassion. This is the link we must find between ourselves and the planet that gives us life."[28]

But how does this relate to the perception that it is not an absence of love that is killing the national parks but too much love? Are we not loving our parks to death? The best way to approach this is to delve into what love is. On Earth Day 1999, I had the unexpected pleasure of exploring this topic with geneticist, author and activist David Suzuki. At one point he blamed the environmental crisis on Christianity, particularly the notion of domination set forth in Genesis. I asked him to elaborate on the importance of spirituality and sacredness. My question triggered an intriguing and passionate response: "I think it easier to suppose that love is a precondition which is built into the very stuff of life. It's just there. We don't understand it, but it is just there. You know, if you look at the big bang, out of nothing came matter and energy; and even as those bits of matter were rushing away from each other, they were exerting a tiny force of attraction. Even cells are drawn together and their membranes will fuse when they come into contact. All this is to say that love may be built right into our genes." Moments later he laughed and said that anybody overhearing us would think he had gone off the deep end. Maybe so, but Harvard's E.O. Wilson, an international authority on ants and other insects in tropical rain forests, has advanced a similar theory, called "biophilia," which he says is the "innate tendency to focus on life and lifelike processes."[29]

One of the most discerning definitions of love was offered by psychoanalyst Eric Fromm, who declared: "Love is the active concern for the life and the growth of that which we love."[30] Matthew Fox, author of *A Spirituality Named Compassion*, concurs and adds, "True compassion extends to all creatures." Furthermore, "it is this love of Nature *for its own sake* that distinguishes true compassion from 'its spurious, sentimental form.'"[31] Quoting from the last lecture given by the Christian mystic Thomas Merton, Fox writes: "The whole idea of compassion is based on a keen awareness of the interdependence of all these living beings, which are all part of one another and all involved in one another."[32] For Fox, compassion implies deep caring, which means "doing and relieving the pain of others, not merely emoting about it.[33] To this, Fromm adds responsibility, respect and knowledge. Responsibility is a voluntary act, and it means to be ready and able to act. Respect arises from seeing another for what they truly are and wanting to nurture and foster their uniqueness, free from exploitation. And to respect and care for another is only possible through knowing them—not in some abstract way, but in a deeply experiential way that resonates through mind and body.

What all this means in terms of humanity's relationship with the planet has been eloquently summarized by the title character in novelist Thomas Mann's *The Confessions of Felix Krull: Confidence Man*, who said: "He who really loves the world, shapes himself to please it."[34] True love comes with maturity, the ability to transcend one's own ego; and to be fully mature is to accept and affirm the need for self-imposed limitations so as not to do harm to that which we love. With it and in it, we experience reverence for the sacredness of Creation and wildness. Humility, not arrogance, then informs our daily decisions and actions.

Clearly, this is not what we are doing. In fact, we are doing just the opposite. Is it possible, therefore, to learn how to love the wild? I certainly believe it is. However, it should be borne in mind that what is to be learned cannot be taught; it must be discovered or realized by each individual in a "Aha, now I get it!" flash of insight. Education can play an important role in facilitating this process, but it must be of a very different kind than we currently have. As the American environmental educator David Orr has pointed out, some of the world's most highly educated people are its worst enemies. So what kind of education must it be? This much is clear: it must be profoundly transformative, enabling learners to change themselves.

Until we learn to love, what are we to do? I give the last word to psychoanalyst Scott Peck, who says: "Genuine love is volitional rather than emotional. The person who truly loves does so because of a decision to love. This person has made a commitment to be loving whether or not the loving feeling is present. If it is, so much the better; if it isn't, the commitment to love, the will to love, still stands and is still exercised."[35]

The wild will only be saved if we learn to love it. To love it requires the realization that we and the wild are two sides of the same coin. There is no either-or choice to be made between people and the planet when it is finally comprehended that what is ultimately in our best interests is also in the best interests of the wild, and vice versa. As I said earlier in this chapter, we and it are interpenetrated, that is, we live as much in the wild (although we are bent on domesticating or destroying it) as it lives in us (although its call has been greatly muted under the suffocating layers of modern life). John Livingston, author of the award-winning book *Rogue Primate*, eloquently speaks to this latter point while describing the experience of watching a hunting lioness:

> The experience of the lioness was the fleeting, elusive, bittersweet recognition of wildness. Not a recollection of the mind, but a tingling, prickling, participatory kindling of the flesh. For a precious instant I have rejoined. For one moment of arrested infinity, my human alienation dissolves. I am home, and when I feel it I recognize it instantly. I recognize also, with terrible sadness, that I had forgotten to miss it.[36]

At our core, we are still wild; hence it is in our self-interest to do all that we can to keep the wild alive. As Henry David Thoreau knew only too well, in wildness is the salvation of the world.

All that is necessary to protect and restore wildness in our national parks is the willingness to learn how truly to love them, and the readiness to embark upon a profoundly exciting cultural transformation that shifts us from unsustainable and lethal values of anthropocentrism to respectful and caring values of ecocentrism. The dimensions of this transformation are being scoped out by deep ecologists, conservation biologists, systems theorists, religious and spiritual communities, and environmental groups. We know enough now to begin to make the necessary attitudinal and behavioural changes.

TEN

# The Big Picture

Canada has changed dramatically since the first national parks were conceived one hundred and fifteen years ago in the minds of people more concerned about tourism and profits than about protecting wilderness and wildlife. To a certain degree, their priorities are understandable given that, in no small way, the parks and their facilities represented islands of civilization within a vast sea of wildness. Although logging, mining, ranching and the newly laid railway were beginning to push back the frontier, its retreat was seen not as a cause for concern but as a reason for celebration. The rapid conversion of natural capital into financial capital was good for the country's economy. Besides, there seemed to be so much wilderness and wildlife; the thought that either could vanish in the not so distant future likely never crossed their minds. Within just two decades, however, many wildlife populations in Western Canada were in serious trouble and large areas of wilderness had been reduced to tattered remnants. In the span of my grandmother's lifetime—she is almost a hundred—the national parks have become islands in a sea of domestication, their wildness threatened by a wave of progress that began in Atlantic Canada only a few centuries earlier.

Rather than seeing their vulnerability to the persistent and escalating threats, the common tendency is to regard the national parks as fortresses or like jars of preserves, with everything inside safe from harm by whatever is happening outside. Nothing could be further from the truth. As was seen in previous chapters, the wildness of the national parks is being degraded by human activities in, around and well beyond their boundaries. In the previous chapter I argued that, to reverse this trend, we must learn to genuinely love the wild and our national parks, and to adopt an ecocentric world view; only by doing so will we address the root causes of the threats to their ecological integrity. Everything else is merely re-arranging the deck chairs on a sinking Titanic.

In conjunction with this change of heart and mind, we also must change our basic perceptions of the national parks, which are dominated by three major metaphors: parks as preserves, parks as playgrounds or parks as profit producers. Each of these metaphors is the source of serious problems for maintaining and restoring wildness in the national parks. In this chapter and the next I will propose alternative metaphors, which more accurately reflect the crucial ecological and social roles that the national parks can, and indeed must, fulfil as a new millennium dawns.

The idea of parks as preserves reflects and reinforces the same old dualistic thinking that sets humanity against the wild. In this case, the underlying assumption is that parks are somehow separate from the surrounding landscape. The assumption is perpetuated by the boundaries that mark off their perimeter. The tendency is to see everything inside them as protected behind an invisible wall. Within Parks Canada, this has led to the development of the "guardian syndrome": *we* will protect the public's parks for *them* (yet another dualism!). Among the Canadian public, it has bred a blind faith and a false sense of security.

"The problem is that parks have been oversold," fumed my friend Bill Swan, who is a naturalist living in the West Kootenays of British Columbia. When he is not working for Parks Canada as a park interpreter, he is leading ecotourism ventures around the world. "It's like a reversal of Smokey the Bear. Instead of thinking all wildfires are bad, we seem to think that parks will protect ecosystems and species no matter what we do outside of them. Neither one of them is right."

Another friend, Kevin Van Tighem, who also works for Parks Canada as an ecologist, wrote a passionate and highly controversial article in the mid-1980s that went even further, contending that parks and protected areas may even encourage destructive land-use practices outside their boundaries. "They have encouraged us to believe that conservation is merely a system of trading environmental write-offs against large protected areas," he said, before pointing out that their presence leads us to believe that "outside the parks, in those places not fortunate enough to be protected from our alien influence, Nature must be—at least to a large extent—written off."

"Destructive development? Unwise land use? That's the nature of the beast, after all; thank God that at least we have our national parks," Van Tighem quipped. "It seems that we have cheated ourselves, with our penchant for easy either/or decisions. We have chosen to draw lines on maps and to write regulations. We have zoned one area for preservation, another for development, another for exploitation; and we have convinced ourselves that this is a rational approach to conservation."[1] Pretty harsh words from someone I know deeply cares about national parks and people.

If parks are not fortresses or preserves, then what are they? Here is how conservation biologists are starting to see them: "the core of a hierarchically connected representative network including satellite natural areas, linkages, and compatible surrounding land (and water) use . . . designed as a part of a planned land use mosaic . . ."[2] Although this leading-edge concept borders on gobbledegook for some, the ideas are not too difficult to understand, especially if one keeps in mind the discussion on systems theory in the previous chapter. What it amounts to is this: national parks are seen as a system within a larger protected areas system, which in Canada's case would include provincial, territorial, regional and municipal parks along with ecological reserves, wildlife sanctuaries and designated wilderness areas. Each of these is perceived as a system unto itself, but all are interconnected. Wildlife moving between Riding Mountain National Park and the Duck Mountains Provincial Park in Manitoba, for example, don't stop to consider the political implications; the only real concern to them is habitat availability and quality at either place, as well as adequate cover while travelling between the two parks. Hence the need to link the various protected areas with wildlife corridors—strips of land left in as natural a state as possible. Finally, parks are viewed as being embedded within the greater ecosystem and the regional landscape; so much so, that it is now increasingly accepted among ecologists that keeping the wild alive depends more on human activities in the surrounding matrix than in the parks and protected areas themselves. As a consequence, fostering compatible land uses adjacent to and between protected areas is viewed as critical to their success.

Connecting existing and potential protected areas with one another by means of corridors is currently believed to be necessary to effectively conserve biodiversity. Corridors have been defined as "linear landscape features that facilitate the biologically effective transport of animals between larger patches of habitat to accommodate daily, seasonal and dispersal movements."[3] They can be created on a variety of scales, ranging from the very small—a wooded ravine running through a subdivision linking two municipal parks—to the very large. An example of the latter would be the Yellowstone to Yukon or "Y2Y" Initiative, which aspires to a continuous corridor spanning the Rocky Mountains and running nearly 3,200 kilometres, from Yellowstone National Park in Wyoming to the Mackenzie Mountains in the Yukon. In total, the project encompasses more than 1.2 million square kilometres of territory on both sides of the border, and has garnered the support and involvement of over 170 Canadian and American conservation organizations and individuals.

On a recent visit to Banff National Park, I met with the project's co-ordinator, Bart Robinson, at his office in Canmore. As a former

editor of *Equinox*, one of Canada's leading environmental magazines, he was an excellent choice for the job: not only does he have
a passion for all things wild, but also essential media and communication savvy. Knowing that I was gathering research material for
this book, he was eager to talk about the Y2Y project.

"We've been very active over the past couple of years," he said
with quiet pride. "We've produced an atlas that will enable us to
better understand the biophysical and cultural aspects of the corridor. We have divided it into a number of smaller regions and
have begun to develop conservation plans for each of them." To
assist with the implementation of the conservation plans, an outreach co-ordinator has been hired to build understanding and
support among First Nations, rod and gun clubs, ranchers and
other sectors of the population. "We're finding that the concept is
really easy to get," enthused Robinson, "and generally there is
growing support for it." As evidence, he pointed out that the
Alberta government was about to announce some new protected
areas east of Canmore and that the British Columbia government
had just recently created the Muskwa–Kechika protected area,
consisting of six parks totalling over a million hectares and surrounded by more than 3 million hectares of special management
area. Furthermore, the American and Canadian national parks
services had signed an agreement committing them to promoting
the Y2Y Initiative. He did, however, acknowledge that not everyone was excited about the idea; the Forest Alliance of British
Columbia, an influential lobby organization, branded the initiative
another land grab.

"What really gives me hope that we can pull this project off are
the success stories coming in from elsewhere," Robinson stated.
"Florida was in danger of losing the panther, and the public was
clear that they didn't want that to happen, so the state government
voted in a $3-billion bond to save the cat. Corridors are an impor-
tant part of the recovery plans."

In accordance with the principles of conservation biology, the
Yellowstone to Yukon Initiative will consist of protected areas

linked by corridors and surrounded by transition zones, in which human activities are harmonized with the goals of conserving biodiversity and wildness. It is a well-established fact, and just plain common sense, that park ecosystems cannot be protected as islands encircled by incompatible land uses. The key is to reduce the contrast between one side of the boundary and the other. For this reason, there has been considerable discussion about the creation of buffers or zones of co-operation around core protected areas. The idea probably arose during the late 1960s out of the Man and the Biosphere program of the United Nations Educational, Scientific and Cultural Organization (UNESCO). The program was established specifically to foster harmonious relationships between people and the environment, and one of the key project areas is the creation of a worldwide network of biosphere reserves. This new category of protected area embraced both preservation and conservation by surrounding a core zone of predominantly undisturbed, self-sustaining natural systems with a zone of co-operation, in which human settlements and enterprises were to be managed, on a voluntary basis, to minimize their impacts on native ecosystems and species, especially those within the core zone. More simply put, the biosphere reserves were envisioned as models of sustainable development.

Canada's first biosphere reserve was established in 1978 at Mont-Saint-Hilaire in Quebec to conserve one of the last minimally disturbed remnants of the Great Lakes–St Lawrence forest. Since then, five more have been designated: Waterton Lakes National Park in southwestern Alberta (1979); Long Point in southern Ontario (1986); Riding Mountain National Park in southwestern Manitoba (1986); Charlevoix in Quebec (1986); and the Niagara Escarpment, also in southern Ontario (1990). A seventh biosphere is expected to be designated soon in the Clayoquot Sound on Vancouver Island's west coast.

The key to the success of the biosphere reserves is local involvement. Without it, there can be no co-operation. At Waterton Lakes and Riding Mountain national parks, park staff and local citizens have formed management and technical committees to address issues such as the spread of the highly invasive plant knapweed, and problems of flooding caused by beaver. The issues are tackled through research, education and demonstration projects, which attempt to develop mutually acceptable solutions and to encourage sustainable human activity on the lands adjacent to or near the respective parks.

By the mid-1980s, under the visionary leadership of superintendent Bernie Lieff, Waterton Lakes Biosphere Reserve encompassed a zone of co-operation that extended approximately twenty-five kilometres beyond the park's boundaries. But the possibilities were even greater, as Lieff was reminded while giving a talk about biosphere reserves to a local school. After carefully explaining the biosphere reserve program at Waterton, he asked the children what they thought the zone of co-operation was. One little boy at the back of the room instantly stuck up his hand and frantically began waving it, so Lieff asked him for his answer. "It's all the area between national parks," the young lad blurted out. How does that old saying go? Something about out of the mouths of babes come words of wisdom? In a few simple words the boy captured the scope of what was required if the wild is to survive even in our highly protected national parks.

Regrettably, the biosphere reserve program has remained underfunded and understaffed from its inception. As a consequence, the program has not been able to realize its potential, prompting an ongoing search for another way of encouraging land uses compatible with the conservation of biodiversity. In 1997, Adrian Phillips, the chair of the World Commission on Protected Areas, put forth an intriguing idea at a conference of scientists and managers aimed at building linkages between protected areas and working landscapes, that is, landscapes devoted to human settlement and enterprises. He began by noting that there were at least six kinds of protected areas officially recognized by the International Union for the Conservation of Nature (IUCN): strict nature reserves, national parks, natural monuments, habitat or species management areas, protected landscapes and seascapes, and managed resource protected areas (multiple-use areas). He pointed out that the first four categories have tended to be the priority for protected area establishment around the world. Phillips then argued for the expansion of protected area systems to include the fifth category, that of protected landscapes or seascapes, which he believed could serve as critically important buffers around the more highly protected areas.

As with the zone of co-operation in the biosphere reserve program, protected landscapes or seascapes are areas managed primarily for conservation as opposed to preservation. They have been developed and used extensively in Europe, composing two-thirds of all the continent's protected areas. The national parks of England and Wales, which cover nearly 10 percent of the two countries, encompass highly protected areas such as nature reserves surrounded by protected landscapes, which are lived in and worked on. According to Phillips, the approach has not yet made significant inroads in North America because of narrow thinking among conservation biologists and environmentalists, who remain fixated on protecting large, unaltered areas. If the idea were embraced, it would mean a host of benefits. As Phillips contends: "More areas, and a higher proportion of a nation's biodiversity, would be protected; national protected area systems would be more representative; national networks of protected areas could be created incorporating those from a range of categories . . ." along with closer alliances between people and protected areas, and between conservation and sustainable rural development.[4] A big cautionary flag needs to be raised here: while sustainably managed lands like a timber licence area do fall within IUCN's family of protected areas, they should not be used as an excuse for not setting aside more highly protected lands.

Protected landscapes do not necessarily need to be a part of a national park per se; they can be formed from private land through such mechanisms as voluntary management agreements or legally binding conservation easements. The latter approach involves attaching certain restraints to property rights to protect natural ecosystems and species. The exact nature of the prohibitions are negotiated between the landowner and a land trust organization, such as the Nature Conservancy of Canada. Once attached to the property title, the prohibitions remain with it indefinitely, no matter who may own the land down the line.

Even without entering into an agreement with another party, whether a government agency or a non-profit organization, private landowners can incorporate conservation into their daily decision making. Recall the ideas put forward by farmer and chair of Riding Mountain National Park's biosphere reserve management committee John Whitaker in Chapter 3. His suggestions for the farming community include bringing hay bales into the barnyard for the winter and not planting alfalfa next to the park's boundaries, so as not to attract elk out of the park. The same principle holds when setting out beehives, which can create problems with park bears. Recreational or residential homeowners can ensure that they properly dispose of garbage for the same reasons. They can also refrain from clearing native vegetation and putting up fences on their property, both of which practices destroy and fragment wildlife habitat. Municipalities can incorporate wildlife needs into land use zoning and offer incentives for landowners to maintain critical habitat. Logging and mining companies can create minimal disruption to wildlife and ecosystems by fully embracing the precautionary principle in the planning and management of their operations. This principle states that the lack of scientific evidence of ecological impact should not be used as justification for proceeding with proposed development. Another way of putting this was offered by a whale biologist who said: "In managing natural resources, we have tended to see how much we can get away with. It's time to start seeing how little we can get away with."

Zones of co-operation, corridors and covenants can do much to ensure the maintenance of a protected area's biodiversity. However, still more is possible and indeed necessary given the extent of damage to natural systems across vast stretches of the landscape. A growing number of ecologists are beginning to realize that maintaining biodiversity is probably not achievable without addressing the damage already done. Out of this realization is emerging a new field of ecology called "restoration," which aims to re-establish "viable communities of plants and animals in their natural diversity."[5] In practice, it consists of activities that "contribute to the re-establishment of the processes which define, shape and maintain a given ecosystem . . ."[6] In other words, ecological restoration is about the recovery of ecosystems after they have lost biological diversity, whereas conservation biology is primarily focused on protecting and conserving ecosystems before such losses have occurred[7].

I received hands-on experience in ecological restoration on a sunny, warm Thanksgiving afternoon while staying with my friend Ted Mosquin. Ted owns an exquisite one-hundred-acre (forty-hectare) piece of land in the heart of Lanark County, near Ottawa. A small, sparkling clear river runs through a corner of his land, and much of the surrounding gently rolling countryside is still clothed in maple forests. In the past, a farmer had succeeded in clearing large portions and attempted to create fields from the unruly land. However, the Canadian Shield lay just below the surface and defied his puny efforts. It is marginal land, at best, for crop growing; it is just right, though, for the maple forests.

After a hearty breakfast, Mosquin invited me to join him in replanting a portion of one of the old fields. Following him into the forest, I soon found myself down on my knees, gently pulling up young maple seedlings that littered the forest floor. In a matter of minutes we had stuffed several plastic bags, which Ted said would be enough for the area he had in mind. With that, he charged off through the woods with me scrambling to keep up. Moments later, we plunged into the field and began to plant the little sprouts in the ground. The procedure was simple: I would slice the earth with a spade wherever Mosquin directed; he would take a seedling from one of the bags, stick it into the cut and step on the dirt to close the earth around the roots. Within a few hours, the bags were empty and we were able to stand and look with satisfaction at the tops of 150 young green trees bobbing among the brown weeds and grasses. It will be several decades before a grove of maples replaces the ill-conceived field, to be sure, but the process of recovery has begun.

The planting of "Rick's Grove," as Mosquin graciously called it, resembles most restoration projects to date. They tend to be small and localized, usually defined by the area of direct destructive impact.[8] As a result, ecological restoration has sometimes been cast as little more than a band-aid solution. "In fact, in the long run it is likely that restoration will be successful *only* if it can be undertaken in large-scale terms," says Donald Falk, the executive director of the Society of Ecological Restoration. Others worry that restoration could be used as a justification for ecologically destructive practices. After all, if we can fix broken ecosystems, why should we worry about what we do to them? The Worldwatch Institute answers: "Restoration is not a substitute for vigorous efforts to preserve natural areas. It cannot be expected to recover the full range of natural diversity on converted lands."[9] It cannot be expected to do so because ecosystems are highly dependent on the conditions that give rise to them; a change in conditions after a disturbance will result in a different ecosystem. Hence, the best restoration can do is to approximate an ecosystem; it can never faithfully replicate it.

Despite these limitations and concerns, ecological restoration is still widely viewed as a powerful tool for the conservation of biological diversity. It is capable of re-weaving tattered webs of life and healing wounded landscapes. Through ecological restoration, the seemingly impossible can occur, that is, the re-establishment of "landscape-scale connectivity and an ecologically friendly matrix" to safeguard protected areas.[10] Falk sees this as the central challenge for the new field and suggests that protected areas be a priority for restoration. "[S]ome Restoration Priority Areas might be adjacent to our highest-quality core reserves, around which they could serve as the much discussed (but rarely created) buffer zones for which

many conservation biologists have argued," he says.[11] The suggestion makes good sense. As the Worldwatch Institute points out: "A
national park, surrounded by farmland, pasture, or any sort of
development, cannot pick up its boundaries and move when conditions no longer favor the array of organisms it was designed to
protect. Restoration may help add habitat to existing parks and
reserves, or help establish species and ecosystems outside their previous range to buffer the biological uncertainties that will come
with a $CO_2$-induced warming."[12] Similarly, restoration priority
could be assigned to important stopover points, migratory routes,
seasonal habitats or spawning streams. The possibilities are limitless.
The key is to think long-term and on a large scale.

There is another priority area for ecological restoration, and
that is inside the protected areas themselves. While many of the
national parks have ecosystem conservation plans, Point Pelee has
an ecosystem restoration plan, the only one of its kind in Canada.
Established in 1918 to protect a crucial continental migratory
stopover for songbirds, the park, covering barely fifteen square
kilometres, is the second smallest national park in the system after
St. Lawrence Islands. Before its protection as a national park, the
point experienced a long history of environmental impacts; ironi-
cally, things went from bad to worse with the creation of the park.
No sooner had the land been converted from a naval reserve than
the National Parks Branch built campgrounds, picnic grounds and
a change house, since the park boasted a long sandy spit jutting out
into Lake Erie. The park was an instant hit. Visitation went from
zero to twenty-five thousand a year in just seven years. Owners of
private land that had been encompassed by the park quickly began
realizing windfall profits by subdividing their property for cottages.
Soon there were several hundred in the park, mostly owned by
Americans. By the early 1950s, more than half a million people
poured through the tiny park's gate each year.

Caught in the crush of people determined to get the best swim-
ming and sunbathing spots, the forest cover was being destroyed.
A few small changes were made to lessen the impact, but these

were rendered largely ineffective by the development of other services designed to accommodate higher use. The crisis continued to build and finally came to an embarrassing head in the late 1960s, when there was serious discussion within government of removing the park from the system because of the rampant development and the degraded state of the ecosystems. Fortunately, that idea was rejected in light of Point Pelee's biological importance. Instead of selling or giving away the park, it was agreed that it should be restored. The parks branch began buying up properties and removing cottages, refreshment stands and other facilities. Over four hundred structures have been removed to date. Only three cabins remain in the park, and Parks Canada is currently negotiating to buy one of them. In the early 1970s, Point Pelee became the first national park in the system to establish a vehicle exclusion zone by shutting off traffic to the south end of the park; as a substitute, visitors would now be conveyed to this popular area by pubic transit.

In the 1980s, park staff developed a plan to guide further restoration work, which would focus on three critical issues: exotic plants, hyper-abundant whitetail deer and human impact. Given that more than a third of the park's vegetation were non-native species, a decision was made to tackle only the most aggressive ones, such as the white mulberry tree, which was introduced to Canada from Europe and which can interbreed with the native red mulberry tree. The latter is found only in small localized populations and has been classified as an endangered species. The control and possible elimination of exotic plants is very labour-intensive, demanding lots of digging, pulling and cutting. Herbicides are used only where necessary and only very sparingly. As a consequence, this kind of restoration work is extremely expensive.

The overpopulation of whitetail deer has been dealt with through culling. Since 1990, the park has been closed four times to allow wardens to shoot some of the deer. For the past three years they have not had to cull deer, as the population appears to have stabilized, at least for the moment.

Dealing with Point Pelee's other overabundant species—humans—has led to some of the boldest restoration moves anywhere in the entire national park system. The park's management plan in 1995 called for the removal of park facilities to assist with the restoration work. As a consequence, all but one road has now been removed. Pushed on by studies revealing high levels of DDT and other toxic materials in the soil, a community camp, warden headquarters and maintenance yard have also been closed. The camp, consisting of several small bunkhouses and a dining hall, has been relocated and will become part of an existing group campground. An addition is being built onto the visitor centre to house the wardens, and a new maintenance yard is being constructed outside the park. Even the administration building is slated to be moved out of the park. By the summer of 2000, the visitor centre will be the only Parks Canada building left in the park.

Restoration work has also gone on outside the park. Point Pelee is a part of Essex County, one of the most densely populated regions in southern Ontario. Less than 4 percent of it remains as natural habitat, mostly in scattered tiny woodlots. Recognizing that the park is an ecological island, park staff teamed up with a variety of naturalist groups, businesses and other government departments to begin replanting native species throughout the county. This partnership, called the Natural Habitat Restoration Program, is now being run largely by the Essex County Field Naturalists.

Throughout the national park system, there are countless examples of facilities being taken out of use and the land they once occupied being restored to natural conditions. At Riding Mountain National Park, the outdoor roller rink, which was owned by a family friend and which had been an important part of our lives, was removed after he sold it to the government. In Kootenay National Park, staff housing was relocated because it had been built smack dab in the middle of a bighorn sheep meadow many years before. Even though these examples are small in scale, they can add up to significant areas being restored. What they suggest is that if we are truly concerned about maintaining the wild in our national parks, we should carefully assess all existing facilities with an eye to their possible decommissioning. Not only would this make more room for natural ecosystems and species, but it would also save money that otherwise must be spent on repairs or replacements.

While we're at it, why not start putting limits on use, most critically in those parks reporting significant ecological damage from overuse? Again, the idea is not without precedent in the national park system. One of the most notable examples is almost at my back door: the West Coast Trail in Pacific Rim National Park, where use is capped at eight thousand a year. To register for the trail, would-be hikers must often spend several days on the phone for the peak-season slots, and then spend over $100 in a variety of fees. What could be done to turn things around in Banff National Park if facilities were slowly decommissioned, limits on use—both in terms of numbers of people and the kind of activities engaged in—put in place, and a shuttle system developed such as that in Point Pelee? Certainly, the ecosystems and species of smaller parks, such as Waterton, Kouchibouguac and Fundy, would greatly benefit from this approach.

Sound impossible? If it does, it may be because most of us still believe that it is our right to have access to the national parks pretty much whenever we want. The funny thing is, we don't expect this with hotels, theatres or restaurants. When the sign says *full*, we may not like it, but we generally accept the fact and move on elsewhere. It is clear that we cannot continue to appropriate more and more space in the parks and still expect the wild to exist.

If we do not act quickly and wisely, we may well be forced to adopt drastic measures enshrined in strict legislation and policy in order to protect what little wildness remains in our national parks. The key to turning things around before it is too late is to see the national parks for what they truly are: more like cells surrounded by a permeable membrane than fortresses made with invincible walls. To maintain their health, cells must be interconnected and embedded within a nurturing environment; so too for parks.

Without these factors, the parks will continue to lose their eco-logical integrity and wildness no matter what measures are enforced within their boundaries.

Maintaining and restoring the wild in Canada's national parks requires "big picture" thinking and extraordinary effort on every-one's part. Recalling a concept introduced in the previous chapter, the field of care must imbue all human activity around and beyond the national parks if they are to achieve their vitally important eco-logical mission.

# ELEVEN

# Re-creation

At the beginning of the last chapter I said that our perception of national parks is dominated by three metaphors: parks as preserves, parks as playgrounds and parks as profit producers—all of which create problems for maintaining and restoring ecological integrity. Over the course of the chapter I set forth an alternative to the metaphor of parks as preserves, demonstrating how they are more like living cells. In this chapter I want to propose alternative metaphors to replace those of parks as profit producers and parks as playgrounds.

Let me begin by tackling the first metaphor. As I pointed out in Chapter 5, running parks as profit-producing businesses is creating severe impacts on ecological integrity. The alternative I wish to propose is a return to the notion of the national parks being a public trust. The Parks Legacy Panel (not to be confused with the aforementioned Panel on Ecological Integrity) recently recommended the same thing for B.C.'s provincial park system. The panel was established to "provide government with practical suggestions and recommendations to enhance the long-term planning and management of protected areas"[1] and was to accomplish this through extensive public consultation. In its final report to the government, the panel recommended as a first principle that "protected areas are maintained in perpetuity as public lands"; therefore, "as an inalienable public good, these areas must not be sold, commercialized or privatized."[2] A public trust they defined as "a public property right or public ownership, wherein the property owner (the Province) becomes a custodian of the land in question and of the associated values that, in essence, belong to future generations of British Columbians. It embodies the concept that the government is the trustee of protected areas and protected area values, with the obligation to preserve these elements for the benefit of current and future citizens."[3] To address B.C. Parks' cash crunch, which is many times more desperate than that of Parks Canada, the panel called for a significant increase in the park budget through a variety of mechanisms, including increased government appropriations (from revenue collected through personal and business taxes), fee adjustments, linking a portion of the gas tax to funding for parks, holding a "green" lottery and phasing in an annual park pass. Nowhere did it suggest running parks more like a business; in fact, just the opposite.

One of the most outspoken opponents of running government services as profit producers is Henry Mintzberg, an internationally renowned Canadian management expert who teaches at McGill University. "In my view, we have confounded the whole relationship between business and government," he says provocatively, "and we had best clear it up before we end up no better off than the Eastern Europeans once were . . . Business is in the business of selling us as much as it possibly can, maintaining an arm's length relationship controlled by the forces of supply and demand," he continues. "I have no trouble with that notion—for cars, washing machines or toothpaste. But I do for health care."[4] This and other services typically provided by government, like maintaining a national system of parks or protected areas, are exceedingly complex, and businesses are not well equipped to provide them. "I'm not a mere customer of my government, thank you," protests Mintzberg. "I expect something more than arm's-length trading and something less than the encouragement to consume."[5] In the end he concludes: "Business is not all good; government is not all bad. Each has its place in a balanced society alongside co-operative and non-owned organizations. I do not wish to buy my cars from government any more than I wish to receive my policing services from General Motors."[6] The fundamental difference is that one provides public goods, the other private goods.

This is not to say that public and private don't cross over; they do from time to time, as Mintzberg has pointed out: "Our national parks, for example, provide customer services (to tourists) and professional client services (to tourists stranded on mountain faces). Parks are also part of the public infrastructure we enjoy as citizens, and that fact requires us, as subjects, to respect the environment of the park."[7] However, he warns, "when it comes to citizen and subject activities, we should stray beyond the state-ownership model only with a great deal of prudence."[8]

The message from both Mintzberg and the Parks Legacy Panel is clear and simple: while the national parks do provide some goods and services that can be made to generate revenue, such as camping, firewood or parking, we should not forget they are ultimately a public trust and are easily violated in the narrow-minded, bottom-line drive to make them more profitable. Part of the problem arises from confusion over what constitutes "essential and basic" services. As the environmental philosopher Arne Naess has pointed out, the provision of more parking space is often taken as satisfying an essential and basic need. Modern society, with its addiction to consumerism and materialism, too often confuses vital needs with compensatory needs. The former are things like food, water and shelter, as well as love, play, creative expression and spiritual growth. Compensatory needs can best be illustrated with an example. I overheard a conversation in a fast-food court of a large mall in which one of the people said, very seriously, "I woke up this morning feeling depressed, so I decided to come here for some shop therapy." Compensatory needs can be defined as the things or experiences we purchase, consume or desire in order to fill what is actually "a hole in our soul." Feeling something missing in our lives, we are driven to acquire status symbols such as new clothes, new cars or bigger houses to make ourselves feel better. The drive is encouraged and perpetuated by advertising that promises us happiness and fulfilment if we purchase the things that other people have. Keeping up with the Joneses is not good enough; one must strive to stay ahead. The trouble is that the root problem is spiritual in nature and no amount of material things can ever satisfy it. The sooner we recognize this and address it, the sooner we will begin to restore our personal well-being as well as that of the rest of humanity and the planet.

All of this shouldn't be taken to infer that I don't think there is a place for revenue generation within the national parks. I happen to agree with Mintzberg and the B.C. Parks Legacy Panel that reasonable fees can be charged for some services. However, the parks should not be expected to generate large amounts of revenue. Instructing the national parks to offset recent budget cuts in excess of 25 percent through revenue generation is driving them towards Disneyfication. The recommendations of the B.C. Parks Legacy Panel with respect to revenue are equally applicable to Parks Canada. I would only add that many other innovative ways of funding the national parks could be considered, such as a national bond, much like a Canada Savings Bond, the proceeds of which would go directly to support the establishment and management of the national parks; or a small tax on international visitors, to be levied when they land at any of the major airports. As a public trust or, better yet, a sacred trust, Canada's national parks deserve to have a base-line budget adequate to meet the difficult and crucial challenge of maintaining ecological integrity through protection, education and "appropriate" visitor services.

This brings me to the metaphor of parks as playgrounds. Parks Canada has always wrestled with the question of what constitutes "appropriate" forms of recreation. The National Parks Act is largely silent on the matter, saying only that the parks are for the "benefit, education and enjoyment" of Canadians and "shall be maintained and made use of so as to leave them unimpaired for the enjoyment of future generations." The first edition of the National Parks Policy, released in 1964, acknowledged that this clause was too general, resulting in an all too common interpretation favouring the development of the parks as lucrative resorts, providing a wide range of "artificial recreations," such as golf courses, tennis courts, lawn bowling greens or downhill skiing operations (interestingly, many of the same facilities and services that Harkin had promoted). It stated that, from then on, these forms of recreation would be considered "secondary uses" and would only be permitted as long as they didn't detract from the basic purpose of the national parks, which was to protect ecosystems and species.[9] Likening the parks to a museum or art gallery, the policy pointed out that "[t]hey do not allow activities . . . which are out of harmony with their real purpose."[10] These activities the policy termed "urban type recreational facilities," and they were to be encouraged to locate outside the parks.

The 1979 edition of the National Parks Policy stated that Parks Canada had a responsibility to "ensure that those facilities and services which are essential and appropriate for public access, understanding and enjoyment" were provided.[11] It went on to state:

> In responding to visitor needs for services, facilities and outdoor recreation activities, Parks Canada must act with care and imagination. All Canadians have a right to appreciate their natural heritage but the means of doing so and the facilities provided will depend on the sensitivity of the environment to human impact. National parks offer rare and outstanding opportunities to experience and learn about the natural environment in a wilderness setting. They cannot, however, provide for every kind of use requested by the public.[12]

Warning against the dangers of overuse, improper use and inappropriate development, the policy directed Parks Canada to encourage "simplicity in facilities" and "self-reliance on the part of visitors."

The most recent policy, issued in 1994, says that "opportunities will be provided to visitors that enhance public understanding, appreciation, enjoyment and protection of the national heritage and which are appropriate to the purpose of each park."[13] Going one step further, it adds that only "essential and basic services" will be provided, so as to maintain ecological integrity and avoid incremental, cumulative impacts.

At first glance there seems to be plenty of guidance within the policy as to what constitutes appropriate use. Why, then, has tourism and recreation development become a major threat to so many of the national parks? There is no simple and easy answer. Certainly, the perception of parks as profit producers has contributed to the problem, but so has the perception of parks as playgrounds. If the national parks are to remain wild, then our understanding of outdoor recreation must change as well.

Recreation embraces a wide variety of activities that are engaged in during leisure time, which is typically thought of as time left after work, sleep and the performance of personal chores.[14] More than specific activities, it is a state of mind. People choose recreation for a multitude of reasons: excitement, solitude, stress reduction, socialization, catharsis or relaxation.[15] Geoffrey Wall, a geographer at the University of Waterloo, suggests that a continuum exists between work and leisure. At one end is the Protestant work ethic, which holds that the only justifiable form of recreation is that which re-creates the person so that they are better able to perform at work. At the other end are the hedonists, who "live for leisure, and who regard work as a necessary evil which must be endured if they are to accumulate sufficient resources to recreate to the full."[16] In a similar vein, an American professor of political science and forestry suggests that recreationists can be categorized along a continuum of spartanism to hedonism. "A spartan," he says, "is a person whose life style admits few luxuries and is conducted in a relatively unbuffered environment."[17] This person is predisposed towards "self-imposed discipline," "simplicity" and "physical exertion." A hedonist, on the other hand, is "oriented primarily toward the exploitation of the pleasure potential of his physical and social environments" and is given to "a high consumption of material goods."[18] This latter group, he notes, also tend to be aficionados of adult toys, such as recreational vehicles, ATVs, dirt bikes, snowmobiles, Jet Skis and speedboats. In fairness, it should be acknowledged that even the spartans can be a little like the adult-toy aficionados. I should know, as I am of the spartan clan, and yet each year when the Mountain Equipment Co-op catalogue comes out, I find myself wistfully thumbing through the pages of the latest innovations in backpacking gear, probably in the same way that a boating enthusiast would linger over the most recent models of Evinrude, Johnson or Yamaha outboard motors. Little wonder that outdoor recreation has become big business.

The similarities between the two groups are quite superficial, however. Probing beneath the surface of recreational choices and behaviours, one finds some fundamental differences in attitudes towards the environment. Edgar Jackson, a geographer at the University of Alberta, suggests that recreationists fall into two general categories: conservers or consumers. The latter tend to be geared for mechanized activities, such as driving, snowmobiling or motorboating, which "impose severe impacts on the natural environment and place heavy demands on natural resources, especially energy."[19] For these recreationists, the natural environment is merely a backdrop for their activity, or something against which to pit machine and muscle. Conservers, like spartans, take pleasure in simple, self-propelled, non-mechanized recreation, such as hiking or canoeing, which has minimal impact on the environment as compared to the activities of the consumers. Not surprisingly, conserver recreationists tend to exhibit stronger pro-environmental attitudes than do consumer recreationists.[20]

The significance of these differences in terms of determining what are appropriate forms of recreation in a national park or wilderness area did not escape Aldo Leopold back in the late 1940s. The closing essay of his classic book *A Sand County Almanac* is a stinging indictment of the prevailing dominance of consumer recreation. He wrote angrily:

Like ions shot from the sun, the week-enders radiate from every town, generating heat and friction as they go. A tourist industry purveys bed and board to bait more ions, faster, further. Advertisements on rock and rill confide to all and sundry the whereabouts of new retreats, landscapes, hunting-grounds, and fishing-lakes just beyond those recently overrun. Bureaus build roads into new hinterlands then buy more hinterlands to absorb the exodus accelerated by the roads. A gadget industry pads the bumps against nature-in-the-raw; woodcraft becomes the art of using gadgets. And now, to cap the pyramid of banalities, the trailer. To him who seeks in the woods and mountains only those things obtainable from travel or golf, the present situation is tolerable. But to him who seeks something more, recreation has become a self-destructive process of seeking but never quite finding, a major frustration of mechanized society.[21]

"This is Outdoor Recreation, Latest Model," he says bitingly.

The new recreationist wishes to return from his or her activity with a trophy—something that attests to its possessor having been somewhere and done something. It could be anything from a photograph of a string of trout to rows of park stickers across the back of a recreational vehicle. What matters almost as much as the experience is the trophy. The trophy-recreationist must "possess, invade, appropriate" in order to enjoy. "He is the motorized ant who swarms the continents before learning to see his own back yard, who consumes but never creates outdoor satisfactions."[22] It is for this type of recreationist, Leopold alleges, that parks and wilderness areas are made more artificial through mass-use and development. He fumed:

It is clear without further discussion that mass-use involves a direct dilution of the opportunity for solitude; that when we speak of roads, campgrounds, trails, and toilets as 'development' of recreational resources, we speak falsely in respect to this component. Such accommodations for the crowd are not developing (in the sense of adding or creating) anything. On the contrary, they are merely water poured into an already-thin soup.[23]

As an alternative to recreation focused on trophies, Leopold proposes that it be reoriented to promote perception through "nature study" of the land, living things and the ways they maintain their existence.[24] He ends the essay with a plea that is even more relevant today than when he wrote it. "It is the expansion of transport without a corresponding growth of perception that threatens us with qualitative bankruptcy of the recreational process," he laments. "Recreational development is a job not of building roads into lovely country, but of building receptivity into the still unlovely human mind."[25] "Unloving" would perhaps have been a more accurate description than "unlovely," but it's a small point. Except for this minor quibble over his choice of words, I can only add "amen."

What's really critical here is Leopold's contention that outdoor recreation should promote receptivity within the human mind to the protection and conservation of biological diversity. This is what J.B. Harkin believed as well. "The farther we have been removed from nature, the more we need to get back to the natural and even primitive life," he once said. "Such a life allows a man to resume his relationship with wild animals, a relationship as old as man himself and which every man takes pleasure in renewing."[26] Elsewhere he remarked: "Those who penetrate them on foot or horseback enjoy an experience which those who whiz through them in cars can never know . . . Wonder, reverence, the feeling that one is nearer the mystery of things—that is what one feels in places of such sublime beauty."[27] In other words, through the right kind of outdoor recreation, people can rejuvenate body, mind and spirit while simultaneously reconnecting with nature.

Historian Theodore Roszak echoes this theme, proposing that the modern urban-industrial complex is a flight from the primitive driven by the imperative to progress beyond nature. Our progress can be measured by the degree to which we render the world artificial. What we are forgetting is that nature is the source from which we as a species arose. Hence, we are taking some big risks. As Roszak warns:

Any cultural goods we produce which sunder themselves from this traditional, lively connection with the non-human, any thinking we do which isolates itself from, or pits itself against the natural environment is—strictly speaking—a delusion, and a very sick one. Not only because it will lack ecological intelligence, but because, more critically still, it will lack psychological completeness.[28]

In other words, the urban-industrial imperative is creating a society of "sick souls" who are increasingly out of touch with the root of their humanity.

A couple of years ago I had the delightful experience of pursuing this theme in depth with Canadian naturalist and author John Livingston. Although recovering from a difficult operation, he invited Di and me out to his home near Carp, Ontario. At the time, we were visiting with Ted Mosquin and his family in Lanark County, only an hour or so away by car. Following his instructions, we turned off the highway north of Carp, a small Ottawa Valley village, onto a narrow dirt track that climbed a low aspen-covered ridge. Continuing along its crest, we passed a couple of homes on large acreages, barely discernible through trees aflame from a brush with the advancing autumn. At the end of the road we came to a lane, which wound down to a large, modern-looking home, which Livingston had said would be his.

We pulled up in front of the house. A pair of large dogs came racing around the corner, and unsure of their attitude, Dianne and I closed ranks. However, it quickly became apparent that they were more interested in playing than in attacking. One in particular kept nudging and licking my hand, wanting me to toss a well-slavered stick. Just as I was bending down to pick it up and throw it, Livingston appeared at the door and called the dogs to him, while greeting us with a gruff, gravelly voice. The dogs obeyed instantly and swirled past him into the house. He shook our hands and led us through the door and up a flight of stairs to the main living area. The view from the top was stunning. Before us, over a sun-drenched expanse of wood, furniture, plants and rugs, upon which reclined the two dogs, large windows offered a sweeping vista of the little valley out of which we had just climbed. Allowing us a few moments to take in the beauty of the setting, he then led us into a bright and spacious kitchen, where he proceeded to make us tea and coffee.

"The problem is cultural," Livingston said categorically after I explained that I was in the process of gathering material for a book about the loss of wildness from Canada's national parks. "We've got to understand the cultural/historical context of how we got to where we are. What I'm talking about is an inherited ideology. These ideas I've put forward in my book *Rogue Primate*."

I had recently read the book, and had found it filled with unvarnished and insightful observations mixed with a healthy dose of moral outrage over the ecological damage the human species was creating. It is Livingston's contention that the planet is suffering from "a growing, creeping and crawling *sameness* that is the utter antithesis of ecological and evolutionary process."[29] Like Roszak, Livingston sees this process of domestication being driven by a cultural imperative that appears intent on remaking the earth and all other life forms in the human image.

"The moment you see a species or ecosystem as a resource," he said, pouring the hot beverages, "by reducing them to this, they lose all inherent worth and become only something to be used to meet human needs. At which point, you can kiss it goodbye.

"Management, whether of wildlife, wilderness or parks, only perpetuates the ideology," he continued between sips. "When management begins, so does domestication. We should not manage nature; we should leave it alone. Same goes for the national parks. We should just be protecting nature until we can kick the people out and expand the parks.

"Does that sound elitist?" he shot at me from over the rim of his cup. I suddenly felt uncomfortable. On one hand I agreed with everything he was saying about the inherent worth of nature and that to manage it as a resource only leads to either its domestication or its demise; yet on the other hand, it seemed to me that parks provided a unique opportunity for people to reconnect with nature and learn to appreciate, respect and care for it. "There's no avoiding appearing to be elitist," he said, sensing my hesitation, "if you truly care about maintaining and restoring the wild. Besides, people don't need to be in the national parks to reconnect with or to experience the wild. Most of them can do it right where they are. There's wildness to be appreciated in a chickadee, an aspen tree or in a hawk circling overhead. These things can be found even in the most densely populated regions of Canada.

"In fact," said Livingston with a glint in his eye, "the wild is within each and every one of us, only waiting to be recovered once again. But we must learn how to throw off the bonds of domestication."

I was still feeling uneasy with Livingston's extreme position on banishing people from the national parks, but while listening to him I was reminded of one of my favourite quotes by Wallace Stegner: "We simply need that wild country available to us, even if we never do more than drive to its edge and look in. For it can be a means of reassuring ourselves of our sanity as creatures, a part of the geography of hope."[30] Maybe at some point it will become necessary to prohibit human use of the parks in order to protect what wildness remains, but I do not believe we are at that point yet in most of Canada. The key seemed to me to be in Livingston's last comment, about learning to recover the wildness within ourselves, and I said so to him.

"You are more positive than I am," he replied. "I don't know that the crisis can be turned around quickly enough. You can't take kids, line them up and say 'experience nature!' Nor can you work with adults, they're too full of crap. But more importantly, what's to be learned can't be taught. It can only be experienced."

One of the most crucial obstacles to overcome in this recovery of wildness is the old dichotomy of "self" versus "other," wherein the former has come to mean "individual self" rather than an inclusive sense of self, which Livingston called "whole self" or "wild wholeness." Notwithstanding his pessimism, he still believes that, despite the layers of domestication that enshroud our consciousness, we all retain "the capacity for wildness" and experience an urge to reconnect with it. Within the urban environment, however, where almost everything we encounter is an artifact, it takes an extraordinary effort to keep from becoming numb and deadened to the call of the wild.

Part of the challenge, we agreed, was to make time for solitude in nature. In solitude, remarkable things can happen. First, the mind becomes still as the winds of thought die down; thinking gives way to being. Second, in this state we encounter the world in a very immediate, sensual way. There is no need to name or explain things, only to be totally in the moment and to accept things as they are. Third, awe and wonder become the only appropriate responses. In the direct, uninterpreted encounter with the wild other, we experience something that is ultimately inexpressible, but for which the words "sacred" or "divine" act as passable stand-ins. If all this sounds religious, it could be because it is, in the truest sense of the word. After all, the word "religion" means "to bind back to the source." Hence, to return to the solitude of nature is to seek the source of our being.

After a couple of hours of stimulating discussion, Dianne and I had to leave in order to return to the Mosquins' in time for supper. As we were putting on our coats, Livingston returned from a back room with an autographed copy of *Rogue Primate*, which he gave to me while wishing me good luck with my own book. Driving back towards Carp, I continued to ponder the idea of the ancient bond linking us to wild places and species. "Wild places help us to connect with our own deep self," eco-philosopher and martial artist Alan Drengson has written. "To recover a sense of the sacred in embodied life requires us to know the wild source within Nature, and hence our own nature."[31] He suggests that wilderness areas, such as may be found within the national parks, should more rightly be viewed as holy places, and treated accordingly. "Wilderness and its preservation are necessary for the preservation and realization of whole humans as well as for its own inherent goodness," says Drengson. "We come home to our natural selves in communion with communities of other beings . . . We live in simple gratitude with deepening compassion and respect for others. We are in harmony with the universe."[32]

If you have ever lost yourself in the flame orange hues of a wood lily, in the nervous enthusiasm of a chickadee or in the sparkling clarity of a mountain lake, you will know what Drengson is trying to communicate. It is not something that can be easily explained; wholeness and its profound connection with nature and wildness has to be experienced before it can be understood.

The next morning I rose early and took Livingston's book down to a grassy bank of the river below the Mosquin home for some further contemplation. "The human achievement has been breathtaking in its suddenness, total in its scope," I read. "This could only be the work of a placeless-being—in an ecological sense, one utterly lacking in both intrinsic inhibitions and extrinsic controls."[33] To this Livingston added: "The loss of ecologic place applies to the total population of a particular kind of domesticated mammal. For the individual within that population there is the parallel loss of what I have called the sense of 'at-one-ship' with other members of a community, and with it the awareness of 'being-a-place.'"

Several months earlier I had had a discussion with Kevin Van Tighem, who is the park ecologist at Waterton Lakes. "I believe that national parks represent a different response to the homesickness that plagues, at least subconsciously, the rootless people of modern North America," he said. "National parks help us to become native not by re-creating North America in our own image, but by re-creating ourselves in its image. They do so by celebrating that which is native to this place, and providing opportunities for us to experience, learn about and come to identify with the nature of this place we call Canada." In his mind, national parks exist partly to make modern urban-industrial Canadians more native—more a part of nature. "To the degree to which they succeed, there is hope for the future of natural biodiversity, healthy landscapes, and we humans," he added firmly and passionately. "Our bottom line must always be the mission of the national parks themselves: to enable people to see, understand, care about and take into their deepest selves the nature of this place. If we succeed, the ecological integrity of not just these national parks but all of Canada will be much closer to being assured—because all Canadians will treasure all of Canada. Canadians will look at their newly native land and see not a hostile wilderness, or a place that needs to be remade to a British, Japanese or German model, but a familiar, deeply loved home. They will visit national parks to learn more about themselves . . . And in so doing, they will see that to degrade their parks, or to fail to sustain the living wealth that is Canada, would be to mutilate or degrade themselves." There is a patriotic aspect to his vision as well. "It should be impossible to visit a national park without coming away from that visit a little more Canadian than we were when we started."

Van Tighem is not alone in this perspective. Across the border, secretary of the interior Bruce Babbitt has said much the same. "Our national parks are important because they are a gateway to the conservation ethic," he argues. "In these, our most precious sites, we can engage our people in a discussion of natural conditions, and of our place in relation to them. The prospect for a heightened environmental ethic . . . depends, in large measure, on how we use our national parks."

So, when the dust settles, what are we left with? In the early part of this chapter I stated that parks are not profit producers but rather are sacred trusts. They are not to be treated as a commodity to be bought, sold and consumed; nor are they resources to be managed. They are, as Harkin knew full well, holy places. Their primary purpose is the protection of the inherent worth of Creation. And just as we recoil from the desecration of churches, mosques or synagogues, all of them sanctuaries for the spirit, so too must we learn to honour and protect the national parks. As Stan Rowe rightly maintains, it's about people serving parks rather than the other way around. This does not mean that we cannot visit and use the parks; however, we must keep in mind that use is purely secondary and should be carried out only with the utmost care and respect. As befits a holy place, the only use that is appropriate is that which reconnects us to the wildness that dwells within their boundaries and that lies waiting to be released at the core of our souls.

Re-creation—not recreation—is the goal: activities that foster reconnections with our true selves and with the land community. "When the self recognizes its source, the sanctity of Nature is restored," says Stan Rowe.[34]

# TWELVE

# Crisis of Spirit

My purpose in writing this book is to do what I can to save the wildness of Canada. Although wildness is sometimes defined in pejorative terms such as desolate, barbaric, unpredictable, uncontrolled or unregulated, I am convinced that it is precisely this quality that is, as Thoreau said many years ago, the preservation of the world. What do I mean by this? Simply that the frightening destruction of the planet's biological diversity is ultimately a crisis of the human spirit. Through the mists of time, likely beginning when we first emerged as a species on an African savannah, we have steadily lost contact with the wellspring of our fragile and ephemeral existence, the ground of our being.

This is particularly so in the Western world, which reached its ascendancy on brute power conferred by the holy trinity of science, technology and capitalism. Like the sorcerer's foolish apprentice, however, we have let loose forces that we now seem incapable of controlling. Not only are entire species and ecosystems crushed beneath our mad rush of progress, but so too are those of our own kind who can neither keep up nor get out of the way, such as the homeless and destitute who haunt the inner-city cores of North America, or the hunting and gathering tribes displaced by the destruction of the Amazonian rain forest in South

America. "We are, in ways that have been expertly rationalized, pressing forward to create a monocultural world-society in which whatever survives must do so as the adjunct of urban industrial civilization," says historian Theodore Roszak. "But we are being diminished by our destructive insensitivity in ways that cripple our ability to enjoy, grow, create. By becoming so aggressively and masterfully 'human,' we lose our humanity."[1] If this trend is to be reversed, we must find our way back to that sense of at-oneness with the essential Self, which identifies with others, including non-human life forms and the planet; and then we must act accordingly.

A few years ago, Dianne and I were sitting on a beach on the north shore of Clear Lake in Riding Mountain National Park. It was about midday and we had just finished a picnic lunch. Feeling pleasantly full and a little drowsy, I decided to lie back for a snooze. As I was reclining, I suddenly became aware that we were being watched. Not much more than twenty metres away, a pair of green eyes blinked and gazed intently over a fallen log that lay across the trail. From the tufts of hair on the tips of the ears, the whiskers and tawny fur, I quickly recognized it as a lynx, one of the most reclusive and secretive animals of the boreal forest. With a gentle nudge and a whisper, I alerted Dianne to its presence and then let myself melt into its fiery green gaze.

When confronted with any phenomenon, we have two choices: we can either explain it or accept it. If we do the former, we immediately run the risk of taking the phenomenon for granted, as just "another instance of the same old thing."[2] The rush of excitement eventually fades and is replaced with apathy or boredom. If, on the other hand, we simply observe it and accept it "in its full individuality," without naming or judging—as I was doing with the lynx—then something quite magical can happen. Neil Evernden has described this experience with extreme insight and eloquence, calling it a "sheer absolute wonderousness that transcends thought," a "most immediate, most incommunicable experience of the 'sacred,'" and an "acknowledgment of mystery."[3]

It is to encounter the "wild other," which is "self-willed, independent, and indifferent to our dictates and judgments."[4] At the same
time, he says, wildness "lies beyond the objects in question, a
quality which directly confronts and confounds our designs. At
root, it is *wildness* that is at issue: not wilderness, not polar bears,
not whooping cranes or Bengal tigers, but that which they as individuals exemplify."[5] Ultimately, he maintains, wildness is nameless. And it is rapidly being overwhelmed by a human tidal wave.

Eventually, the lynx grew weary of watching us and stood up
from its crouched position, stretched and sauntered off into a
nearby hazel thicket. As it disappeared, I felt a pang of sadness for
the loss of all that it represented. The planet today is being bled of
its wildness. The best estimates place the current rate of extinctions
at between 50 and 250 species a day.[6] Only five other times in the
earth's history has there been such an unprecedented loss of
species. We are in a period of mass extinction. Unlike the previous
periods of mass biological impoverishment, however, the current
one is driven almost entirely by one species: humans. Our global
population has reached nearly 6 billion and continues to grow at
approximately 1.8 percent a year. To put this in perspective, the
world's population has doubled in my lifetime of nearly fifty years
and is projected to double again before I die.

The region in which I live, which geographers refer to as the
Georgia Basin, encompassing Victoria, Vancouver and Seattle, is the
fifth fastest-growing region in the world.[7] Although I don't see evidence of this growth in my quiet Victoria neighbourhood, it confronts
and shocks me each time I leave its confines, and especially when I
visit Vancouver. At present, the city is growing by slightly more than
22 percent annually.[8] Michael Harcourt, a former premier of British
Columbia and now a senior associate of the Sustainable Development
Research Institute at the University of British Columbia bluntly points
out that in the next millennium, and for the first time in human history, more people will live in cities than in the countryside.

Meanwhile, a ravenous consumption of raw materials is also
inflicting a staggering toll on the planet. This is especially true in

the more developed countries, which "account for only about 20 percent of global population, yet they consume 86 percent of the world's aluminum, 81 percent of its paper, 80 percent of its iron and steel, and 76 percent of its timber."[9] Mining now tops all the world's rivers combined in the transport of soil and rock, and the world's consumption of paper has increased fivefold since 1950.[10] Not surprisingly, the rate of industrial logging has doubled during this same time period. As a result a little more than half of the planet's original forest cover remains, mostly in small, scattered fragments.[11] All this serves to keep the global economy ticking along, funnelling ever more profits back into the vaults of the large transnational corporations, predominately located in the United States, Europe, Canada and Japan.

The upshot is simple to understand: increasing populations and resource consumption result in habitat destruction, habitat fragmentation, overkill and the spread of invasive species. These impacts are occurring on all scales, from the global to the local. Here on the West Coast, the federal Department of Fisheries and Oceans has invoked drastic measures, including closures, in an attempt to bring the coho salmon back from the edge of extinction; and biologists bite their lips praying that a captive breeding program will save the world's most endangered mammal, the Vancouver Island marmot. The first is largely a victim of habitat destruction along its natal rivers and streams, and overkill by deadly efficient fishing boats. The marmot has suffered from habitat destruction and fragmentation, primarily due to industrial forestry. Meanwhile, broom, gorse and daphnia—three highly invasive plants—have spread throughout the parks and green spaces around Victoria.

Over the past 3.5 billion years, evolution has unfolded naturally, but that is rapidly changing. As never before, the fate of virtually every species on the planet rests upon the choices we make. World-renowned biologist Norman Meyers puts the matter this way: "No generation in the past has faced the prospect of mass extinction within its lifetime, the problem has never existed before.

No generation in the future will ever face a similar challenge: if this present generation fails to get to grips with the task, the damage will have been done and there will be no 'second try.'"[12] Because we are capable of prediction and of control over our actions, we are not like an ice age, a meteor or any other natural catastrophe. We can make different choices; we have an evolutionary responsibility.

There are many reasons for assuming this responsibility. The prominent biologist E.O. Wilson argued in 1984 that our actions must be grounded in self-interest. People, he says, will "conserve land and species fiercely if they foresee a material gain for themselves, their kin, and their tribe."[13] A couple of years later, the World Commission on the Environment and Development echoed his perspective. As the commissioners wrote in their final report:

> The diversity of species is necessary for the normal functioning of ecosystems and the biosphere as a whole. The genetic material in wild species contributes billions of dollars yearly to the world economy in the form of improved crop species, new drugs and medicines, and raw materials for industry. But utility aside, there are also moral, ethical, cultural, aesthetic, and purely scientific reasons for conserving wild beings.[14]

The commissioners urged governments to embark immediately upon aggressive programs of park expansion, suggesting that at least 12 percent of the world should be set aside in order to stem the loss of species.

Stan Rowe soundly rejects utilitarian arguments as they ultimately reinforce the very values that cause species extinction and habitat destruction. Instead, he takes a very commonsensical approach. "The reasons for safeguarding wilderness are intensely ecologic," he says, "embedded in bone, body and brain, because we are earth creatures . . . The Noah Principle states it another way: Everything that exists has a right to exist, and ought to be helped to survive the human deluge."[15] Further, he declares: "We are nature made conscious, participating in an ongoing creative process. We are, or ought to be, the conscience of the world."[16]

The creation of parks and protected areas is the principal means of fulfilling our responsibility to protect ecosystems and species. At present there are nearly ten thousand scattered around the globe, comprising almost 6.5 percent of the land area.[17] Is this enough to stave off a mass extinction? Hardly. As managers and biologists know all too well, protected areas are still too few, too isolated and too internally fragmented to withstand human-driven change within, around and well beyond their boundaries. A survey of 135 national parks in 61 countries resulted in the documentation of over 1,600 kinds of threats, with 65 to 75 percent of these being human-caused.[18] Not surprisingly, parks and protected areas worldwide are losing species and ecosystems they were intended to protect.

Closer to home, William Newmark, a biologist from California, has studied the collapse of species within the national parks of western North America since their establishment. These parks include Yosemite, Yellowstone, Grand Teton, Rocky Mountain, Glacier, Waterton, Kootenay, Banff, Jasper and Yoho. According to his most recent calculations, twenty-nine populations of mammals have become extinct, while only seven have colonized the parks.[19] A major contributing factor is the increasing insularization of the parks by adjacent land uses such as logging, mining, agriculture or urbanization. This process is especially deadly for carnivores such as wolves, grizzlies or cougar, which utilize large territories extending well beyond the safety of park boundaries.

The State of the Parks 1997 report on Canada's national parks presents an equally grim portrait of the wild and the prospects for it. It lists twenty-nine different stresses, including park infrastructure, heavy-metal pollution, acidic precipitation, exotic species, urbanization, tourism facilities, mining, agriculture and forestry, that are contributing to the demise of numerous species. Point Pelee has lost twenty-three; Fundy reports the disappearance of twelve and Prince Edward Island has nine fewer.[20] At least ten species no longer occur in the Bow Valley of Banff or are of such low numbers that they are considered to be among the "walking dead," doomed to disappear. Meanwhile, national park ecosystems are being invaded by exotic animals and plants. A tiny fragment of the nearly extinct Carolinian forest, located within Point Pelee, has been overrun by more than 230 alien plant species. St. Lawrence Islands and Bruce Peninsula have each received nearly 200 plant invaders, and twelve other parks have documented cases of anywhere between 100 and 160 exotic plants. When their influence is added together, they do not bode well for the future of wildness within Canada's national parks. Indeed, the prognosis is one of increasing domestication of the parks unless these stresses can be alleviated—and very quickly.

So who's responsible for this shameful crisis? The short answer is: everybody. From the beginning, politicians, the elected representatives of the Canadian public, have promoted and exploited the national parks as profitable playgrounds. It is only very recently that the minister responsible for them has categorically stated that there are limits to growth and that protection must be made the top priority. Yet, despite this decree from on high, development crawls on, increment by increment—a process I described in Chapter 1 as death by a thousand cuts. While the Hon. Sheila Copps says slow down and stop, many of her colleagues in Ottawa, particularly those responsible for industry and tourism, are saying hurry up, promoting ever more visitation and adjacent land development. Furthermore, for there to be any real improvement, the government would have to stop running the country as if it were a business. There is no doubt that recent budget cuts have greatly reduced Parks Canada's managerial effectiveness, especially in the areas of enforcement, research and education.

Parks Canada too must be held accountable. It may be possible to forgive the organization for the honest mistakes made in the past, based on a lack of scientific understanding, such as the eradication program aimed at carnivores and other undesirable species or the construction of numerous roads and facilities in environmentally sensitive areas. But this time has long since passed. While not perfect, our collective understanding of ecosystems and species has revealed a complexity that surpasses anything we could have previously imagined. In the wake of this realization, scientists now strongly counsel a precautionary approach, which encourages decision making to err on the side of environmental protection even when data and facts are uncertain. They also firmly believe that parks and protected areas can only fulfil their role as refuges for the wild and native biological diversity when managed as a part of a greater ecosystem, as part of a greater whole.

In many respects, Parks Canada is a world leader in this new approach, often called ecosystem management. Over the past three decades it has developed internationally recognized expertise in the application of state-of-the-art ecosystem science and conservation biology principles and practices. Current research efforts are directed towards the identification of indicators for ecological integrity, such as the presence of large carnivores or levels of human disturbance. Once identified, these indicators can be monitored to establish long-term trends and to provide the basis for corrective action if necessary. As a result of this and related work, Parks Canada staff are frequently called upon to advise other park systems around the world.

However, ecosystem management is more than just a way of managing parks; fundamentally, it is about managing people— even those within Parks Canada itself. As a 1996 document setting forth standards for ecosystem management makes very clear, "Ecosystem-based management is the way legislation and policy direct *everyone* in Parks Canada to do business."[21] Regrettably, there is a disturbing lack of agreement within the organization as to what its business is. The document says that the National Parks Act directs Parks Canada to adopt an ecocentric philosophy, which "considers the human use of resources to be secondary in importance to the primary goal of maintaining ecological integrity."[22] But it is painfully obvious that not everyone within the organization agrees with this direction. How else can we explain such contradictory behaviour as the damage Parks Canada inflicted on P.E.I.'s Greenwich Dunes, the upgrade of Cape Breton's golf course or the expansion of the Château Lake Louise in Banff? These, and many other examples, make it readily apparent that too many Parks Canada personnel hold an anthropocentric philosophy, which puts human use of parks ahead of maintaining ecological integrity.

Little wonder that intense frustration and anger seethes below the cool professional facade that the organization projects. As recently as a few weeks ago I heard many fed-up employees accuse their organization of not walking the talk. They dare not say anything, however, out of fear of retaliation by those in positions of power. Despite rhetoric to the contrary, the organizational culture discourages healthy debate on controversial issues, rather than encouraging commitment to the mandate of maintaining ecological integrity. Those who are committed to this goal are often marginalized.

The values and principles at issue strike at the very core of Park Canada's identity. What is it? Provider of recreation and tourism opportunities? Profiteer from natural amenities and park products? Protector of wild species and native ecosystems? As I am continually reminded, the answer very much depends on who you ask. There is no shared vision. In its place is not a vacuum but a crisis of the spirit. There is a disagreement over core values throughout all layers of the organization, from headquarters down to the field. Disciplining or even firing a few key people, while probably necessary, is not enough. What the organization desperately needs is some kind of cultural transformation that brings about an alignment with its legally required mandate of maintaining ecological integrity. This is something that must become second nature to everyone within the organization.

As urgent as it is to address the serious problems within Parks Canada, it must be recognized that the responsibility for maintaining the wildness of the national parks is too great for Parks Canada to bear alone, even if it had a clear vision and was backed by supportive politicians. The current reality is that the Canadian public has to engage in some serious soul-searching as well. As long as we remain ambivalent about our relationship with the wild northern frontier that is the original nature of Canada, we will continue to either destroy or degrade it. Until we have made the switch from an anthropocentric perspective, which ultimately says that people come first everywhere and in all cases, to an eco-centric one, which rightly holds that we are but one species among millions and that we are all interdependent on each other and on the life-sustaining ecosphere, we will lack the necessary humility to stop our insane drive to domesticate and control the planet. I shudder when I think about what kind of world that would be.

While there may be resistance to recognizing the inherent worth of wildness and biological diversity, it is not "hard-wired" into our brains or genes; instead, I am compelled to believe that it is a learned response, and so the possibility exists for a switch in world views. What's called for is a special kind of education. In the words of E.F. Schumacher, a compassionate and wise economist, the primary task of education must be "the transmission of ideas of value," for "more education can help us only if it produces more wisdom."[23] He was utterly convinced that education had to unearth and challenge the inherited, largely unexamined "life-destroying ideas" that underpin modern society. Regrettably, this is not the kind of education most people experience.

Clearly, there is some unlearning and relearning that Canadians must undergo. What is to be unlearned and relearned? Almost fifty years ago, Aldo Leopold had this to say on the question: "Education, I fear, is learning to see one thing by going blind to another."[24] As I have argued, we have come to perceive the national parks as profit producers, playgrounds or preserves. Each of these old metaphors must be relinquished in favour of alternative ones that more accurately address the current ecological crisis. The national parks, I have contended, are a sacred trust, holy places, sanctuaries for the wild that is emblematic of Creation and that is at the root of our soul. I have also said that there are serious problems that arise from perceiving the national parks as fortresses surrounded by invisible moats and walls, and well guarded by Parks Canada. The national parks are not fortresses. Rather, they are living systems, like cells defined by a permeable membrane that permits two-way exchanges with its surrounding environment. Since parks of sufficient size to support viable populations of many species are few and far between, the wild can only survive within them as long as it is also allowed to exist outside the parks and to travel between them. In other words, national parks—and all other protected areas for that matter—must be embedded within a buffered landscape and be well connected by wildlife corridors.

Nor are parks playgrounds in the usual sense of the word. While Canada's national parks were conceived as tourism resorts, the idea was already being questioned in the early twentieth century. Although he frequently used the word "playground" to describe the national parks, J.B. Harkin, the first commissioner, had very particular ideas about what he meant by it. He saw what would happen if the demands for "cheaper forms of amusement [and] commercial exploitation" were satisfied: the parks would "lose the very thing that distinguished them from the outside world."[25] Re-creation of the human body, mind and spirit is what he had in mind, not a frivolous recreation that only perpetuated the exploitation and desecration of nature.

Contrary to appearances, the national parks are not in good health. There is a tendency to view their problems like acne—small, localized blemishes that can be easily treated—when in fact they are more like cancer, insidiously and quietly spreading throughout the entire system. We must learn to see the populous elk around Banff townsite as a sign not of a healthy ecosystem but of a dysfunctional one, just as we need to learn to see what is not there, such as wolves, grizzlies, moose and beaver in the lower Bow Valley. With a little practice it doesn't take too long before the eye can pick out the imbalances in species composition or ecosystem processes, whether they be alien plants or acidified lakes.

Finally, we need to unlearn our naive trust in Parks Canada. I'm willing to bet that if we were to compare the values of Parks Canada employees with those of the Canadian public, we would find that the former are decidedly greener than the latter. However, this does not in any way mean that they couldn't make substantial improvements. There are many extremely dedicated people within the organization, but they are overpowered by others who compromise on protection of ecological integrity in favour of immediate, short-term human interests. Consequently, our naive trust must give way to concerned attentiveness and a readiness to either criticize or celebrate, as the need be.

What's called for here is a new, deeper kind of environmental education. As commonly defined, environmental education strives to produce "a citizenry that is knowledgeable concerning the biophysical environment and its associated problems, aware of how to help solve these problems, and motivated toward their solution."[26] After almost forty years of conventional environmental education, the best we've accomplished is an environmentally concerned citizenry which is still very hazy on basic ecological knowledge. An even greater problem is attitudinal. As I have stressed earlier in this book, we hold values and beliefs that are not ecologically sound. Thus, while we may line up to support recycling programs, our overall consumption and waste continues to increase. To be more effective, environmental education must show the connections between individual decisions and ecological impacts, and do this in a way that encourages a shift in basic attitudes, values and beliefs. Equally importantly, it must be made relevant and engaging to the adults who are the decision makers of today. It is neither fair nor sound to pass off environmental responsibility to the next generation.

Even if environmental education was to achieve these things, it still wouldn't be enough. Somehow, it must help us address the root cause of the current global crisis, which is fundamentally a crisis of the spirit. Environmental education, if it is to have any real and lasting effect, must help us come to know who we truly are and what we are to do with our lives. "Know thyself"—this two-thousand-year-old Delphic motto is just as relevant today as when it was first coined. Eco-philosopher and plant ecologist Stan Rowe puts the matter this way: "Who people believe they are in relation to the rest of creation and what they believe to be important in their lives will channel their actions constructively or destructively within this one and only planetary Home."[27] With this, he challenges: "Who in the World do you think you are? What on Earth are you doing?"[28] Only in coming to know on a deeply felt level that our true identity lies beyond the ego can we cultivate the necessary wisdom to live in harmony with the rest of Creation. No one can be forced to undertake this spiritual work; the desire must come from within. Environmental education's role, then, becomes one of stimulating and facilitating a process of self-discovery and consciousness raising.

So what's the motivation? Why would people want to engage in this kind of process? In Chapter 9, I wrestled with the idea that love is the motivator. I still think this is true. However, I wish to add a few more thoughts to this notion. Like many other writers, I have been captivated by the ideas of Paul Shepard presented in his thought-provoking book *Nature and Madness*. Toward the end of it, he asks rhetorically what the prospects are for the future of the world given the psychopathology currently gripping the human race. His answer is as hopeful as it is surprising. "An ecological harmonious sense of self and world is not the outcome of rational choices," he argues. "It is the inherent possession of everyone; it is latent in the organism . . ."[29] In other words, there is in all of us a "genuine impulse" that seeks "authentic expression." To the degree that we allow the impulse to direct our lives will we achieve a harmonious relationship with the planet.

What is this "genuine impulse?" It is wildness. And wildness is the essence of life.

Somehow it doesn't seem right to end this book without saying something about personal responsibility and choice. The wild will only be kept alive in and around our national parks if we do all that we can to reduce or eliminate our impacts on it, and encourage others to do likewise. The struggle to save the wild that is the very essence of the national parks may seem overwhelming, but if we give up, we only hasten its demise. We must not let this happen; too much is at stake. Change is possible and absolutely crucial, and we must start now. Those of us who sense or know the importance of the wild, not just to the national parks but also to the human spirit, have a special responsibility to make changes in our own lives and then encourage and support others to do the same.

I do not use the word "responsibility" lightly. If you break the word down, it literally means "the ability to respond." We all have the ability to make the necessary changes in our lives that will respect the inherent worth of the wild. This ability grows through a simple three-step process, beginning with awareness of the urgent need for change, then learning about the threats to the wild, and lastly, carefully examining all of our decisions and choices in light of what we have learned. I hope my book will serve to stimulate this process of awakening and change.

Throughout the book I have emphasized the very serious nature of the crisis facing the wild in our national parks, and I have laced it with ideas, big and small, of what individuals, groups or organizations can do to address this crisis. Let me briefly recap some of these ideas and add a few more.

## Parks Canada

The organization must:

- embark on a complete cultural transformation, with leadership, a renewed sense of direction and purpose among employees, and a reframed corporate plan, that align with the mandate of maintaining ecological integrity
- reinvigorate interpretation and public outreach by ensuring that they are adequately funded and staffed, and that they incorporate state-of-the-art techniques in social marketing and adult education
- ensure that park management decision making is driven by ecosystem and social science
- bolster ecosystem science funding and staffing to levels adequate to meet management needs within and adjacent to the national parks
- embark upon a process of limiting use, particularly in the most popular parks, that includes decommissioning of facilities and restoration of damaged ecosystems
- direct field staff to become active participants in adjacent-land-use management, and support them when park values conflict with these outside uses

## Federal Government

The federal government must:

- direct Parks Canada to embark upon cultural transformation to bring it more into alignment with the mandate of maintaining ecological integrity
- ensure that Parks Canada is provided with sufficient funding to carry out its core responsibilities: the establishment and pro-

tection of the national parks and the delivery of public education programs
- demonstrate leadership in the protection of wildlife within and between national parks by encouraging provincial and local government co-operation in the development of policies designed to reduce the ecological impacts of current human activities
- provide financial incentive for private land stewardship, such as covenants

## Provincial and Local Governments

Provincial and local governments should:
- develop and implement land-use plans that support the establishment of wildlife corridors and zones of co-operation around and between the national parks
- resist the temptation to encourage subdivision of land into smaller and smaller lots, which fragments critical wildlife habitat
- offer incentives to landowners who wish to keep sections of their land as wildlife habitat
- designate lands adjacent to national parks and other protected areas as special management zones, in which land use activities will be managed to reduce impacts on wildlife and wilderness
- work with each other and with landowners towards the establishment of wildlife corridors between parks and protected areas

## Resource Industries

Farming, mining, logging and all other exploitive industries, and their associated processing/manufacturing industries, must:
- adopt standards of doing business that go beyond mere compliance with federal or provincial environmental protection laws
- avoid large-scale disruptions or destruction of habitat and movement corridors
- restore wildlife habitat wherever possible
- keep roads and utility corridors to a minimum, and close them as soon as possible to limit habitat fragmentation

- reduce and eliminate production and/or use of toxic chemicals
- reduce and eliminate the consumption of natural capital, especially non-renewable resources

## Local Communities
Local communities should:
- strive to embody the highest levels of environmental stewardship in all their activities
- take an active interest in the welfare of their neighbouring national parks, offering assistance and support wherever possible
- protect significant and sensitive habitat from development
- pass by-laws that promote land stewardship

## Urban Dwellers
City dwellers, whether in Vancouver, Toronto, Montreal or Halifax, have a profound impact on the broader landscape and on the national parks by virtue of their consumption of resources. Therefore, they must:
- become more aware and knowledgeable about the ecological consequences of their choices
- seek to minimize their environmental footprint by reducing consumption in addition to reusing and recycling materials and products

## Park Visitors
Park visitors can contribute substantially to keeping the wild alive. They must:
- reduce the ecological footprint of their activities, moving from mechanized, consumptive forms of recreation to self-propelled, conserver forms
- support the establishment of limits on numbers and kinds of use, as well as the decommissioning of facilities in the most popular parks
- become informed and caring users of a park by learning about the threats to it and then acting accordingly

## Individuals

The National Parks and Conservation Association (NPCA), the only non-profit organization in the United States dedicated to protecting, promoting and enhancing public understanding of the national parks system, published a book called *Our Endangered Parks* (San Francisco: Foghorn Press, 1994, ISBN 0-935701-84-2), which is packed with solid ideas on how individuals can help protect the parks. It is definitely worth picking up. Here are some of the ways they suggest an individual can help.

### *With a few hours a month*

- Read and research. Park-related issues and stories are covered by most national and local newspapers, magazines, and television and radio stations. More information can be obtained from public and university/college libraries, environmental groups and Parks Canada. Individual action needs to be informed action, so become knowledgeable on the issues.
- Get on your park's mailing list. This is another great way to become informed about the specific issues facing a park.
- Join a local or national park advocacy organization. Park advocacy groups rely on active membership bases to support programs, produce educational materials, and increase the visibility of park issues among the media, elected officials, Parks Canada and the general public. Most groups provide their members with newsletters. A partial list of park advocacy groups is presented in Appendix A.
- Write a letter or make a phone call to an elected official. Raise the level of awareness of your elected officials about park issues by writing, phoning, faxing or e-mailing them for their position. This will let them know that their constituents care about the problems facing national parks and are interested in how government works to solve these problems. An informed and alert constituency creates a heightened political response to park problems.

- Write a letter to the editor of a local or national newspaper or magazine. The news media can be a crucial help in raising the visibility of park issues and in stirring the support of local and national communities.

### With one day a month
- Attend the meeting of your local park group. These meetings provide an opportunity to meet other park advocates and to become well informed on park issues.
- Visit your park. Become familiar with it, and pay attention to details so that you are able to detect when the park is being improved, neglected or altered in any way. When you do notice a problem, be sure to alert park management. Also alert the local or national park advocacy group.

### With a few days a month or more
- Volunteer. Become a volunteer with Parks Canada, park advocacy groups, historical societies or co-operating associations.
- Participate in park planning. Parks Canada policies require public involvement. The general management plan is the comprehensive plan for your park and should guide day-to-day decisions made by park staff. Ask when the plan is scheduled to be revised, and become familiar with the existing document so that you can have a point of reference for any activity occurring in the park.
- Build a network of people in your community who are interested in protecting parks. If there is a park advocacy group in your area, become an active member and help recruit other interested park supporters. Seek to develop a well-rounded coalition that represents all aspects of the community. Include neighbourhood leaders, local politicians, the chamber of commerce, members of local environmental groups and other park users. Reach out to people who might not think of themselves as park supporters or environmentalists.

**Parks Canada**
25 Eddy Street
Hull, Quebec K1A 0M5
Web site: www.parkscanada.pch.gc.ca

**Canadian Parks and Wilderness Society**
880 Wellington Street, Suite 506
Ottawa, Ontario K1R 6K7
Tel.: (613) 569-7266
Toll free: 1-800-333-WILD (9453)
Fax: (613) 569-7098
Web site: www.cpaws.org
E-mail: info@cpaws.org

**World Wildlife Fund Canada**
245 Eglinton Ave. East, Suite 410
Toronto, Ontario M4P 3J1
Tel.: (416) 489-8800
Toll free: 1-800-26-PANDA (267-2632)
Fax: (416) 489-3611
Web site: www.wwfcanada.org

**Canadian Nature Federation**
1 Nicholas Street, Suite 606
Ottawa, Ontario K1N 7B7
Tel.: (613) 562-3447
Toll free: 1-800-267-4088
Fax: (613) 562-3371
Web site: www.cnf.ca
E-mail: cnf@cnf.ca

**Nature Conservancy of Canada**
110 Eglinton Avenue West, Suite 400
Toronto, Ontario M4R 1A3
Tel.: (416) 932-3202
Toll free: 1-800-465-0029
Fax: (416) 932-3208
Web site: www.natureconservancy.ca
E-mail: nature@natureconservancy.ca

**Sierra Club of Canada**
412–1 Nicholas Street
Ottawa, Ontario K1N 7B7
Tel.: (613) 241-4611
Fax: (613) 241-2292
Web site: www.sierraclub.ca
E-mail: sierra@web.net

**Western Canada Wilderness Committee**
227 Abbott Street
Vancouver, BC V6B 2K7
Tel.: (604) 683-8220
Toll free: 1-800-661-WILD (9453)
Fax: (604) 683-8229
Web site: www.wildernesscommittee.org
E-mail: info@wildernesscommittee.org

## Preface

1. Michael Valpy, "The parks in the market," *The Globe and Mail*, March 14, 1996.

## Chapter 1

1. Parks Canada, *State of the Parks 1994* (Ottawa: Minister of Supply and Services, 1995), 34.
2. Robert Ornstein and Paul Ehrlich, *New World, New Mind: Moving Towards Conscious Evolution* (New York: Doubleday, 1989), 3.
3. Ibid. 10.
4. Bill McKibbon, *The End of Nature* (New York: Random House, 1989), 8.
5. Government of Canada, *National Parks Act* (Ottawa: Minister of Supply and Services, 1990), 3.
6. Ibid.
7. Canadian Heritage, Parks Canada, *Guiding Principles and Operational Policies* (Ottawa: Minister of Supply and Services, 1994), 16.
8. Aldo Leopold, *A Sand County Almanac* (San Francisco and New York: Sierra Club/Ballantine, 1970), 262.
9. Reed Noss, *Maintaining Ecological Integrity in Representative Reserve Networks*, a discussion paper for the World Wildlife Fund Canada and World Wildlife Fund United States (Toronto and Washington, 1995), 20.
10. Ibid., 21.
11. Ibid., 22.

12. Daniel B. Botkin, *Discordant Harmonies: A New Ecology for the Twenty-First Century* (New York and Oxford: Oxford University Press, 1990), 9.

13. For excellent discussions of this idea see Paul Shepard's *Nature and Madness* (San Francisco: Sierra Club Books, 1982), and Theodore Roszak's *The Voice of the Earth* (New York: Simon & Schuster, 1992).

14. Noss, *Maintaining Ecological Integrity*, 27.

15. Neil Evernden, *The Social Creation of Nature*, (Baltimore and London: The Johns Hopkins University Press, 1992), 120.

16. Ibid., 121.

17. John A. Livingston, *Rogue Primate: An Exploration of Human Domestication* (Toronto: Key Porter Books, 1994), 5.

18. J.B. Harkin, "Reflections of a Park Administrator," *Park News* 23, no. 5 (1988): 11.

19. Parks Canada, *Guiding Principles and Operational Policies* (Ottawa: Minister of Supply and Services, 1994), 16.

20. Canadian Heritage, "Mitchell creates Panel on Ecological Integrity in Canada's National Parks," press release, November 10, 1998.

21. Harkin, "Reflections," 11.

22. Stan Rowe, *Home Place: Essays on Ecology* (Edmonton: NeWest, 1990), 49.

23. Ibid., 52.

24. Ibid., 40.

25. Ibid., 32.

## Chapter 2

1. David Bernard, Charlie Pacas and Nancy Marshall (compilers), "State of the Banff–Bow Valley Report," prepared for the Banff–Bow Valley Study, August 26, 1995.

2. If you add in all those who are simply passing through on the Trans-Canada, the annual visitation rises to approximately 8.5 million.

3. Banff–Bow Valley Study, "Banff–Bow Valley: At the Crossroads," Summary Report of the Banff–Bow Valley Task Force (Ottawa: Minister of Supply and Services Canada, 1996).

4. Banff Community Plan, "Development and Land Use Issues Background Report," Technical Appendix, August 1996.

5. Banff Community Plan, "Development and Land Use Issues Background Report," Final Report, August 1996.

6. Bernard et. al., "State of the Banff–Bow Valley Report," 6–14.

7. This is known as the "need-to-reside" policy, and it includes people who lease lands within the park, and their descendants.

8. Banff–Bow Valley Study.

9. Leslie Bella, *Parks for Profit* (Montreal: Harvest House, 1987), 14.

10. Banff–Bow Valley Study, 46.

11. Banff Community Plan, Sept. 1998, 20.

12. Carey Elverum, "Elk-Human Conflicts in Banff National Park," *Research Links*.

13. Bernard et al., "State of the Banff–Bow Valley Report."

14. Parks Canada, *Ecosystem Conservation Plan (Draft): Riding Mountain National Park*, Revised and Updated Version, Dec. 2, 1996.

15. Parks Canada, *Clyburn Watershed Management Plan: Terms of Reference*, July 1997.

16. Ibid., 35.

17. "Copps moves to save Banff from extinction," *The Globe and Mail*, Oct. 8, 1996. As the Banff–Bow Valley Task Force put the matter: "Park managers, caught between the aspirations of environmental organizations and of the business community, allowed both groups to proceed with their plans and expectations. Parks Canada backed away from addressing the contradictions between the two positions and let each feud with the other in public. When the tensions threatened to get out of hand, the Minister appointed the Banff–Bow Valley Study." (Banff–Bow Valley Study, 17.)

18. Banff–Bow Valley Study, 14.

19. Ibid., 19.

20. Ibid., 19.

21. Ibid., 64.

22. Ibid., 32.

23. Ibid.

24. Sheila Copps, PC, MP, "Speaking Notes: Release of the Banff–Bow Valley Task Force Report," October 7, 1996.

25. Kevin McNamee, "Heritage Minister takes action to save Banff National Park," *Nature Alert* 7, no. 1 (Winter 1997): 1–2.

26. "Banff growth reined in," *Calgary Herald*.

27. Ibid.

28. Auditor General of Canada, "Canadian Heritage—Parks Canada: Preserving Canada's Natural Heritage," (November 1996), 31-9–31-10.

29. "The battle over Banff: millions of tourists may be threatening a treasured national park," *The Edmonton Journal*, August 4, 1997.

30. Under this latter principle, new business applications and developments would only be considered if they could demonstrate that they were appropriate to the community and the park. The principle was to be achieved by only allowing projects that were within the limits

established by community plans, that were within established growth limits, and that embraced business practices that reduced or eliminated environmental impacts.

31. Parks Canada, "Copps and Mitchell Announce New Protection Measures for Canada's National Parks" press release, June 26, 1998.

32. Catherine Ford, "Wildlife vs. People: Ottawa makes the correct decision," *Calgary Herald*.

## Chapter 3

1. Parks Canada, *Ecosystem Conservation Plan (Draft): Riding Mountain National Park*, December 2, 1996, 17.

2. Ibid., 10.

3. Val Werier, "Hands Off Duck Mountains!" *Winnipeg Free Press*, December 14, 1995.

4. Ibid.

5. Ibid.

6. There is a saying among the First Nations of North America: "A pine needle dropped in the forest. The deer heard it; the eagle saw it; and the bear smelled it." The incredible keenness of the bear's nose has also been observed by Andy Russell, mountain man and gifted writer. He attests that a stone kicked off a high ridge by a person's boot carries enough scent for a bear to detect at the bottom.

7. Parks Canada, *Ecosystem Conservation Plan*.

8. University of New Brunswick Faculty of Forestry and Environmental Management, "State of the Greater Fundy Ecosystem," Greater Fundy Ecosystem Research Project, May 7, 1998, iv.

9. Ibid., iv.

10. Parks Canada, *State of the Parks 1997 Report* (Ottawa: Minister of Public Works and Government Services, 1998), 43.

11. Thomas R. Stanley, Jr., "Ecosystem Management and the Arrogance of Humanism," *Conservation Biology* 9, no. 2 (1995): 256.

12. Alanna Mitchell, "Canada's parks facing crisis," *The Globe and Mail*, Oct. 18, 1999.

13. Ibid.

14. Ibid.

## Chapter 4

1. Kejimkujik National Park consists of two portions: an inland and a seaside adjunct. The seaside portion was added to the park in 1988. Visitation to the small stretch of coastline has been slowly and steadily increasing, although Parks Canada has not made a strong effort to pro-

mote it in order to ensure better protection of the piping plover population found there. Just ten years ago, Kejimkujik's seaside adjunct boasted Nova Scotia's largest population of this endangered species; since then, the habitat destruction caused by storms and an increase in predation by crows, gulls and raccoons have begun to reduce the piping plover population. In addition to not strongly promoting the existence of the seaside adjunct, sensitive areas have been fenced and signed to minimize human disturbance, and nests have been protected from predators with wire enclosures. (From Canadian Heritage, Parks Canada, *Kejimkujik National Park Management Plan*, 1995.)

2. David Orr, *Earth in Mind: On Education, Environment and the Human Prospect* (Washington: Island Press, 1994), 1.

3. David Bernard, Charlie Pacas and Nancy Marshall, *State of the Banff–Bow Valley Report*, compiled for the Banff–Bow Valley Study, August 26, 1995, 3-3.

4. David A. Castillon, *Conservation of Natural Resources: A Resource Management Approach* (Dubuque, IA: Wm. C. Brown Publishers, 1992), 74.

5. David Welch, "Air Quality Issues, Monitoring and Management in Canadian National Parks," in *Linking Protected Areas with Working Landscapes Conserving Biodiversity*, eds. Neil W.P. Munro and J.H. Martin Willison. Proceedings of the Third International Conference on Science and Management of Protected Areas (Wolfville, Nova Scotia: Science and Management of Protected Areas Association, 1998), 367.

6. Stan Rowe, "National Parks and Climatic Change," Occasional Paper No. 4 (Ottawa: National Parks Branch, Canadian Parks Service, Environment Canada, 1989).

7. Ibid.

8. Environment Canada, "Getting Environmental Results on Climate Change," from Environment Canada's Web site, last updated July 1998.

9. Martin Mittelstaedt, "Climate Shift wrecks bird habitat," *Times-Colonist*, Nov. 29, 1998.

10. Stan Rowe, "National Parks and Climate Change."

11. "Global warming slowed," *Times-Colonist*, January 24, 1999.

12. Stan Rowe, "National Parks and Climate Change."

13. "Global warming slowed."

14. Environment Canada, "Getting Environmental Results on Climate Change."

15. Ibid.

16. Ibid.

17. Ibid.

18. David Anderson, PC, MP, speaking notes for speech delivered to Alliance for Responsible Environmental Alternatives' 1999 National Climate Change Conference, October 7, 1999.
19. Ibid.
20. Malcolm Curtis, "Anderson pledges tough action," *Times-Colonist,* October 25, 1999.
21. "The road too heavily traveled: crawling around Toronto," *The Globe and Mail,* editorial, October 27, 1999.
22. Sierra Club of Canada, "100 groups urge action on Climate Change," press release, October 27, 1999.

## Chapter 5

1. Peter Newman, *The Canadian Revolution 1985–1995* (Toronto: Viking, 1995), 281.
2. At the time, Parks Canada was a part of the Department of Environment.
3. Kevin McNamee, "Back Page," *Park News* 20, no. 4 (Winter 1984/85): 40.
4. The Canadian Wildlife Service, within Environment Canada, was not so fortunate: they lost their entire interpretive program. Their interpretive centres were turned over to non-profits to run, and where no new owner could be found, the centres were sold. The Prairie Wildlife Centre west of Swift Current was sold to a local golf course to serve as its clubhouse.
5. Tom McMillan, notes for remarks to the Annual General Meeting of the Canadian Parks and Wilderness Society, Toronto, September 26, 1986.
6. Ibid.
7. Parks Canada, "National Business Plan for Parks Canada," April 21, 1995.
8. D'Arcy Jenish, *Money to Burn: Trudeau, Mulroney, and the Bankruptcy of Canada* (Toronto: Stoddart, 1996), 56.
9. Ibid., 59.
10. Ibid., 74.
11. Ibid., 81.
12. Ibid., 87. According to Jenish, the list of departmental cuts included: "$1.6 billion from defense; $1.4 billion from transport; $900 million from human resources development; $900 million from industry; $600 million from natural resources; $550 million from international assistance; $450 million from agriculture; and $200 million from fisheries. Subsidies to business were slated to tumble to $1.5 billion from $3.8 billion over the same three years. Grain transportation subsidies

for Western farmers, which had emerged out of the Crow rate of 1897, were eliminated. Transfers to the provinces for health care, post-secondary education, and social assistance were set to fall by $4.5 billion by 1997-98."

13. Alvin Finkel, *Our Lives: Canada after 1945* (Toronto: James Lorimer & Company, 1997), 304.

14. D'Arcy Jenish, *Money to Burn*, 78.

15. Canadian Parks Service, "A Study of Canadian Attitudes Toward Canada's National Parks," prepared by Angus Reid Group, Inc., 1993, ii.

16. Parks Canada. "National Business Plan 1995/1996–1999/2000," Canadian Heritage, April 21, 1995, 14.

17. Canadian Heritage, "Parks Canada into the Future: Highlights," n.d.

18. Parks Canada, "National Business Plan 1995/1996–1999/2000," 1.

19. Such was not to be the case, as the development of the Greenwich Dunes and other environmentally sensitive sites throughout the national parks continue to show.

20. Canadian Heritage, "Parks Canada into the Future: Highlights."

21. Michael Valpy, "The parks in the market," *The Globe and Mail*, March 14, 1996.

22. Pat Carney, "How priceless our parks?" *The Vancouver Sun*, October 4, 1996.

23. Canadian Heritage, "Parks Canada into the Future: Highlights."

24. Anne McIlroy, "North celebrates new park as privatization sweeps South," *The Globe and Mail*, June 27, 1996.

25. Anne McIlroy, "Staff vows to fight national park plan," *The Globe and Mail*, April 10, 1996.

26. Auditor General of Canada, "Canadian Heritage-Parks Canada: Preserving Canada's Natural Heritage," Minister of Public Works and Government Services, November 1996, 31-14.

27. Ibid.

28. Nephan Consulting, "Review of Parks Canada Public Education Programming," Draft, November 1997, 5.

## Chapter 6

1. Parks Canada, "Prince Edward Island National Park to be Expanded," Press Release, February 7, 1998.

2. Ibid.

3. Parks Canada, "Development Concept Approved for Greenwich, Prince Edward Island National Park," Press Release, December 22, 1998.

4. "Cavendish II on the Greenwich Dunes?" News Release, Prince Edward Island Environmental Network, February 18, 1999.

5. Ibid.

6. Nancy Willis, "Criticism of Greenwich plans gets reaction from MacAulay," *The Guardian* (Charlottetown), October 20, 1999, 3.

7. Dave Lipton, Field Unit Superintendent, Parks Canada. Interview on *Maritime Noon*, CBH-FM, Nova Scotia, October 18, 1999.

8. Ibid.

9. Ibid.

10. The Department of Environment also came very close to forcing Parks Canada to give up its historic sites because they didn't fit with the department's goals.

11. Parks Canada, "A Parks Canada Agency: A Discussion Paper," 1996.

12. Sheila Copps, Deputy Prime Minister and Minister of Canadian Heritage, Address to the Park Ministers Meeting, Charlottetown, September 30, 1996.

13. Ibid.

14. Anne McIlroy, "Parks to get legal guardian in new Canadian agency," *The Globe and Mail*, February 6, 1998, A4.

15. Ibid.

16. Francis J. Gouillart and James N. Kelly, *Transforming the Organization* (New York: McGraw-Hill, 1995), 4.

17. Ibid., 2.

18. Edward Grumbine, "Reflections on 'What is Ecosystem Management?'" *Conservation Biology* 11, no. 1 (February 1997): 45.

19. Katherine L. Jope and Joseph C. Dunstan, "Ecosystem-Based Management: Natural Processes and Systems Theory," in *National Parks and Protected Areas: Their Role in Environmental Protection*, ed. R. Gerald Wright (Cambridge, Mass.: Blackwell Science, 1996), 45.

20. Ibid., 48.

21. Auditor General of Canada, "Canadian Heritage—Parks Canada: Preserving Canada's Natural Heritage" and "Canadian Heritage—Parks Canada: Management of Historic Canals," Minister of Public Works and Government Services, 1996, 31-12.

## Chapter 7

1. National Parks Act (Amended), Government of Canada, October 1989, Section Four, 3.

2. W.F. Lothian, *A History of Canada's National Parks*, vol. IV (Ottawa: Minister of Environment and Minister of Supply and Services, 1981), 16.

3. Ibid.

4. Gifford Pinchot, as quoted by Janet Foster, *Working for Wildlife* (Toronto: University of Toronto Press, 1978), 35.

5. Gifford Pinchot, "Ends and Means," in *The American Environment: Readings in the History of Conservation*, 2nd ed., ed. Roderick Nash (Reading, Mass.: Addison-Wesley Publishing Company, 1976), 59.

6. Ibid. 60.

7. John Muir, in Stephen Fox, *John Muir and His Legacy: The American Conservation Movement* (Boston and Toronto: Little, Brown and Company, 1981), 53.

8. J.B. Harkin, "Reflections of a Parks Administrator," *Park News* 23, no. 5 (1988): 11.

9. Ibid.

10. Ibid.

11. Ibid.

12. Parks Canada, *Parks Canada Policy* (Ottawa: Minister responsible for Parks Canada, 1979), 7.

13. J.B. Harkin, quoted by Janet Foster, *Working for Wildlife*, 222.

14. Ibid., 79.

15. J.B. Harkin, "Reflections of a Parks Administrator," 11.

16. W.F. Lothian, *A History of Canada's National Parks*, 121.

17. Ibid., 92.

18. Ibid., 103.

19. Alvin Finkel, *Our Lives: Canada after 1945* (Toronto: James Lorimer and Company, 1997), 8.

20. Fred Bodsworth, "Beauty and the Buck," *Maclean's*, March 1963. Excerpted in *Parks News* 5, no. 1 (February 1969): 13.

21. Ibid., 13–14.

22. National Parks Branch, *National Parks Policy* (Ottawa: Department of Northern Affairs and National Resources, 1964), 5.

23. Ibid.

24. "Statement by the Hon. Jean Chrétien Re: Village Lake Louise," *Park News* 8, no. 4 (July 1972): 15.

25. Gavin Henderson, "Village Lake Louise," *Park News* 8, no. 2 (March 1972): 5.

26. "Statement by the Hon. Jean Chrétien," *Park News*, 15.

27. Parks Canada, *Parks Canada Policy*, 11.

28. Parks Canada Employees for Ethical Service to Parks, n.d.

## Chapter 8

1. Angus Reid, "A Study of Canadian Attitudes Toward Canada's National Parks," 1993, iii.

2. For an example discussion of this problem see Larry M. Gigliotti, "Environmental Education: What Went Wrong? What Can Be Done?" *Journal of Environmental Education* 22, no. 1 (1990).

3. The best reference on this fascinating topic is *The Golden Bough* by Sir James Frazer, originally published between 1890 and 1915.

4. Paul Shepard, *Nature and Madness* (San Francisco: Sierra Club Books, 1982), 3.

5. John A. Livingston, *One Cosmic Instant: A Natural History of Human Arrogance* (Toronto: McClelland and Stewart, 1973), 125.

6. Ibid., 129.

7. Ibid., 132.

8. Genesis 26.

9. From *The Norton Anthology of Poetry* (New York: W.W. Norton & Company, 1970), 532.

10. Ibid., 588.

11. W.L. Morton, *The Canadian Identity* (Madison, WI: The University of Wisconsin, 1961), 4.

12. Ibid., 4.

13. Bruce Litteljohn and Jon Pearce, Eds., *Marked by the Wild* (Toronto: McClelland and Stewart, 1973), 216.

14. Margaret Atwood, *Survival* (Toronto: Anansi Press, 1972), 32.

15. Ibid., 49.

16. Ibid., 60.

17. Grey Owl, *Tales of an Empty Cabin* (Toronto: Macmillan of Canada, 1989), vii–viii.

18. "Cutbacks, infighting hurt pesticide control efforts, environment boss says," *Times-Colonist*, May 26, 1999.

19. Environics International Ltd., "Environmental Monitor Top Line Findings: Environment Canada Omnibus Survey Fielded February 1999," May 21, 1999.

20. Environics International Ltd., "Concern About Wilderness Issues Resurges in BC, Atlantic Provinces," press release, March 24, 1999.

21. Statistics Canada, Household Environmental Practices, Catalogue no. 11-526-XPB, 1996.

22. Environics International, "Concern About Wilderness Issues Resurges."

23. Robert Fife, "Razing habitats of at-risk animals to be criminalized," *National Post*, November 8, 1999, A1.

24. Stan Rowe, *Home Place* (Edmonton: NeWest, 1990), 39.

## Chapter 9

1. Rick Searle, *Population Growth, Resource Consumption, and the Environment: Seeking a Common Vision for a Troubled World*, (Victoria: Centre for Studies in Religion and Society, 1995), 22.
2. Ibid.
3. Ibid., 23.
4. J. Baird Callicott, "Traditional American Indian and Traditional Western European Attitudes Towards Nature: An Overview," n.d.
5. Annie I. Booth and Harvey M. Jacobs, "Ties that Bind: Native American Beliefs as a Foundation for Environmental Consciousness," *Environmental Ethics* 12, n.d.
6. Rick Searle, *Population Growth*, 26.
7. Ibid.
8. Ibid., 40.
9. Ibid., 41.
10. Ibid., 45.
11. Ibid., 34.
12. Ibid., 35.
13. Ibid., 31.
14. Matthew Fox, *A Spirituality Named Compassion* (San Francisco: Harper, 1990), 10.
15. Fritjof Capra, *The Web of Life* (New York: Doubleday, 1996), 29.
16. James Gleick, *Chaos: Making a New Science* (New York: Penguin Books, 1988), 3.
17. Fritjof Capra, *The Web of Life*, 32.
18. Ibid., 33–34.
19. Ibid., 35.
20. Ibid.
21. Neil Evernden, *The Natural Alien* (Toronto: University of Toronto Press, 1986), 45.
22. Ibid., 64.
23. Bill Devall and George Sessions, *Deep Ecology* (Salt Lake City, Utah: Gibbs M. Smith, Inc., Peregrine Smith Books, 1985), 67.
24. Aldo Leopold, *A Sand County Almanac* (San Francisco and New York: Sierra Club/Ballantine, 1966), 240.
25. Stan Rowe, *Home Place* (Edmonton: NeWest, 1990), 25–26.
26. Ibid., 52.
27. Theodore Roszak, *The Voice of the Earth* (New York: Simon & Schuster, 1992), 38.
28. Ibid., 39.

29. E.O. Wilson, *Biophilia* (Cambridge, Mass.: Harvard University Press, 1984), 1.

30. Eric Fromm, *The Art of Loving*, 33rd ed. (New York: Bantam Books, 1956), 22.

31. Matthew Fox, *A Spirituality Named Compassion* (San Francisco: Harper, 1990), 18.

32. Thomas Merton, "Marxism and Monastic Perspectives," in *A New Charter for Monasticism*, ed. John Moffatt (Notre Dame, Indiana: University of Notre Dame Press, 1970), 80.

33. Matthew Fox, *A Spirituality Named Compassion*, 7.

34. Thomas Mann, *The Confessions of Felix Krull: Confidence Man*, tr. Denver Lindley (New York: Knopf, 1955).

35. Scott Peck, *The Road Less Traveled* (New York: Simon and Schuster, 1978), 119.

36. John A. Livingston, *Rogue Primate* (Toronto: Key Porter Books, 1994), 5.

## Chapter 10

1. Kevin Van Tighem, "Have Our National Parks Failed Us?" *Park News* 22, no. 2 (Summer 1986): 31–33.

2. Neil Gilson, Lois Pittaway and Grand Ross, "'Defensive Driving for Protected Spaces' or 'Don't Get Cut Off'—Anticipating the Need for Wildlife Corridors and Greenspace Buffers for the Ann and Sandy Cross Conservation Area," in *Linking Protected Areas with Working Landscapes: Conserving Biodiversity*, ed. Neil W.P. Munro and J.H. Martin Willison, Proceedings of the Third International Conference on Science and Management of Protected Areas (Wolfville, Nova Scotia: Science and Management of Protected Areas Association, 1998), 278.

3. Adrian Phillips, "Working Landscapes and Protected Areas: The Agenda for the 21st Century," in *Linking Protected Areas with Working Landscapes*.

4. Edward C. Wolf, *On the Brink of Extinction: Conserving the Diversity of Life*, Worldwatch Paper no. 78 (Washington: Worldwatch Institute, 1987), 28.

5. T.A. White and K.S. Hashisaki, "Taking a Broader View: Seeking Common Ground for the Restoration Paradigm," in *The Role of Restoration in Ecosystem Management*, ed. David L. Pearson and Charles V. Klimas (Omnipress, Wisconsin: Society of Ecological Restoration, 1996), 6.

6. Edward C. Wolf, *On the Brink of Extinction: Conserving the Diversity of Life*, 29.

7. Donald A. Falk, "Choosing a Future for Ecological Restoration," in *The Role of Restoration in Ecosystem Management*, 211.

8. Edward C. Wolf, *On the Brink*, 36.
9. Donald A. Falk, "Choosing a Future," 214.
10. Ibid.
11. Ibid.
12. Edward C. Wolf, *On the Brink*, 36.

## Chapter 11

1. Parks Legacy Panel, "Sustaining Our Protected Areas System: An Interim Report," Ministry of Environment, Lands and Parks, July 1998.
2. Parks Legacy Panel, "Sustaining Our Protected Areas System: Final Report," Ministry of Environment, Lands and Parks, February 1999, 12.
3. Ibid., 12–13.
4. Henry Mintzberg, "The Myth of Society Inc.," *Report on Business Magazine* (October 1996): 113–14.
5. Ibid., 114.
6. Ibid., 116.
7. Henry Mintzberg, "Managing Government, Governing Management," *Harvard Business Review* (May–June 1996): 78.
8. Ibid.
9. National Parks Branch, *National Parks Policy* (Ottawa: 1964), 4.
10. Ibid.
11. Parks Canada, *Parks Canada Policy* (Ottawa: Minister responsible for Parks Canada, 1979), 14.
12. Ibid., 42–43.
13. Parks Canada, *Guiding Principles and Operational Policies* (Ottawa: Minister of Supply and Services), 18.
14. Geoffrey Wall, ed., *Outdoor Recreation in Canada* (Toronto: John Wiley & Sons, 1989), 3.
15. Ibid., 4.
16. Ibid., 5–6.
17. John Baden, "Neospartan Hedonists, Adult Toy Aficionadoes, and the Rationing of Public Lands," in *Managing the Commons*, ed. Garrett Hardin and John Baden (San Francisco: W.H. Freeman and Company, 1977), 241.
18. Ibid.
19. Edgar Jackson, "Perceptions and Decisions," in *Outdoor Recreation in Canada*, ed. Geoffrey Wall (Toronto: John Wiley & Sons, 1989), 109.
20. Ibid., 110.
21. Aldo Leopold, *A Sand County Almanac* (San Francisco and New York: Sierra Club/Ballantine, 1970), 280–81.

22. Ibid., 294.

23. Ibid., 289–90.

24. Ibid., 290.

25. Ibid., 295.

26. Janet Foster, *Working for Wildlife: The Beginning of Preservation in Canada*, 2nd ed. (Toronto: University of Toronto Press, 1998), 87.

27. J.B. Harkin, "Reflections of a Parks Administrator," *Park News* 23, no. 5 (Summer 1988): 11.

28. Theodore Roszak, *Where the Wasteland Ends* (Garden City, New York: Doubleday & Company, 1973), 7.

29. John A. Livingston, *Rogue Primate* (Toronto: Key Porter Books, 1994), 39.

30. Wallace Stegner, "The Meaning of Wilderness in American Civilization," in *The American Environment* ed. Roderick Nash (Reading, Mass.: Addison-Wesley Publishing, 1976), 197.

31. Alan Drengson, "Wild Journeying Way," *The Trumpeter* (Fall 1996).

32. Ibid., 6.

33. John A. Livingston, *Rogue Primate*, 51.

34. Stan Rowe, *Home Place* (Edmonton: NeWest, 1990), 77.

## Chapter 12

1. Theodore Roszak, *The Voice of the Earth* (New York: Simon & Schuster, 1992), 70.

2. Neil Evernden, *The Social Creation of Nature* (Baltimore and London: The John Hopkins University Press, 1992), 117.

3. Ibid.

4. Ibid., 120.

5. Ibid., 121.

6. David W. Orr, *Earth in Mind* (Washington: Island Press, 1994), 7.

7. Michael Harcourt, in a keynote address at "Your Business and the Environment: A Profitable Alliance" conference, Victoria, July 7, 1999.

8. Ibid.

9. John E. Young and Aaron Sachs, "Creating a Sustainable Materials Economy," in *State of the World 1995*, ed. Lester Brown (New York and London: W.W. Norton & Company, 1995), 77.

10. Ibid., 79.

11. Dirk Bryant, Daniel Nielsen and Laura Tangley, *The Last Frontier Forests: Ecosystems and Economies on the Edge* (Washington: World Resources Institute, 1997), 1.

12. Norman Meyers, quoted in Edward C. Wolf, *On the Brink of Extinction:*

*Conserving the Diversity of Life*, Worldwatch Paper no. 78 (Washington: Worldwatch Institute, June 1987), 37.

13. E.O. Wilson, *Biophilia* (Cambridge, Mass., and London: Harvard University Press, 1984), 121.

14. World Commission on the Environment and Development, *Our Common Future* (Oxford University Press, 1987), 13.

15. Stan Rowe, "Why Preserve Wild Areas and Species?" *Park News* 18, no. 3 (Fall 1982): 12.

16. Ibid., 15.

17. David Quammen, "Planet of Weeds," *Harper's* (October 1998): 62.

18. Gary E. Machlis and David L. Tichnell, *The State of the World's Parks* (Boulder, Colorado, and London: Westview Press, 1985), 51.

19. William D. Newmark, "Extinction of Mammal Populations in Western North American National Parks," *Conservation Biology* 9, no. 3 (June 1995): 518.

20. Parks Canada, *State of the Parks 1997* (Ottawa: Minister of Public Works and Government Services, 1998), 25.

21. Parks Canada, "Principles and Standards for Ecosystem-Based Management for Parks Canada," prepared by Geomatics International Inc., Guelph, Ontario, December 1996, 1.

22. Ibid., 3.

23. E.F. Schumacher, *Small is Beautiful* (London: Abacus, 1974), 66.

24. Aldo Leopold, *A Sand County Almanac* (San Francisco and New York: Sierra Club/Ballantine, 1970), 168.

25. James B. Harkin, "Reflections of a Parks Administrator," *Park News* 2, no. 1 (January 1966).

26. W.B. Stapp et. al., "The concept of environmental education," quoted in Larry M. Gigliotti, "Environmental Education: What went wrong? What can be done?" *Journal of Environmental Education* 22, no. 1 (1990): 9.

27. Stan Rowe, *Home Place*, 62.

28. Ibid.

29. Paul Shepard, *Nature and Madness* (San Francisco: Sierra Club Books, 1982), 128.

For those wishing to learn more about some of the topics and ideas presented in this book.

Atwood, Margret. *Survival*. Toronto, Anansi Press Limited. 1972.

Bella, Leslie. *Parks for Profit*. Montreal, Harvest House. 1987.

Capra, Fritjof. *Web of Life*. New York. An Anchor Book, Doubleday. 1996.

Evernden, Neil. *The Social Creation of Nature*. Baltimore and London, John Hopkins University Press. 1992.
– *Natural Aliens*. Toronto, University of Toronto Press. 1986.

Foster, Janet. *Working for Wildlife*. Toronto, University of Toronto Press. 1978.

Grey Owl. *Tales of an Empty Cabin*. Toronto, MacMillan of Canada. MacMillan Paperback Series. 1989.

Harmon, David. *Mirror of America: Literary Encounters with the National Parks*. Boulder, Roberts Rinehold Publisher. 1989.

Litteljohn, Bruce and Jon Pearce (Eds). *Marked by the Wild*. Toronto, McClelland and Stewart. 1973.

Livingston, John. *Rogue Primate*. Toronto, Key Porter Press. 1994.
– *Fallacy of Wildlife Conservation*. Toronto, MacClelland and Stewart. 1981.

Nash, Roderick. *The American Environment: Readings in the History of Conservation.* 2nd Edition. Reading, Mass. Adison-Wesley Publishing Company. 1976.

Ornstein, Robert and Paul Ehrlich. *New World, New Mind.* New York, Doubleday. 1989.

Orr, David. *Earth in Mind: On Education, Environment, and the Human Prospect.* Washington, DC. Island Press. 1994.

Rodney, William. *Kootenai Brown: his life and times.* Sidney, British Columbia. Gray's Publishing. 1969.

Roszak, Theodore. *The Voice of the Earth.* New York, Simon and Schuster. 1992.

Rowe, Stan. *Home Place: Essays on Ecology.* Edmonton, NeWest. 1990.

Russell, Andy. *Grizzly Country.* New York, Ballantine Books. 1967.

Shepard, Paul. *Nature and Madness.* San Francisco, Sierra Club Books. 1982.

Wilson, E. O. *Biophilia.* Cambridge, Mass. and London, England. Harvard University Press. 1984.

Wright, Gerald R.. *National Parks and Protected  Areas: Their Role in Environmental Protection.* London, Blackwell Science. 1996.